CONSTITUTIONAL CONVENTIONS IN WESTMINSTER SYSTEMS

Conventions are fundamental to the constitutional systems of parliamentary democracies. Unlike the United States, which adopted a republican form of government – with a full separation of powers – and codified constitutional structures and limitations for executive and legislative institutions and actors, the United Kingdom and subsequently Canada, Australia and New Zealand have relied on conventions to perform similar functions. The rise of new political actors has disrupted the stability of the two-party system, and in seeking power the new players are challenging existing practices. Conventions that govern constitutional arrangements in the United Kingdom and New Zealand, and the executive in Canada and Australia, are changing to accommodate these and other challenges of modern governance. In Westminster democracies, constitutional conventions provide the rules for forming government; they precede law and make law-making possible. This prior and more fundamental realm of government formation and law-making is shaped and structured by conventions.

BRIAN GALLIGAN is a professor of political science at the University of Melbourne. He is the author or co-author of eight books on Australian politics and political economy, including *Beyond the Protective State* (1992), *A Federal Republic* (1995), *Citizens without Rights* (1997) and *Australians and Globalisation* (2001). He is the joint author of *Australian Citizenship* (2004) and *Becoming Australian* (2014) and co-editor of *The Oxford Companion to Australian Politics* (2007) and *Human Rights in Asia* (2011).

SCOTT BRENTON is a lecturer in political science and the Director of the Doctoral Academy at the Melbourne School of Government. He has published extensively on Australian politics, particularly on altering traditional forms of governance and challenging, or rather adapting, existing conventions. He has contributed to several major Australian Research Council projects, including the Parliamentary Accountability Project, the Democratic Audit of Australia and Strengthening Parliamentary Institutions.

CONSTITUTIONAL CONVENTIONS IN WESTMINSTER SYSTEMS

Controversies, Changes and Challenges

Edited by

BRIAN GALLIGAN

and

SCOTT BRENTON

CAMBRIDGE
UNIVERSITY PRESS

CAMBRIDGE
UNIVERSITY PRESS

University Printing House, Cambridge CB2 8BS, United Kingdom

Cambridge University Press is part of the University of Cambridge.

It furthers the University's mission by disseminating knowledge in the pursuit of education, learning and research at the highest international levels of excellence.

www.cambridge.org
Information on this title: www.cambridge.org/9781107100244

First published 2015

A catalogue record for this publication is available from the British Library

Library of Congress Cataloging-in-Publication Data
Constitutional conventions in Westminster systems : controversies, changes and challenges / edited by Brian Galligan, Scott Brenton.
pages cm
ISBN 978-1-107-10024-4 (Hardback)
1. Constitutional history–Australia. 2. Constitutional history–Canada.
3. Constitutional history–Great Britain. 4. Constitutional history–New Zealand.
I. Galligan, Brian, 1945- editor. II. Brenton, Scott, editor.
K3161.C665 2015
342.02′92–dc23 2015005491

ISBN 978-1-107-10024-4 Hardback

CONTENTS

NOTES ON CONTRIBUTORS

NICHOLAS ARONEY is a professor of law and an Australian Research Council Future Fellow at the Centre for Public, International and Comparative Law at the University of Queensland. His research under the fellowship involves a systematic comparison of the Australian federal system with other systems of multi-level governance throughout North and South America, Europe and Asia. Nicholas has published widely in the fields of constitutional law, comparative constitutional law and legal theory, including several books and numerous journal articles and book chapters. He is a former editor of *The University of Queensland Law Journal* (2003–2005) and *International Trade and Business Law Annual* (1996–1998), past secretary of the Australian Society of Legal Philosophy and a current member of the Governing Council of the Australian Association of Constitutional Law.

ANDREW C. BANFIELD is Head of the School of Politics and International Relations at the Australian National University. His research examines political institutions in Canada and Australia, with a specific focus on courts, legislatures and federalism, and he has published widely in these areas. Andrew was an instructor in the Department of Political Science at the University of Calgary, Canada, and has been a visiting scholar at the University of Melbourne (2007), and a graduate fellow at the Institute for Advanced Policy Research at the University of Calgary (2005–2007).

NICHOLAS BARRY is a lecturer in politics at La Trobe University. His research and teaching interests are in the areas of Australian politics and political theory. He is currently working on a defense of luck egalitarianism, which is a responsibility-sensitive, luck-insensitive theory of justice, and he is also examining the links between contemporary egalitarian theory and policy debates over disadvantage and welfare reform. Nicholas is also working on human rights protection in

Australia, with a particular focus on Australia's National Human Rights Framework, and he has future work planned on constitutionalism, democracy and judicial politics.

ANDREW BLICK is Lecturer in Politics and Contemporary History at King's College London. He was formerly Senior Research Fellow in the Centre for Political and Constitutional Studies at the Institute of Contemporary British History (ICBH) and Senior Research Fellow at the Democratic Audit, University of Liverpool. Andrew has acted as a consultant on constitutional issues for organisations, including the United Nations Development Programme and the UK National Audit Office, and has undertaken research projects for the Rowntree trusts, Carnegie UK Trust, the German Marshall Fund and the Madison Trust. He has extensive experience of devising and implementing research projects. Andrew has written numerous books, articles and pamphlets, and provided written and oral evidence to parliamentary committees. He has worked in Parliament and closely with parliamentarians on various occasions. In 1999 he was an administrative assistant at Number 10 Downing Street.

SCOTT BRENTON is a lecturer in political science at the Australian National University. He previously worked at the Australian Parliament House and published a research monograph through the Parliament on the representative duties of parliamentarians (*What Lies Beneath: The Work of Senators and Members in the Australian Parliament*, 2010). He has published extensively on Australian politics and public policy, particularly on issues of accountability and the fragmentation and the rise of minor parties and new political actors. Scott has published fourteen peer-reviewed publications on areas related to this book, most recently a journal article titled 'Ministerial accountability for departmental actions across Westminster parliamentary democracies' in the *Australian Journal of Public Administration*.

GRANT DUNCAN is an associate professor in the Politics Programme at Massey University of New Zealand. His research and publications have covered general changes in social policy and public management in New Zealand, specialising in accident compensation legislation and policy. He has analysed the means by which policy institutions construct and administer populations, with a focus on work-capacity and chronic-pain disability. He also has a special interest in the political uses of happiness.

BRIAN GALLIGAN is a professor of political science at the University of Melbourne, and was previously a professor in the Research School of Social Sciences at the Australian National University. He has published extensively on Australian politics and political economy, including four books as single or co-author with Cambridge University Press: *Beyond the Protective State* (1992), *A Federal Republic* (1995), *Citizens without Rights* (1997) and *Australians and Globalisation* (2001). He has co-authored *Australian Citizenship* (2004), and is the co-editor of *The Oxford Companion to Australian Politics* (2007) and *Human Rights in Asia* (2011).

ROBERT HAZELL holds a personal chair as Professor of Government and the Constitution and is the Director of the Constitution Unit at University College London. Robert is a former barrister and worked at the Home Office as a policy-making civil servant, contributing to immigration, police, prisons, broadcasting, race relations, drugs and criminal justice policy. He was the Director of the Nuffield Foundation, and in 2006 was awarded the Commander of the Order of the British Empire (CBE) for his services to constitutional reform. He has published widely on devolution in Scotland, Wales and the English regions; freedom of information; parliamentary reform and Lords reform; a British bill of rights; referendums; electoral reform; the Crown and royal prerogative; constitutional watchdogs; and the process of constitutional reform.

JENNY MENZIES is a member of the Commonwealth Grants Commission and Director of the consultancy Policy Futures. She has over twenty years' experience in policy and public administration in both the state and commonwealth governments. As a senior executive within the Queensland Department of the Premier and Cabinet, she developed the government's strategic policy agenda including the Smart State Policy. She was Cabinet Secretary from 2001 to 2004 and the inaugural Secretary for the Council for the Australian Federation from 2007 to 2009. She has published in the fields of caretaker conventions, federalism and intergovernmental relations.

NARELLE MIRAGLIOTTA is a senior lecturer in Australian politics at Monash University. She has a comprehensive publication record in the field of Australian politics and is emerging as one of the country's leading experts. She has broad teaching and research interests in various aspects of Australian politics, including the politics of the Australian media, green political parties and Australian elections and electoral systems.

J.R. NETHERCOTE is Adjunct Professor at the Canberra Campus of the Australian Catholic University. A former officer of the Department of the Senate, he edited *Parliament and Bureaucracy* (1982) and jointly edited *The House on Capital Hill* (1996). He oversaw the publication of J. R. Odgers' *Australian Senate Practice*, 6th edition (1991), and contributed to the preparation of Odgers' *Australian Senate Practice*, 7th edition (1993). From 2000 to 2003, he was editor of *Australasian Parliamentary Review*.

PETER H. RUSSELL is a professor emeritus of political science at the University of Toronto where he taught from 1958 to 1997. Considered one of Canada's most respected political scientists, Peter was Director of Research for the McDonald Commission on the Royal Canadian Mounted Police, a member of the Federal Task Force on Comprehensive Land Claims, and President of the Canadian Political Science Association. He chaired the Research Advisory Committee for the Royal Commission on Aboriginal Peoples. His recent publications include articles on constitutional politics, judicial independence and Aboriginal peoples. He is the author of *Two Cheers for Minority Government: The Evolution of Canadian Parliamentary Democracy.*

CAMPBELL SHARMAN is an adjunct professor at the University of British Columbia and was previously a senior political scientist at the University of Western Australia. He is an expert on federalism and the effect of institutional rules, both electoral and constitutional, on the political and governmental process in parliamentary systems. He is involved in a continuing project analysing long-term trends in parties, representation and government in Australia based on the Australian Politics and Elections Database. During 2004 he was Associate Research Director for the BC Citizens' Assembly on Electoral Reform and has undertaken projects for the Centre for the Study of Democratic Institutions.

ANNE TIERNAN is a professor in the School of Government and International Relations at Griffith University. She is Director of Griffith's Executive Masters in Public Administration (EMPA) program. Her research focuses on the work of governing. Her scholarly interests include: Australian politics and governance, policy advice, executive studies, policy capacity, federalism and intergovernmental coordination. She has written extensively on the political-administrative interface, caretaker conventions, governmental transitions and the work of policy advising.

Prof Tiernan is author of books including: *Lessons in Governing: A Profile of Prime Ministers' Chiefs of Staff and The Gatekeepers: Lessons from Prime Ministers' Chiefs of Staff* (both with R.A.W. Rhodes, Melbourne University Publishing, 2014), *Learning to be a Minister: Heroic Expectations, Practical Realities* (with Patrick Weller, Melbourne University Press, 2010) and *Power Without Responsibility: Ministerial Staffers in Australian Governments from Whitlam to Howard* (UNSW Press, 2007).

Prof Tiernan is a member of the Member of the Public Records Review Committee of the Queensland State Archives. Between 2008 and 2012 she was a member of the Board of Commissioners of the Queensland Public Service Commission.

PATRICK WELLER has been professor of politics at Griffith University since 1984. He holds the Premier of Queensland Chair in Governance and Public Management. He has a BA from Exeter College Oxford, an MA from Oxford University, a PhD from the Australian National University and a D.Litt. from Griffith University. He is also an adjunct professor in the Australia and New Zealand School of Government. He is an Officer of the Order of Australia (AO) and a fellow of the Academy of Social Sciences of Australia. He has published several books on cabinet government and the public service.

ACKNOWLEDGEMENTS

We would like to acknowledge the generous financial support provided by the Academy of the Social Sciences in Australia and the School of Social and Political Sciences at the University of Melbourne. Scott Brenton was also supported by a University of Melbourne Early Career Researcher grant.

We are grateful to our contributors and workshop participants as these ideas and debates have developed over a number of years and through numerous productive exchanges. Our tireless Research Assistant, Angela Merriam, has been invaluable in the final stages. Finally, the editors and assistants at Cambridge University Press have been great to work with.

Introduction

In recent years there has been renewed public and practitioner interest in constitutional conventions that govern so much of the operation of Westminster systems. Yet surprisingly, given their importance and the extent of changes that have occurred or been proposed, constitutional conventions have been relatively neglected by scholars. Our book remedies this, explaining the character of conventions with comparative and up-to-date accounts of four of the main Westminster countries: the United Kingdom, Canada, Australia and New Zealand.

Comparing Westminster countries flourished in earlier times (Brady 1947) but became 'an intellectual backwater', according to Rhodes, Wanna and Weller (2009: 17). Their book *Comparing Westminster* signals a revival of this rich field for comparative study. Westminster countries provide a paradigm grouping of 'most similar' nations, 'related by history, belief systems, and inclination. They form a loose family of governments, not clones of one another. Westminster was, and remains, useful shorthand to identify their origins and some of their basic characteristics' (Rhodes, Wanna and Weller 2009: 230). Comparing conventions in Westminster systems also flourished earlier on with the classic accounts of H.V. Evatt (1936) and Eugene Forsey (1943). These became authoritative texts that were referred to when the occasional issue arose during the post-war decades. For the most part, however, conventions were pretty much taken for granted, attracting only occasional attention and comparative updating (Marshall 1984; Butler and Low 1991).

A second reason for the relative neglect of conventions over the last half century has been the dominance of law that focused, not surprisingly, on legal aspects of Westminster systems. Following Dicey, many constitutional lawyers spoke disparagingly of 'mere conventions', or more recently as 'soft laws' that approximated some of the preferred attributes of law. Our book provides a corrective account of conventions as primary political institutions that rely on political and social support.

Chapter 1 sets out our political account of conventions, and something of their nature, legitimacy and flexibility. Chapter 2 by constitutional lawyer Nicholas Aroney is complementary, showing the complexity and interconnectedness of constitutional law and convention.

The book is comparative but restricted to the four Westminster countries with the 'most similar systems', the United Kingdom, Canada, Australia and New Zealand. Comparing Westminster conventions enables us to identify the highly comparable features in the executive and legislative branches of government, and the variations due to differences in historical development, political culture and circumstances, and institutional choices. Our selection of these four countries was limited by considerations of comparability in the closeness of shared traditions of government, and constraints of space and manageability. A much larger study or further volumes would be required to cover all of those countries with Westminster-derived systems of government, including 'Eastminster' countries such as India, a vast democratic republic, and Malaysia, with its strong Islamic heritage, as well as smaller Pacific and Caribbean countries such as Papua New Guinea and Trinidad and Tobago. Our study of constitutional conventions in the four 'most similar' countries might provide a comparative model for exploring the development of constitutional conventions in these other more varied Eastminster and smaller Pacific and Caribbean countries.

The structure of the book is as follows. The first two chapters define the character of conventions and how they compare with law. This is followed by three thematic chapters on key institutions of executive government: the basic institutions and rules of responsible government in Chapter 3, cabinet government in Chapter 4 and caretaker conventions in Chapter 5. These chapters are comparative but selective in their coverage with individual authors focusing on aspects and examples that illustrate their narrative. Chapter 6 explains how changing party political arrangements and the prevalence of minority and multi-party governments have sparked renewed interest in constitutional conventions. Chapters 7 and 8 focus on the parliamentary conventions that govern parliaments and restrict upper houses. The cluster of country studies, Chapters 9 through 12 on the United Kingdom, Canada, Australia and New Zealand, give succinct profiles of the current state of play in each of the four countries. The final two chapters are concerned with codifying (Chapter 13) and reforming conventions (Chapter 14). A brief conclusion brings out some of the overall themes of the book.

In discussing conventions that govern Westminster parliamentary systems and previewing the detailed work of subsequent chapters, it is worth distinguishing two broad types of conventions that we might term 'core' and 'customary' or 'administrative'. This is not meant to be a sharp distinction of an essentialist kind, but a way of facilitating discussion of the different types and attributes of institutions and practices encompassed by the umbrella term of convention. Core conventions are the more fundamental ones that determine the institutional structure and procedures for forming governments and specifying relations between the political or real executive and the formal head of state. They include the complementary conventions that privilege the lower house of parliament where the executive is primarily based. Core conventions are underpinned by, and give effect to, fundamental democratic values and their breach would be a violation of such values.

Core conventions that cover the executive and relations between the chambers in bicameral systems are manifest in the four countries under consideration, and testified in the country studies in Chapters 9 through 12 on the United Kingdom, Canada, Australia and New Zealand, respectively. These studies show that, for the most part, core constitutional conventions work in predictable and comparable ways in all four countries, with variations being exceptions explained by different circumstances and events. The Canadian prorogation crisis of 2008 was exceptional, but not unknown as New Zealand was faced with a similar proposal to suspend parliament by a beleaguered minority premier back in 1910. The New Zealand attempt was aborted by the wise counsel of an authoritative governor-general as Grant Duncan recounts in Chapter 12, while the recent Canadian prorogation was achieved by a dominant prime minister. Nevertheless, despite ongoing dispute about the rights and wrongs of 2008 that Peter Russell explains in Chapter 13 and proposals for codifying the conventions at play in this explosive episode, government practice continues in 'the peaceable kingdom', as Andrew Banfield calls his beloved country of origin in Chapter 10, in conventional ways.

There is a common conventional discourse across these countries deriving from the original British model and its adoption and retention as the dominion countries became equal Commonwealth countries and autonomous in their national government. Conventions relating to the responsible government executive and the monarchic and vice-regal head are highly comparable in all four countries, as discussed in Chapter 3. The dominance of the elected lower house of parliament – New Zealand being unicameral – over the appointed upper houses in Britain and Canada, complements the executive arrangements. This primacy of the lower or popularly elected house is brought out by J. R. Nethercote in Chapter 7 on parliament and by Campbell Sharman in Chapter 8 on upper houses. Government is formed by those who have the confidence, or majority support, in the lower house. Executive and legislative institutions without democratic legitimacy – the Queen, the House of Lords and the appointed Canadian Senate – are the ones most neutered by controlling conventions. In the Canadian case, convention trumps written text, marginalising an appointed chamber that has enormous paper powers but lacks democratic legitimacy.

Despite its elected Senate, Australia also has a standard responsible government executive, although one that was compromised somewhat during the 1975 constitutional crisis when the Senate blocked supply and the governor-general dismissed a prime minister who had the confidence of the House of Representatives. As with Canadian prorogation in 2008, the Australian crisis of 1975 is the stand-out exception where sharp disagreements about the way conventions should have operated in that instance continue. Nevertheless, the more routine processes of forming governments, including the minority Gillard Labor government in 2010, and changing prime ministers, from Gillard to Rudd in 2010 and back to Rudd just before the 2013 election, continue on. Despite the 1975 crisis, Barry and Miragliotta conclude in Chapter 11 that there is broad consensus on constitutional conventions and little enthusiasm for their codification in Australia.

The more customary or administrative conventions are the ones that facilitate and expedite executive decision making, structure legislative process and facilitate government transitions. Across all of these aspects of government, there are well-recognised formalities and practices that give a certain dignity to proceedings while at the same time allowing for flexibility and robust political behaviour. For example, parliaments have elaborate standing orders and formal processes, but these can be readily suspended to expedite government business, as J. R. Nethercote brings out in Chapter 7. Cabinet conventions that structure the collective decision making of government are broadly comparable in all four countries, yet differ in detail and are adjusted and changed to suit prime ministerial preference. They are also changed to accommodate new arrangements for minority and multi-party government that Scott Brenton details in Chapter 6. Cabinet practices of secrecy and solidarity are examples of established practices that facilitate executive decision making but can be changed. Secrecy could be reversed and replaced with full disclosure of proceedings, according to Marshall (1984: 7), without any violation of 'constitutional morality'. While that might enhance public accountability, it would inhibit frank discussion so secrecy is maintained. Solidarity, however, has been modified to accommodate multi-party government.

Conventions can change in all sorts of ways, and can be articulated and codified in various forms by executive, legislative and judicial instruments. Andrew Blick in Chapter 14 points out the various forms that reforming conventions can take, and the consequences that can be either advantageous or limiting. As Blick comments, conventions are a vital part of any constitution, but often go unnoticed. Such opaqueness causes a serious democratic deficit, according to Peter Russell in Chapter 13, which was evident in Canada's 2008 prorogation crisis and could best be remedied through codification. Unlike laws, however, conventions can lack precision and their practical application can remain contentious even when codified. Authors can vary in their approach to conventions, as the following chapters show, even if there is broad consensus on key conventions.

New Zealand and the United Kingdom have been leaders in the codification stakes for somewhat different reasons. Both lack written constitutions like those of Canada and Australia, so there is more scope and perhaps greater need for codification. Both have experienced major political changes to their constitutional systems: New Zealand in adopting mixed-member proportional (MMP) voting that often ensures multi-party government, and the United Kingdom in updating arcane practices and granting devolution. With entrenched written constitutions, Canada and Australia have far more extensive codification of the legislature, the federal division of powers between national and provincial or state governments and aspects of the executive, so there is more limited scope and need for further codification.

Codification in its various forms captures and records rather than creates conventions and conventional change. Conventional change often occurs under the mantle of continuity. Cabinet manuals are obvious examples: they spell out the accepted procedures of operation, but are adjusted by successive governments to accommodate changes. The New Zealand Cabinet Manual that has become something of a model for codification advocates is approved at the first cabinet meeting of a new government, and is varied to suit the needs of that government. For example, the novel Labour–Alliance coalition that Prime Minister

Helen Clark put together in 1999 allowed for the minor partner to express publicly a differing view on certain matters to allow for 'party distinction'. As Duncan points out in Chapter 12, the New Zealand Cabinet Manual was amended accordingly. Weller in Chapter 4 gives the example of Prime Minister Bob Hawke having his department secretary revise the definition of collective responsibility to allow a left-wing minister opposed to the mining and export of uranium to debate the issue in party caucus while remaining a minister but not a cabinet minister. Hazell in Chapter 9 documents the flurry of conventional documentation that has occurred in tracking the myriad of conventional changes in UK government.

Caretaker conventions facilitate government transitions, ensuring that important policy decisions and appointments are not made around election time when the new or continuing government has not been determined. Although much of the detail of caretaker conventions is administrative in character, and often formulated by senior officials, these conventions give effect to the underlying democratic principle of government having the confidence of the house that represents the will of people. During the election period when this is not known, the old government is quite properly restrained in what it can do, as Menzies and Tiernan document in Chapter 5. As in other areas, there is both continuity and change in constitutional conventions that operate during this waiting period. The basic rule is that new policies not be implemented or important decisions made until the outcome is clear with the new or renewed government having a supportive mandate reflected by its having the confidence of the newly elected lower house of parliament.

Conventions are essential to all constitutional systems, but especially Westminster ones. They vary in form, with some being fundamental for democratic government and others adopted for administrative facility. They are political in character, and even if codified in various ways provide flexible institutions for ensuring continuity but allowing for change in constitutional arrangements. We trust our book will make this better known and appreciated.

References

Brady, Alexander 1947. *Democracy in the Dominions*. Toronto University Press.

Butler, David and Low, D.A. (eds.) 1991. *Sovereigns and Surrogates: Constitutional Heads of State in the Commonwealth*. London: Macmillan.

Evatt, H.V. 1936. *The King and His Dominion Governors*. Oxford University Press.

Forsey, Eugene A. 1943. *The Royal Power of Dissolution of Parliament in the British Commonwealth*. Oxford University Press.

Marshall, Geoffrey 1984. *Constitutional Conventions*. Oxford: Clarendon Press.

Rhodes, R.A.W., Wanna, John and Weller, Patrick 2009. *Comparing Westminster*. Oxford University Press.

1

Constitutional conventions

BRIAN GALLIGAN AND SCOTT BRENTON

This opening chapter addresses the foundational questions of what is a convention, what gives a convention its legitimacy and how conventions remain stable yet adaptable. Conventions are often defined negatively, in terms of not being law, or in political terms with the implication that they are inferior to law. We contend that conventions occupy a more fundamental realm: government and the rules for forming government precede law and make law-making possible. In other words, conventions are more fundamental than laws; they govern the formation and basic functioning of government overall and in its key parts, and governments set up the law-making institutions that make, interpret and enforce laws. Hence it is not appropriate to go backwards, as it were, and view conventions from the more precise lens of law, which has been a strong tendency since the nineteenth century.

Hence our starting point is consideration of the origins of systems of government and law, and why they are supported and obeyed. We propose a political approach to explain how conventions derive from fundamental political principles that inform practice. After all, conventions are basic political rules affecting the structure and powers of government that are not enforceable in courts of law, so not amenable to jurisprudential treatment that purports to view them as quasi-laws. While for the most part conventions are not formally codified as laws are, they are broadly accepted as binding by government actors and citizens. They shape government practice albeit with flexibility that allows for development and change.

As a crucial part of Westminster-derived constitutional systems, conventions govern the institutions and operation of most aspects of parliament and responsible government: the offices of prime minister and cabinet, the rules for forming government, the dissolution of parliament, the appointment and removal of ministers, the role of the Queen and vice-regal representatives, doctrines of collective and individual ministerial responsibilities, the transaction of parliamentary business, caretaker government, the independence of the judiciary, relationships with and between the public service, the executive and the legislature and the chain of accountability involving public servants. Conventions are crucially important in countries with 'unwritten' constitutions like those of the United Kingdom and New Zealand, and define the executive parts of partly written constitutions such as those of Canada and Australia.

Conventions attracted more attention in the late nineteenth and early twentieth centuries when parliamentary politics were more fluid and vice-regal offices in Westminster dominions, as they were then termed (Evatt 1936), were filled by UK appointees who played a more active role. The rise and dominance of disciplined party politics for much of the twentieth century usually produced clear electoral outcomes with the vice-regal office, now filled by prominent domestic appointees, becoming more formal. In recent years, however, all four countries have experienced coalition and minority governments with multi-party cabinets, while Canada has a long history of minority government despite a majoritarian electoral system.

Australia has been home to many non-traditional Westminster experimentations, most notably the powerful Senate, and independents and minor party parliamentarians have served in state cabinets. New Zealand, once described as 'more Westminster than Westminster', has radically changed its electoral system and fostered more consensus-style government. There are continuing calls for democratic reform in the United Kingdom and Canada, particularly in the upper house, while both countries also grapple with how to accommodate nationalist and separatist movements. Democratic reform, at least for some (Marsh and Miller 2012), requires a multi-party system to better represent today's more complex postmodern society.

While the United States adopted a republican form of government, with a full separation of powers, codified constitutional limitations and democratic mandates for executive and legislative institutions and actors, the United Kingdom and subsequently Canada, Australia and New Zealand relied on conventions to perform similar functions. Conventions were used to curtail executive power, formally the prerogative of the monarch, and to regulate executive–legislative relations. In recent decades there have been consistent calls for greater democratisation and enhanced oversight and scrutiny of the executive in all four countries. Implicit is a critique of responsible *party* government, with the major political parties, traditionally the guardians of the 'rules of the game', being challenged by new political actors.

The United Kingdom and New Zealand, with unitary systems of government and without entrenched written constitutions, have been leading the charge. New Zealand adopted a new system of voting, MMP, that produces multi-party government, and has pioneered the development of a comprehensive Cabinet Manual to explain how conventions are adapted to its consequences, as Grant Duncan explains in Chapter 12. The United Kingdom has been undergoing a 'twenty-year constitutional revolution', according to Robert Hazell in Chapter 9, that has entailed 'the creation of new conventions; the modification of old conventions; the codification of many conventions; and the demise of conventions rendered obsolete.' The intensity of discussion and development of conventions has been more subdued in Canada and Australia, except for flash points such as Canada's prorogation crisis in 2008 and Australia's constitutional crisis of 1975. In these two countries, written federal constitutions, combined with judicial review, structure and oversee legislative and executive power to a far greater extent.

Despite different trajectories, the four countries under consideration have experienced common changes. The most significant changes have been driven by the challenges of forming governments and achieving executive unity sufficient to ensure confidence while allowing for differences. Where governments have been formed through formal agreements, there has also been a steady extension in the scope of policy commitments and significant budget implications. The 'logic of appropriateness' has guided this process, and there is an expectation that judgements, actions and decisions will have to be justified to others (*see* March and Olsen 1989). This historical institutionalist account helps to explain why many conventions have remained so stable. Political actors have responded to various situations in what they considered was most appropriate with regard to their position and responsibilities (Koeble 1995). The most appropriate response in a liberal democracy is generally the one that ensures political stability, but also takes into account the will of the people. For example, the major parties will look for a response that preserves their dominant position while also acknowledging changed political circumstances. Many scholars have described the cartel-like behaviour that major political parties have engaged in (*see* Katz and Mair 1995), with the longer term objective of alternating in government.

While aspects of all of these have been considered by various authors, the field as a whole is relatively neglected: the last authoritative book was Geoffrey Marshall's *Constitutional Conventions* (1984). Most commentary on conventions is by constitutional lawyers who typically work from a legal perspective, for example from Dicey, who first made the sharp distinction between law and convention, to the present day (e.g. Sirota 2011). A legal perspective tends to restrict and often distorts the character of conventions. Our approach is primarily a political one: drawing on political theory, political history and accepted practice in determining the nature of conventions and how they operate. We view constitutional conventions as integral parts of the constitutional system that has broad political and social, rather than legal, foundations (Galligan and Versteeg 2013).

Although constitutional law and the courts that interpret and apply it have a different institutional character, they are also part of that same larger constitutional system. Constitutional law and conventions are not the same, but differ by 'a matter of degree', as Barber (2009: 309) points out: 'Constitutional conventions and laws are two brands of social rule which differ in the extent of their formalization.' So rather than defining conventions in negative terms as being 'not law', we see them as political institutions that are core parts of the constitutional system and govern ongoing political practice.

This first chapter sets out the basic theory and framework of conventions, and outlines their character and the crucial role they play in parliamentary and responsible government in established Westminster systems. It will provide a framework for the overall understanding of conventions. Major institutions, such as the constitutional monarchy, cabinet government, upper houses or caretaker conventions, or developments, such as minority and multi-party governments or codifying conventions in handbooks and cabinet manuals, are discussed in later chapters. We begin with A.V. Dicey's classic view that dominated twentieth-century thinking about conventions and continues to influence constitutional lawyers.

The legal view of conventions: Dicey's legacy

A.V. Dicey, the Vinerian Professor of English Law at Oxford, published the *Law of the Constitution* in 1885, revising subsequent editions over the next thirty years to take account of major developments in UK and Commonwealth governments. The eighth edition was published in 1914, with subsequent editions since his death. Although Dicey has been roundly criticised by political scientists (e.g. McLean 2010), he has cast a long shadow over constitutional thinking in Westminster systems.

Dicey focused on three leading principles: the sovereignty of parliament, the rule of law and the conventions of the constitution (Dicey 1973). Dicey's treatment of all three of these leading principles was from a legal perspective. The sovereignty of parliament was the foundational principle recognised by courts, and the laws passed by parliament were supreme. The parliament was from a legal point of view the absolute sovereign of the British Empire, and every Act of Parliament was binding on courts throughout its dominions.

These sweeping claims were a legal fiction – albeit a powerful one – in Dicey's time, and hardly captured the autonomy of the increasingly independent nations that once were colonial dominions. Nevertheless, the fiction of parliamentary sovereignty in the United Kingdom continued to have legal currency (Goldsworthy 2010), in part because of its restraint in attempting to exercise such sovereignty and in part through a curious transference of sovereignty thinking and discourse to the parliaments of Canada, Australia and New Zealand. The UK parliament had established the constitutional systems of those countries through exercising its sovereign power, it was said, and the national parliaments so established became parliamentary clones in exercising sovereignty in their domains. The sovereignty of dominion parliaments was restricted in leaving much of foreign policy making to the imperial UK parliament, and for federal countries like Canada and Australia domestic sovereignty was said to be divided between national and provincial or state parliaments.

Not surprisingly in this world of legal parliamentary sovereignty and the rule of law, constitutional conventions were only second best. Dicey's mature view is summed up in his answer to the question 'Have there been during the last thirty years notable changes in the conventions of the constitution?' This question is posed in his opening discussion of the conventions of the constitution in the eighth edition of his book. His answer distinguished two sorts of conventions:

> namely, first, new rules or customs which still continue to be mere constitutional understandings or conventions, and, secondly, understandings of conventions which have since 1884 either been converted into laws or are closely connected with changes of law. These may appropriately be termed 'enacted conventions'.
>
> (Dicey [1885] 1973: lxxvi)

So here we have it: mere conventions or customs if they remain as such, or otherwise conventions that have become law or are closely connected to laws. This view colours Dicey's answer to the subsequent question as to why conventions are obeyed and how they are enforced. His answer is not because of political consensus or the power of public opinion but 'nothing else than the force of the law'. The sanction that constrains the 'boldest political adventurer to obey the fundamental principles of the constitution and the conventions in which these principles are expressed, is in fact that the breach of those principles will almost immediately bring the offender into conflict with the Courts and the law of the land' (Dicey [1885] 1973: 445). This is clearly not the case as our subsequent political account of conventions makes clear. Nor is there the sharp distinction between conventions that are customs or 'mere constitutional understandings' and 'enacted conventions' that become law. In Chapter 2 Nicholas Aroney provides a far more nuanced and complex account of law and convention.

Dicey acknowledged the fact that 'political sovereignty' based on the will of the electorate or nation underpinned both the supremacy of the elected House of Commons and the rule that gives the appointment and control of the government mainly to the House of Commons, but treated these as 'understandings' or 'customs'. They comprise the modern code of 'constitutional morality' that 'secures, though in a roundabout way, what is called abroad the "sovereignty of the people" ' (Dicey [1885] 1973: 431).

Dicey influenced the constitutional thinking in Westminster countries for generations, particularly among constitutional lawyers who dominated the study of constitutions. Their focus was on constitutional law and court decisions, viewing conventions as customs or political practices that had inferior status. For the most part conventions were neglected by political scientists as being part of a constitutional lawyers' domain. To properly base conventions, we need to take a more realistic political approach that puts conventions at the core of the constitution with the same basic foundation as constitutional law, both of which are interrelated parts of the constitutional system. To use Dicey's terms we need to go beyond accepting the legal sovereignty of parliament and probe the basis of its political sovereignty. This requires an account of Westminster-style constitutional systems that have parliament and responsible government as primary institutions.

The political view of conventions

The political approach to conventions draws upon the larger political view of constitutional systems that pays primary attention to the nature of constitutions as systems of government that perform the complex process of governing and are accepted by the people, political elites and citizens, in which they operate. Accordingly, the UK constitutional system has at its core the primacy of Parliament, and in modern times, of the House of Commons as the elected house of parliament. Dicey's foundational law principle whereby the courts acknowledge parliamentary sovereignty is the legal recognition of this political state of affairs. There is no prior legal principle or rule that established such sovereignty; nor does the parliament have absolute sovereignty, but rather a politically limited authority and jurisdiction. We might restate these two key points in positive terms: UK parliamentary sovereignty is based on convention, and it is limited by political factors. The evidence for these two propositions is realistic and historical.

The primacy or legislative authority of parliament is based on its general acceptance within the polity of the United Kingdom. This fact is well recognised by the prominent legal scholar H.L.A. Hart, who states that general acceptance is 'a complex phenomena, in a sense divided between official and ordinary citizens, who contribute to it and so to the *existence* of a legal system in different ways'. Hart explained further:

> The officials of the system may be said to acknowledge explicitly such fundamental rules conferring legislative authority: the legislators do this when they make laws in accordance with the rules which empower them to do so: the courts when they identify, as laws to be applied by them, the laws made by those thus qualified, and the experts when they guide the ordinary citizens by reference to the laws so made. The ordinary citizen manifests his acceptance largely by acquiescence in the results of these official operations. He keeps the law. . .
>
> (Hart [1961] 1972: 59/60)

Evidence for the existence of a legal system, Hart argues, depends on the congruence or acceptance of 'two different sectors of social life', the official and the citizens: 'Crudely put, the facts are that the rules recognized as valid at the official level area are generally obeyed' (Hart [1961] 1972: 114). This is the ultimate 'rule of recognition' on which legal systems are based.

While Hart is discussing the foundations of a legal system, his observations that its existence depends on the recognition and acceptance of two groups, officials and citizens, applies more generally to constitutional systems. So also does his example of 'the embryology of legal systems' in the Commonwealth countries. As Canada, Australia and New Zealand became progressively autonomous nations with their legal systems, the legislative authority by the Westminster Parliament was reduced and finally terminated. This was achieved through a series of Commonwealth conferences with decisions formalised in various declarations and legislation at Westminster and in the national parliaments, and recognised by the courts. Legal recognition followed and formally registered political achievement, even if there were unresolved legal conundrums such as a supposed sovereign Westminster Parliament having its sovereignty reduced.

Scottish devolution, and possible secession, is a case where Westminster's authority has been restricted by the political necessity to give autonomy to Scotland and the Scottish Parliament to manage Scottish affairs. While Scottish people recently voted not to separate from the United Kingdom, the decision was theirs to make. It is no longer the case that an oligarchic few could change Scotland's status through an act of union, and the people acquiesce. Nor does a legalist perspective, albeit the 'soft law' one of Aileen McHarg, provide a plausible narrative. In her account that relies on traditional notions of the legal sovereignty of Westminster,

> the Sewell convention gives some recognition to the Scottish Parliament's claim to political sovereignty whilst maintaining the legal supremacy of the Westminster Parliament, just as decades earlier the conventions declared at successive Imperial Conferences acknowledged the growing political equality of the United Kingdom and its Dominions whilst retaining Westminster's formal status as an Imperial Parliament'.
>
> (McHarg 2008: 868)

Exaggerated notions of legal sovereignty and supremacy are retained with political reality allowed in as a soft law qualifier. It is preferable to acknowledge the primacy of changing political reality and constitutional systems, and seek appropriate legal terminology for their formal recognition.

Constitutional systems together with their component conventions and legal systems are political arrangements. In Russell Hardin's mega conventional view that he draws from the eighteenth-century political philosopher David Hume: 'Government derives its power (not its right) to rule by some specific form of coordination that is a convention and the populace acquiesces in that rule by its own convention' (Hardin 2013: 59). In other words, the whole constitutional system, including its legal and conventional parts, is a particular sort of grand coordinating system that is conventional in form. That it is a system of government requires the second convention of recognition and acceptance or acquiescence by those within its jurisdiction. Courts and law are part of this constitutional system, albeit with distinctive organisational form and rules of operation.

Conventions work in ordering the parliamentary legislature constituting the executive government in Westminster parliamentary systems because they are broadly supported, accepted or acquiesced to by both political elites and the people, or at least those who are more engaged and active citizens. That conventions work in a routine but flexible way in shaping legislative and executive government is hardly contestable because the four parliamentary democracies under consideration, the United Kingdom, Canada, Australia and New Zealand, are among the most stable, enduring and well-governed polities. In these countries it is clearly apparent that conventions operate and are broadly supported by political elites and the citizenry. There is some debate in the literature about the character of popular support: whether it really is strong support or weaker acquiescence on the part of the people. For Russell Hardin, '*acquiescence is the compelling fact*' for grounding 'the dual-convention theory of government' (2013: 60; emphasis in original).

Hardin's critical realism that draws on Hume rejects alternative contract theories of government deriving from Thomas Hobbes and John Locke that were prominent in Hume's time, and still have currency today (Ginsberg 2013: 182). Locke had written his influential *Second Treatise of Government* to justify the Glorious Revolution of 1688 when parliamentary oligarchs terminated the absolutist Stewart line in favour of a limited monarchy. According to Locke's account of the origins of government, people who were naturally free and equal came together and agreed to enter civil or political society, exchanging their natural rights for civil or political rights. They agreed to the broad framework of government, and were entitled to change it, or key parts of it, if it became tyrannical and unsuitable for their interests. The formation of government was a solemn agreement or sort of original contract in the first instance and required at least 'tacit' consent for its continuation. Various forms of contract theory informed much of eighteenth-century political thinking and were influential in the constitutional founding of the United States. As Locke made clear, his was a theoretical rather than a historical account of the origins and basis of legitimate government. This was not always acknowledged by subsequent contract theorists reflecting on the constitutional convocations that drafted the American constitution and the rhetoric of articulate founders like Jefferson in drafting the Declaration of Independence that justified severing British rule, and

Madison in explaining and defending the new American constitution in the influential *Federalist Papers.*

The critical realist view has an alternative account of constitutional origins, and a different intellectual pedigree. Hume's account of the constitutional break that brought William and Mary to the throne in 1688 is one of elite action and popular acquiescence: 'it was only the majority of seven hundred, who determined that change for ten millions...[T]he bulk of those ten millions acquiesced willingly in the determination' (Hume [1772/1777] 1994: 191). Hume did allow that the consent of the people would be a just foundation of government, but that it was rare and 'never almost in its full extent'. Nevertheless, as the case of switching monarchic succession to William and Mary showed, constitutional change can be effected and become widely accepted (Hume [1772/1777] 1994: 192).

Such pragmatic empiricism that acknowledges the fact of, and support for, government and basic changes to government structures does need some further explanation. Why do political elites and the people governed continue to support or acquiesce in the system of government that orders and limits their behaviour? Hume's answer to this broad question of allegiance and obedience to the law was 'common interest and utility'. '[I]f government were totally useless, it never could have place' Hume argued, 'and that the sole foundation of the duty of allegiance is the *advantage*, which it procures to society, by preserving peace and order among mankind' (Hume [1777] 1972: 205, 211, emphasis in original). If this seems a weak conclusion, it is in line with the earlier tradition of Hobbes and Locke that people entered political society under government in order to achieve individual security, peace and order. At the end of the day, according to Hume, matters will likely be decided by 'an appeal to general opinion': 'there is really no other standard, by which any controversy can ever be decided' (Hume [1772/1777] 1994: 200). Hume might have added force of arms that often achieve or facilitate, at least in part, the founding of political systems or major changes within them.

Explaining the existence and endurance of systems of government has been a major concern of political science since Renaissance times with Machiavelli, the ultra-realist, finding the explanation in a combination of political circumstances and the character of, and dynamic interrelationship between, the rulers and people. To succeed, Machiavelli's Prince needed to tailor his behaviour to suit the times and the character of the people – ruling for the common good if the people were virtuous, or as a ruthless tyrant if they were corrupt. Similarly for republics, that Machiavelli preferred, provided the people had the qualities that a republic required, rulers needed to curb their ambitions for the public good, as was the case in the ancient Roman republic before Caesar and the emperors. This realist strand was also prominent in the American constitutional founding that assumed the self-interested behaviour of politicians but sought to channel and curb this through clever institutional architecture incorporating the division of powers and checks and balances within and between the branches of government.

According to modern realists like Ran Hirschl, stakeholders abide by constitutional constraints out of self-interest. Although Hirschl is discussing the foundation of constitutions, his observations might apply equally to their ongoing support. Political actors who voluntarily establish institutions that appear to limit their institutional flexibility, Hirschl says, 'must assume that the clipping of their wings' will be compensated for by the limits imposed on rivals and the reduced risk of other non-favourable political developments in the future (Hirschl 2013: 167). Limiting political actors and channelling their actions are functions of conventions to which we now turn.

Conventions that bind

Whether some practice is a convention or not is fundamental for understanding what conventions are and a threshold issue for projects purporting to codify them. We might begin with two basic aspects: conventions are principles and practices of government that are both recognised and binding. The two aspects are necessary: recognition of conventions among key political actors and commentators is an obvious prerequisite; their acceptance as binding is also required if conventions are to govern political activity. This dual requirement has been generally recognised by leading scholars in the past. Sir Kenneth Wheare, the Australian who was prominent at Oxford, defined conventions in his *Modern Constitutions*: 'By convention is meant a binding rule, a rule of behaviour accepted as obligatory by those concerned in the working of the Constitution' (Wheare 1951: 27).

Wheare also reconsiders earlier classifications of constitutions in terms of rigidity and flexibility (*see* Bryce 1884). While the 'procedures' for changing conventions are not rigid like many written constitutions, in practice they are not easy to alter due to the very absence of a tangible and accepted means of immediate change.

Others have given a more extensive set of requirements that have to be met in recognising conventions, with their binding requisite being an integral part. Sir Ivor Jennings proposed a tripartite test that turned on three questions, to which he gave partial answers:

> first, what are the precedents; secondly, did the actors in the precedents believe that they were bound by a rule; and thirdly, is there a reason for the rule? A single precedent with a good reason may be enough to establish the rule. A whole string of precedents without such a reason will be of no avail, unless it is perfectly certain that the persons concerned regarded them as bound by it.
>
> (Jennings 1959: 136)

Jennings' test is significant because it was adopted by the Canadian Supreme Court in deciding the *Patriation Reference* case (1981: SCR 753). Paradoxically for a court of law, but in an advisory opinion, the Supreme Court of Canada advised that there was a convention requiring the federal government to have substantial provincial support before it could properly advise the UK Parliament to make amendments to the Canadian constitution affecting provincial powers. This occurred just prior to the patriation of the constitution when the Trudeau government sought to make amendments without provincial support. Regardless of this weighty endorsement, Jennings' test is hardly definitive and its application depends on judgement and reasonable consensus (Heard 2014: 172ff.). All three parts of Jennings' test are contestable: sorting out legitimate precedents; agreeing on what is a good, or a good-enough reason, to establish a rule; and being satisfied that actors believed they were bound by a rule. In this case the Canadian Supreme Court by a majority decision supported the federalist side in a political dispute about a convention, and that was enough to carry the day.

Geoffrey Marshall, in his classic account of *Constitutional Conventions* (1984), discusses both the recognition and binding character of conventions at some length, but without any crisp resolution. Marshall argues that Wheare's 'emphasis on *obligatory* behaviour ... may obscure the point that the conventions, as a body of constitutional morality, deal not just with obligations or duties but confer rights, powers, and duties' (1984: 7). In summarising his views, Marshall concludes that 'No general reason needs to be advanced to account for compliance with duty-imposing conventions beyond the fact that when they are obeyed ... they are believed to formulate valid rules of obligation' (Marshall 1984: 210). This does not take us very far in determining what are or are not conventions. Saying that a convention requires belief on the part of the observer that they are valid rules of obligation does not preclude mistaken belief. Nor is it clear that we should preclude those where observance is due to political calculation or rational choice rather than belief.

What kind of obligation does a duty-imposing convention impose? Marshall asks this in discussing Jennings' test that actors must believe they are bound by a rule. Marshall's best answer is 'the critical morality of the Constitution' that he prefers to the 'positive morality of the Constitution' because it enables one to judge actual behaviour against what 'the political actors *ought* to feel obliged by' (Marshall 1984: 11–12). Although it follows Dicey and Jennings, this all seems to make the discernment of conventions too much a psychological guessing game. Do we need to know what political actors believe or ought to believe about rules, rather than observing patterns of behaviour and political consensus?

On the recognition of conventions, Marshall is clear that 'If a convention is to be a guide to conduct it must be known what course of action it prescribes' (Marshall 1984: 211). But as he immediately acknowledges, conventions are plagued by vagueness, and he instances the Canadian convention upheld by the Canadian Supreme Court in the *Patriation Reference* case. The Court's decision added weight to the provincial case, and no doubt tipped the political balance in their favour, although dissenting judges took opposing views. In any case, Marshall points out that conventions have a spectrum from clarity to vagueness that other rules of behaviour share: 'namely that what they require in some clear cases is known but what they require in more marginal or arguable cases cannot be stated in advance' (Marshall 1984: 211). As the following chapters show, there are multiple ways and instruments in which conventions can be specified, even if some are contested.

Codification and constitutional reform

Contemporary discussions and debates about conventions often focus on whether to codify and to what extent, which leads to broader issues of constitutional reform. Codes are essentially written forms, and can include codes of conduct, guides, manuals and even legislation. In this volume we make a distinction between this latter form and the others. Codification in written forms other than through legislation and the constitution does not change the status of conventions. While it makes conventions clearer, such formulations are provisional, contentious and subject to adjustment and change. Yet these are the main forms of codification, with only very few examples of political actors seeking to legally or constitutionally codify conventions, unless they are part of other constitutional reforms.

Rather, practitioners and scholars have generally been more interested in forms of codification that can be easily updated, recognising that one of the reasons for creating a code is to help clarify new and at times uncertain situations. Codes articulate how conventions are viewed at a particular time but need to evolve as conventions change. Many contemporary codes are endorsed by each new government, and that provides an opportunity to revise the code and reflect on its previous application (e.g. New Zealand Cabinet Office 2008). However, this process vests power in the major political parties, with other political actors only able to provide input into the process if they are in an influential position during the government formation phase. These factors are all important for understanding the tension between stability and adaptability of conventions.

Calls for codification through legislative or constitutional means generally arise when more significant constitutional reforms are being proposed. These more significant constitutional reforms tend to be ones that democratise, but, at the same time, weaken the political positions of the older major parties. For example, devolution in the United Kingdom and the introduction of the proportionally representative electoral system in New Zealand have brought conventions to the fore, along with a plethora of new political actors that see new political systems as an opportunity to adapt practices that have unduly empowered the incumbents. In these cases, all actors have an interest in clarifying what the practice should be, and legislative or constitutional change is seen to be the best way of guaranteeing ongoing compliance. Codification in New Zealand and the United Kingdom has been more common, where change has been greater and constitutional entrenchment less than in Canada and Australia. It is also no coincidence that these countries lack written constitutions.

While in Australia and Canada it is more difficult to pursue substantial legal or constitutional codification for many reasons, there is also a particular deference to the written constitution and often debates will centre on deciphering the original intentions of the founders. Major crises such as that of Australia in 1975 and Canada over prorogation in 2008 leave little hope of resolution because of the clash of conventions and ongoing dispute over their application. Yet in these countries, proposals for constitutional change still show the inextricable link between democratisation and clarifying conventions through codification. In Canada, such issues include the appointed upper house, accommodating diverse interests in the federation and multi-party power sharing. In Australia, moves towards a republic have raised questions about the mandate of the head of state (whether or not to directly elect) and the reserve powers of the current governor-general. In the following chapters we consider common issues across the four countries, while also focusing on the unique features of each country.

References

Barber, N.W. 2009. 'Laws and Constitutional Conventions', *Law Quarterly Review* 125: 294–309.

Bryce, James 1884. *Constitutions.* New York: Oxford University Press American Branch.

Dicey, A.V. [1885] 1973. *Introduction to the Study of the Law of the Constitution*, 10th edn. London: Macmillan.

Evatt, H.V. 1936. *The King and His Dominion Governors.* Oxford University Press.

Galligan, Denis and Versteeg, Mila (eds.) 2013. *Social and Political Foundations of Constitutions.* Cambridge University Press.

Ginsberg, Tom 2013. 'Constitutions as Contract, Constitutions as Charters', in Galligan, Denis and Versteeg, Mila (eds.), *Social and Political Foundations of Constitutions.* Cambridge University Press, 182–204.

Goldsworthy, Jeffrey 2010. *Parliamentary Sovereignty: Contemporary Debates.* Cambridge University Press.

Hardin, Russell 2013. 'Why a Constitution?', in Galligan, Denis and Versteeg, Mila (eds.), *Social and Political Foundations of Constitutions.* Cambridge University Press, 51–72.

Hart, H.L.A. [1961] 1972. *The Concept of the Law.* Oxford: Clarendon Press.

Heard, Andrew 2014. *Canadian Constitutional Conventions: The Marriage of Law & Politics*, 2nd edn. Oxford University Press.

Hirschl, Ran 2013. 'The Strategic Foundations of Constitutions', in Galligan, Denis and Versteeg, Mila (eds.), *Social and Political Foundations of Constitutions.* Cambridge University Press, 157–81.

Hume, David. [1772/1777] 1994. 'Of the Original Contract', Essay Twenty-Two, in Haakonssen, Knud (ed.), *Political Essays.* Cambridge University Press, 186–201.

Hume, David. [1777] 1972. 'Of Political Society', Section IV, in Selby-Bigge, L.A. (ed.), *Enquiries Concerning the Human Understanding and Concerning the Principles of Morals..* Oxford: Clarendon Press, 205–11.

Jennings, Sir Ivor 1959. *The Law and the Constitution*, 5th edn. University of London Press.

Katz, Richard S. and Mair, Peter. 1995. 'Changing Models of Party Organization and Party Democracy'. *Party Politics* 1(1): 5–28.

Koeble, Thomas A. 1995. 'The New Institutionalism in Political Science and Sociology'. *Comparative Politics* 27(2): 231–43.

March, James G. and Olsen, Johan P. 1989. *Rediscovering Institutions: The Organizational Basis of Politics.* New York: Free Press.

Marsh, Ian and Miller, Raymond 2012. *Democratic Decline and Democratic Renewal.* Cambridge University Press.

Marshall, Geoffrey 1984. *Constitutional Conventions.* Oxford: Clarendon Press.

McHarg, Aileen 2008. 'Reforming the United Kingdom Constitution: Law, Convention, Soft Law', *Modern Law Review* 71: 853–77.

McLean, Iain 2010. *What's Wrong with the British Constitution.* Oxford University Press.

New Zealand Cabinet Office 2008. *Cabinet Manual.* Wellington, New Zealand: Cabinet Office, Department of the Prime Minister and Cabinet.

Patriation Reference 1981. *Reference re: Resolution to Amend the Constitution.* 1 SCR 753.

Sirota, Leonid 2011.'Towards a Jurisprudence of Constitutional Conventions', *Oxford University Commonwealth Law Journal* 11: 29–51.

Wheare, K.C. 1951. *Modern Constitutions.* Oxford University Press.

2

Law and convention

NICHOLAS ARONEY

This chapter focuses on the distinction between law and convention. Is it conceptually coherent? Is it morally justified? Is it borne out by the practices of political actors and courts? There are several ways in which the issue might be tackled. In this chapter, one way it is addressed is by looking at how commentators describe the operation of their political systems and what would-be reformers advocate when they believe that the conventions are not being properly followed. Sometimes they call for an authoritative statement of the conventions, sometimes they promote their codification into binding law and sometimes they call for the courts to recognise and enforce them. Another way to address the matter is to consider how the courts approach cases when they are asked to take the existence of a convention into consideration and sometimes to enforce it. In such cases, it is necessary to consider whether it is meaningful to distinguish between 'recognition' and 'enforcement' of a practical norm in legal adjudication. In the background there are further questions about how we define 'law', and also 'convention': especially by what criteria we identify them, and whether the criteria might in each instance. One's theories of law and of political morality are unavoidably implicated in any such inquiry.

Definitions, distinctions and questions

The modern, technical use of the term 'convention' is a creature of the nineteenth century. Commonly attributed to A. V. Dicey, the term was first used in a recognisably modern sense by an historian, E. A. Freeman, while the underlying concept also appeared in the work of their contemporaries Macaulay, Mill, Bagehot, Hearn, Todd, Anson and Maitland as well as in the earlier writings of Burke (Hood Phillips 1966: 137). In its Old French and Latin roots, the term 'convention' had a very old meaning associated with the idea of a 'convening' or a 'coming together', in the form of a 'meeting' or 'assembly', as well as in the sense of an 'agreement, covenant or treaty'. In the eighteenth century, it also took on the meaning of a general 'practice' or 'customary behaviour', such as the 'customs', 'traditions', 'mores' or 'positive morality' of a particular society (e.g. Hume [1739–40] 2000: III.ii.2). But it was Dicey, drawing on Freeman, who stamped upon the term its current technical sense, when he asserted that the British constitution consists of two kinds of 'rules': first, 'law' or legal rules in the 'strictest sense', that is, rules that are enforceable by the courts, and second, 'conventions, understandings, habits, or practices' which 'regulate [the] conduct' of political actors but are not judicially enforced and have not been codified into law by legislation (1973: lxix, cxlvi).

Dicey's insistence on the distinction between law and convention, and the criteria by which he distinguished them (i.e. enforcement by the courts and legislative codification), provides an indication of the influence of legal positivism on his thought (Waldron 2006). The significance he ascribed to the role of convention is, however, also a measure of the extent to which he sought to integrate the historical perspectives of those like Burke, Hume and Freeman, who emphasised the role of custom and tradition in the evolution of British society and government, with the insights of those like Hearn and Bagehot, who had drawn attention to the vital role of conventions in the contemporary operation of the Westminster system (Phillips 1966; Dicey 1973: 11–20; Berman 1994: 1735–7; Jaconelli 2005: 171). Synthesising these perspectives, Dicey argued that the term 'constitutional law' had to be understood to embrace both 'law' (i.e. that which is enforceable by the courts) and 'convention', which he also referred to as legally unenforceable 'constitutional morality' (Dicey 1973: 21–2).

But in what does this constitutional morality consist? How easily can it be identified as distinct from law? Here, there is a problem according to some critics that conventions are incorrigibly amorphous and ill-defined; they lack a well-settled set of defining criteria and their exact content is often contested. Take the approach of Ivor Jennings as a prominent example. He asked: 'Firstly, what are the precedents? Secondly, did the actors in the precedents believe they were bound by a rule? And thirdly, is there a good reason for the rule?' (1959: 136). Jennings thus proposed three criteria for determining whether a convention exists. Did he understand them to be necessary 'elements' that must all be satisfied for a convention to exist, or did he intend them to be understood as merely indicative 'factors'? He implied the latter when he further said that:

> A single precedent with a good reason may be enough to establish the rule. A whole string of precedents without such a reason will be of no avail, unless it is perfectly certain that the persons concerned regarded them as bound by it.

But if the relevant criteria are only factors to be considered, if the weighing of these factors depends on judgements about the beliefs of political actors and the underlying normative reasons for their existence, and if there is no authoritative process or institution by which these judgements are made, then the very existence and exact content of conventions is often going to be controversial.

Colin Munro put it this way, when he observed of conventions, contrasting them with legal rules:

> There is no authoritative mark of their existence, so that uncertainty abounds. The sources of convention are open-ended and diverse, and no importance attaches to them. Conventions have no unifying feature and so form merely a 'discrete unconnected set'. The existence of a legal rule is shown by reference to a formal sign that it is of a system, but conventions have no system.

Munro's criticism was predicated on a sharp distinction between law and convention, based on the existence of a 'formal sign' by which the rules that form part of the law are identified (Hart 1961: 54–5; Munro 1975: 232–3; Maley 1985: 132). However, the sharp distinction that Dicey proposed and Munro defended has been the subject of much criticism, usually related to doubts about the theory of law upon which the distinction is based. It is said that law is ultimately no different from convention because both law and convention consist of rules which regulate conduct, and law, like convention, ultimately rests on customs, understandings, mores and practices of political morality. From this point of view it is argued that conventions can be treated as if they are law. They can be acknowledged and taken into consideration by the courts. They may even 'crystallise' into law and be enforced as such by the courts.

T. R. S. Allan has presented a very strong version of this line of argument (1986: 312–13; 1993: 244). He has put it this way:

> The distinction between law and convention, derived from Dicey and based on court enforcement, is too dogmatic. It is generally accepted that conventions are 'recognised' by the courts: the many examples of judicial reasoning dependent on the existence and force of convention are well known. No water-tight divide exists, however, between recognition and enforcement. To recognise a convention, in a context where legal doctrine can be invoked in its support, is in practice to enforce it.

> The law/convention distinction, though sometimes convenient for purposes of exposition, provides no real assistance in adjudication. It obscures the important issue: is the situation before the court one which demands a legal remedy? The answer will turn on whether the matter is justiciable and whether an appropriate remedy exists. . . .The justiciability of a constitutional convention will depend on its normative character and its significance as part of the general constitutional-order.

There are multiple claims in this passage that stand out for scrutiny. It is pertinent to ask how well they are borne out in the way that the courts deal with cases involving conventions.

Geoffrey Marshall distinguished several ways in which conventions can become part of the law or used in legal argument (1984: 14–15). Sometimes the content of a convention may be specifically enacted into law. For example, the Parliament Act 1911 (UK) formalised relations between the two houses of the UK Parliament that had formerly been matters of convention. The Statute of Westminster 1931 (UK) similarly enacted into law aspects of the conventional relationship that had developed between the United Kingdom and several of its former colonies. The constitutional statutes of numerous former British colonies also refer to and sometimes specifically enact the content of particular conventions associated with the system of parliamentary responsible government. In other instances, Marshall pointed out, conventions can be said to have an 'indirect' legal effect upon the development of related areas of law. In *Attorney-General* v. *Jonathan Cape* ([1976] QB 752), for example, the convention of the collective responsibility of the Ministry was cited in support of the conclusion that the legal-equitable principle protecting confidential information would apply, in principle, to a breach of cabinet solidarity. However, as Marshall further observed, and not without understatement, 'examples of *direct* conversion or acknowledgement of non-legal rules as enforceable rules of law are hard to find' (1984: 15). Although conventions are sometimes invoked by courts in the application or interpretation of existing rules of law, Marshall insisted that conventions are not direct sources of legal rights and duties (1984: 210–11).

David Feldman has made two salient observations in relation to Allan's claims about the 'crystallisation' of conventions into enforceable law (2013: 112). First, he has pointed out that 'important conventions often contradict rather than complement the formal, legal rules'. To the extent that this is the case, if conventions may sometimes crystallise into law as Allan maintains, and especially if they were specifically to be enforced, then they would produce new rules of law that contradict and displace existing rules of law. This is an outcome that is significantly more far-reaching than the use of conventions in legal reasoning to support arguments about the way in which the common law should develop. Feldman goes on to point out that 'when lawyers make use of conventions, they do not blur the distinction between norms which are identifiably legal as having been made by a legally-authorised institution and those which are not; their roles are quite distinct'. It needs to be acknowledged that conventions are used in judicial reasoning and that, to this extent, the line between law and convention is a permeable one. But beyond this, the most that can safely be said is that the legal enforceability of conventions is a conceptual possibility (Wheare 1962; Maley 1985; Waldron 2006; Barber 2009). An example of legal enforcement remains something of a 'holy grail' (Barber 2009: 302).

The importance of constitutional context

Individual conventions always operate in the context of a larger collection of practices, norms and laws existing in a specific political community or among a group of related communities. Sometimes a particular convention is part of a relatively well-defined set of conventions. The core conventions of parliamentary responsible government operating within Westminster-derived systems are of this kind. Other conventions have a more discrete character. Although these conventions remain system-dependent, we unreflectively refer to them individually, in the singular and not in the plural. Examples include the Sewel convention in the United Kingdom, the patriation convention in Canada, and the presidential two-term convention in the United States (Neale 2009).

Moreover, conventions mean different things in different contexts. Sometimes they operate to clarify the meaning of ambiguous language used in written constitutions or constitutional statutes; other times they supplement incomplete language or gaps in the law with specific procedures or practices necessary to give the law practical effect; and yet other times they contradict or displace the practical operation of rules of law by requiring legally discretionary powers to be exercised in certain ways or in accordance with particular expectations (Jones and Iyer 1989: 407–9). How these different kinds of conventions operate depends a great deal on constitutional context. Within a Westminster setting, the most important conventions are in the nature of duty-imposing rules that control the exercise of legally conferred powers, especially the prerogative powers of the Queen in the United Kingdom and her vice-regal representatives in Canada, Australia and New Zealand (Jaconelli 2005: 154–5; Sirota 2011: 30–1). In the United States, by contrast, conceptions of the executive powers of the president are very different, not least because the institutions of president and Congress are separately established by the Constitution, which provides for their appointment through distinct electoral processes. In this setting, the notion that the president might, by convention, become 'responsible' to the Congress in the Westminster sense is barely imaginable.

Some commentators have gone so far as to claim that such is the authority accorded to the written Constitution in the United States that while conventions may serve to clarify or supplement the language of the Constitution, they cannot contradict or supplant its provisions (Jones and Iyer 1989: 408). Four distinguished American text writers similarly observe that while both the Westminster and American systems rely upon 'text and tradition', in England 'the written constitutional documents are islands of text in a sea of unwritten convention', while in the United States the written constitution 'is like a great continent, a land mass with scattered lakes and rivers and ponds of tradition' (Paulsen et al. 2010: 22). These views may well exaggerate the distinction (Horwill 1925: 7). But the existence of a written constitution does seem to make a difference. For example, the convention that American presidents hold office for only two terms, although supported by practice and political expectation, could be successfully defied by Franklin Roosevelt largely because the Constitution provides for an electoral system that makes no mention of the convention. Roosevelt's re-election prompted a movement to amend the Constitution itself to stipulate that a president could not be elected for a third term (United States Constitution, Amendment XXII, proposed 1947, ratified 1951; Bowden and MacDonald 2012: 400). The 'failure' of the supposed convention thus had to be remedied by formal constitutional amendment. In Westminster systems, however, such matters are regulated in an entirely different way. The length of time that a prime minister holds office is determined ultimately by the parliament (in most if not all such systems, the lower house of the parliament). The parliament could, in theory, enact a law that limited the period of time during which a person could hold the office of prime minister, but there is as yet no felt need to do so, essentially because the parliament retains the capacity to remove a prime minister whenever it wishes. Indeed, movements in Westminster systems to codify the conventions or otherwise to clarify and consolidate their content and application arise precisely when there is concern that legal powers are or may be exercised in a manner thought to be contrary to convention, as occurred in Australia in 1975 in relation to the power of the Australian state premiers to appoint replacement senators to fill casual vacancies, the power of Australian Senate to refuse to pass the annual supply bills and the power of the governor-general to dismiss the prime minister (Sawer 1977; Cooray 1979).

Even among political systems within the Westminster tradition there are important differences. The particular political circumstances of each Westminster-derived polity give rise to numerous specific differences in how individual conventions are understood and practised (Bowden and MacDonald 2012: 394–7). One of the most important distinctions concerns those which operate within the context of a written constitution (e.g. Canada and Australia) and those which do not (e.g. the United Kingdom and New Zealand). Relatedly, there is an important distinction between the United Kingdom and the three other Commonwealth countries in this respect: in the United Kingdom what is fundamentally at stake is the direct, unmediated legal powers of a hereditary monarch and a sovereign parliament, whereas in the former colonies, these original concentrations of executive and legislative power are legally mediated through appointed governors and derivative parliaments (in the case of federal Canada and Australia, multiple governments and parliaments in each country, with executive and legislative powers distributed between them). When this is combined, as in Canada and Australia, with the existence of a written constitution and constitutional judicial review, there is not quite the same urgent necessity to control the 'raw' power of Crown and parliament. Rather, where a written constitution exists, the debate about conventions usually revolves around conceptions of the relatively fixed political order that the constitution authoritatively establishes as a matter of enforceable law. In other words, the existence, nature and scope of a convention is considered, not only in relation to a long-established set of practices and expectations, but in terms of its relationship to the 'plan' of government instituted by the written constitution (Walters 2008: 38; Gardner 2011).

To be sure, in all Westminster-derived systems there are concerns about Executive domination of parliament, a development which has a tendency both to consolidate executive and legislative power in the same hands and to weaken the capacity of the parliament to hold the Executive to account, especially in the absence of an effective upper house (Lord Hailsham 1976; Aroney, Prasser and Nethercote 2008; Baker 2009). Moreover, in all such systems constitutional crises frequently give rise to a great deal of interest in identifying and clarifying the existence and proper operation of the conventions, such as by codification or some other authoritative statement (Bowden and MacDonald 2012: 398). But in the United Kingdom especially, one senses a quite palpable desire among recent commentators to strengthen and extend existing constitutional controls on the Crown and the parliament in the form of both conventions and laws. For, in the absence of a justiciable written constitution, conventions have to do most of the work in constraining political power (Jaconelli 2005: 149; Blick 2012: 1). Allan's work in this area is a very clear example. In much the same vein, Mark Elliot urges judges to enforce conventions in order to place legal limitations on the otherwise sovereign powers of the parliament (2002: 375, 2003: 35–40). As Nick Barber points out, Elliot's argument is open to the interpretation that he is calling on the courts to engage in acts of 'juridification through barefaced judicial *fiat*' (2009: 298). Similarly, Aileen McHarg has argued that recent proposals to promote the acknowledgement and declaration of a whole range of new conventions are best understood as attempts to *influence* constitutional behaviour by way of 'soft' rather than 'hard' law (2008: 856). Marshall put the point very candidly (1985: 39) when he said:

> It would seem better to define conventions as the rules of behaviour that *ought* to be regarded as binding by those concerned in working the constitution when they have correctly interpreted the precedents and the relevant constitutional principles. This definition is better at least for academics. Without it, it would not be possible to say, in the face of a consensus of belief by politicians, that although they believed a convention to exist, they were nevertheless mistaken. What political scientist would want to give up the right to say that?

When one compares the cases and considers the academic literature about the relationship between convention and law in various Westminster countries, perceptible differences in tone, in urgency, and in the structure and presuppositions of argument are noticeable. These differences are, in turn, further variegated when particular cases are considered, whether one is considering conventions in the context of international law, constitutional law, administrative law, statutory law, procedural law or parliamentary privilege, for example. Space does not permit a comprehensive survey of all of these instances, but some short case studies, taken from Canada, Australia, New Zealand and the United Kingdom, can serve to illustrate the importance of broader constitutional context for the operation and evolution of conventions and their use in legal argument.

Parliamentary approval of military action in the United Kingdom

The United Kingdom has recently witnessed an extended debate over whether the House of Commons should be given the opportunity to debate and vote on the deployment of armed forces overseas, and if so, what mechanism should be introduced to secure this (2006 HL 236-I: para. 3; 2007 Cm 7239: paras. 6, 42, 89–110). The issue rose to prominence following the UK government's decision to seek parliamentary approval before engaging in the Iraq war in 2003, a decision which led to calls for a requirement that the government must always do this in the future. Several parliamentary committees have reported on the question, most recently in connection with the debate in the House of Commons in 2013 concerning proposed military action in Syria (2014 HC 892: 6).

A survey of these committee reports and government documents reveals an interesting evolution. In particular, there appears to have been a significant shift in focus from the first report, in 2003, which considered whether 'there should be at least a convention' (2004 HC 422: para. 20); reports in 2006, 2007 and 2008 which contemplated and proposed its deliberate creation (Cm 7170: para. 29; Cm 7239: paras. 6, 20, 90; Cm 7342-I: para. 215); a report in 2011 declaring its existence (HC 923); a report in 2013 recommending against its codification or crystallisation into law (HL 46); and most recently, a report in 2014 expressing concern that despite precedent for the existence of the convention, many of its aspects remain uncertain, (HC 892: paras. 6, 9, citing Professor Gavin Phillipson [PCD 04], who stated at para. 3 that 'some may even still dispute its existence').

Underlying the debate is the remarkable proposition that such a convention could deliberately be brought into being as a desirable compromise between the prospect of formal oversight or none (2006 HL 236-I: para. 93). Several inquiries have gone so far as to specify substantive content for the new convention (e.g., 2006 HL 236-I: para. 110). The undoubted emergence of the Sewel convention in the United Kingdom, which requires that Westminster will 'not normally legislate with regard to devolved matters except with the agreement of the devolved legislature', supports this idea of a deliberately created convention (HL Deb, 21 July 1998, vol 592, col 791; 2013 Cm 5240: para. 13). The Cabinet Manual (discussed later) records the 'acknowledgement' by the Government in 2011 'that a convention had developed in Parliament that before troops were committed the House of Commons should have an opportunity to debate the matter' and that the government 'proposed to observe that convention except when there was an emergency and such action would not be appropriate'. The Foreign Secretary, William Hague, explained that by this emendation the convention had been 'declared' and 'formalised' (2013 HC 649: para. 6).

Nonetheless, fundamental debate over the exact constitutional status of the convention remains. In 2013, the House of Lords Constitution Committee considered that the 'existing convention . . . provides the best framework for the House of Commons to exercise political control over, and confer legitimacy upon' deployment decisions, due to the fact it 'is flexible, effective and consistent with the existing structure of parliamentary scrutiny of the executive' (2013 HL 46: para. 74). It also concluded: 'Parliamentary control over the Government in this area should remain a matter of constitutional convention' (HL 46: para. 74). In respectful disagreement with these recommendations, however, a year later the House of Commons Constitution Committee reiterated its conviction that parliament's role should be 'enshrine[d]' in law and that 'as a useful interim step' a formal parliamentary resolution should be passed in order to better secure the 'current convention' and to clarify 'some of the ambiguities that exist under current arrangements' (2014 HC 892: para. 51; McHarg 2008: 859). For some, there is a growing dissatisfaction with the use of convention alone to regulate practice, and concern that conventions are inherently susceptible to political manipulation (Hough 2000: 360, 376).

Although the same basic issues arise in Canada and Australia, the interest in establishing a corresponding convention or legal rule in these countries seems more subdued. In 2008, the Australian Greens party initiated a bill which sought 'to ensure that, as far as is constitutionally and practically possible, Australian Defence Force personnel are not sent overseas to engage in warlike actions without the approval of both Houses of Parliament' (Explanatory Memorandum, Defence Amendment (Parliamentary Approval of Overseas Service) Bill 2008 [No. 2], 2). However, when reviewing the bill, the Foreign Affairs, Defence and Trade Legislation Committee considered it not to be 'a credible piece of legislation' because 'while well intended, the bill may have unforeseen and unfortunate consequences that need to be identified and resolved' before further consideration could be given to the issue (Foreign Affairs, Defence and Trade Legislation Committee 2010: 2.102). As of yet, Australia has therefore not taken steps to codify the prerogative powers exercised by the governor-general and to make provision for parliamentary approval of troop deployment (Parliamentary Library Background Note 2010). Similarly, a report appraising the situation in Canada noted that practice over time had been inconsistent and casually concluded that 'constitutional requirements are not likely to change', though 'debate will continue' (2006 PRB 00-06E: 13). Likewise, a 2013 policy paper prepared by the Canadian Defence & Foreign Affairs Institute directly engaged with the 'British example', only to conclude that 'Canada's existing practice has many advantages, and that Canadian parliamentarians should be mindful of the risks and costs involved in adopting a constitutional convention to control the executive's military deployment prerogative' (Lagassé 2013: 1).

As the experience in Britain, Canada and Australia suggests, it seems that the absence of a written constitution in the United Kingdom is apt to evoke a greater sense of anxiety to find ways to control the otherwise 'raw' power of the Executive (e.g. 2014 HC 892: para. 9; White [PCD 01]: para. 7). Further examples are the *Governance of Britain* Green Paper issued in 2007, the subsequent White Paper and the Draft Constitutional Renewal Bill published in 2008 (Cm 7170; Cm 7342-I), which were directed to modernising the role of the executive by reducing its powers and making it more accountable to parliament and the people (for more detail and context, see Chapter 9). As McHarg observes, many of the proposed reforms suggest 'a conscious attempt to *influence* constitutional behaviour and thus the development of new constitutional norms, but without resorting to the enactment of formal law' (2008: 855–6). In Canada and Australia, where executive and legislative power is already distributed among federal and provincial or state governments under a justiciable written constitution, the debate over the existence, nature and role of conventions is markedly different. In New Zealand, where there is no written constitution, the context is different again.

Bridling power in New Zealand's 'executive paradise': the Cabinet Manual

New Zealand, like the United Kingdom, does not have a formal written constitution (Palmer 2007: 591).[1] Recent debate about the adoption of a written constitution ended inconclusively (Constitutional Advisory Panel 2013). New Zealand's constitutional evolution has been shaped profoundly by the abolition of its upper house in 1950. Coupled with first-past-the-post voting, this enabled executive governments to dominate the

[1] *The Constitution Act 1986* (NZ) is an ordinary statute of the New Zealand Parliament.

parliament, creating what came to be called an 'executive paradise' (Zines 1991: 47) marked by 'the fastest law in the West' (Palmer 1979). Routine exercise of 'unbridled power' became a matter of such widespread concern that in 1994 mixed-member proportional (MMP) voting was introduced in an effort to rebalance the system (Aroney and Thomas 2012). MMP reduces the capacity of single parties to form governments in their own right. The frequent necessity of forming coalition governments has brought change to the way conventions operate in New Zealand, but many of the new elements of the system still seem to be in a state of political flux (compare Boston and Bullock 2009 and Joseph 2009). Still today, commentators observe that New Zealand's constitutional arrangements are highly flexible, 'uncodified and fluid', and framed more by politics than law (Palmer 2005: 1). These features have fostered concern that constitutional change can occur too easily in New Zealand without public debate (Palmer 2005: 593–6). It appears that New Zealand has a highly pragmatic political culture which usually acquiesces in the many 'unheralded, apparently technical, reforms that simply slip through the system'.

One development especially relevant to the functioning of conventions in New Zealand has been the development of a written cabinet manual (see New Zealand Cabinet Office 2008). When it first appeared in 1979, the New Zealand document, like its earlier Canadian counterpart, the *Manual of Official Procedure of the Government of Canada* (1968), was intended for limited use within government circles as a guide to ministers and senior public servants (McLeay 1999: 11; Bowden and MacDonald 2012: 373–9). However, over time successive versions of the Manual were given wider exposure, so that in 1996 it was bound and sold in bookshops. The Manual is a 'working document' that describes both everyday rules and important constitutional conventions (McLeay 1999: 13).

As such, the Cabinet Manual occupies a paradoxical status in New Zealand constitutionalism. By its own lights, it is adopted by each new government at the first meeting of Cabinet. It thus purports to contain an authoritative statement of the conventions of responsible government that bind those who hold and exercise executive power, but it is itself a document made by Cabinet and is subject to revision by those whose conduct it ostensibly regulates. It is frequently 'updated', often in response to changes in underlying political arrangements between governments and their supporting parties within parliament. It is even relied upon by governments to support actions for which they lack parliamentary support.[2] And it is insisted in New Zealand that its contents are not justiciable (e.g. Kitteridge 2006). However, its adoption and amendment in New Zealand does not generate much public or academic discussion. Commentators seem therefore inclined to emphasise that its authority must depend on more than its promulgation by the executive. As McLeay has insisted, 'it is the conventions that help stamp authority on the Manual, rather than the other way around' (1999: 15). (For more detail on the status and role of the Cabinet Manual in New Zealand, see Chapter 12.)

The New Zealand example has had a particular influence in the United Kingdom. For, as Andrew Blick as observed, in both countries the lack of a written constitution means that greater reliance has to be placed on the conventions as means of controlling and limiting government (2012: 8, 12). The idea that the UK government should itself adopt a cabinet manual seems to have had several motives. Gordon Brown supported its development as part of the debate over whether the United Kingdom should have a written constitution. Further, it was thought that it might provide guidance should the 2010 election result in a minority government. In this context, the adoption of something similar to the New Zealand Cabinet Manual was seen as a means by which government could be made more transparent and accountable (Blick 2012: 2). Modelled on the New Zealand document, the UK Cabinet Manual is meant only to describe, not prescribe, convention (Bowden and MacDonald 2012: 382–3, 389), but it does contain some important innovations (see Chapter 9). It operates as a kind of soft law in its effect on the behaviour of public servants and governments, and offers a written text that can be more readily used by courts where an understanding of the operation of constitutional conventions is deemed relevant to the issues at hand (Blick 2012: 12).

Patriation of the Canadian constitution and the prorogation crisis

The often discussed Canadian *Patriation Reference* (1981 1 SCR 753) illustrates the way in which debate over the existence and content of a

[2] For example, in 1998 the Shipley government proceeded with a Cabinet meeting after coalition partner NZ First party walked out of the meeting. The coalition agreement stipulated that this meant that there was not quorum for the meeting, but the Cabinet Manual did not. The Prime Minister persisted with the meeting on advice that the Cabinet Manual, which states convention, is not overruled by the coalition agreement.

convention will be affected by the existence of a written constitution. In that case the Supreme Court held by majority that constitutional convention constrained the two houses of the federal Parliament of Canada from requesting an amendment that would directly affect federal-provincial relationships without prior consultation with, and substantial (but not necessarily unanimous) agreement of, the provinces (Hogg 1982). The convention was adduced from the practice of provincial consultation and consent in connection with a long series of UK amendments to the *British North America Act* 1865 (UK). As Marshall pointed out, the Supreme Court considered itself able to pronounce upon the existence of the convention because statutory law had given it jurisdiction to furnish advisory opinions on questions of both law and fact. As a consequence, he argued, 'the power to recognise the conventions derived . . . from statute', and he concluded that 'the establishment of such a judicial arbitration may complicate but it does not controvert Dicey's separation of law and convention (Marshall 1985: 16–17)'.

On the 'legal' aspect of the case the majority directly rejected the proposition that conventions may 'crystallise' into law and that this particular convention had done so. Their arguments were of two types: theoretical and precedential. The theoretical arguments concerned the nature of both law and convention. According to the majority, convention, by virtue of its dependency on political recognition and practice, is inconsistent with its legal enforcement. Rules of law are recognised and applied in and through judicial decisions, but no such 'parental' role is played by judicial decisions in relation to conventions. This last point merged into an argument based on precedent. In this respect, the majority pointed out that no case had been adduced where a convention had matured into a rule of law and that, in fact, in several previous cases the distinction between convention and law had been positively affirmed. (Chapter 10 provides further analysis of the decision.)

Reactions to the recent prorogation controversies in 2008 and 2009 further illustrate the significance of constitutional context in understanding the law–convention relationship. As explained in more detail in Chapter 10, the Canadian prime minister advised the governor-general to prorogue parliament on two occasions, first in order to avoid an impending vote of no confidence, and a second time with the effect of dissolving parliamentary committees that were investigating matters potentially embarrassing to the government. These actions provoked extended debate. On one hand, Heard expressed concern that 'a dangerous precedent' was being set which risks 'depriving Parliament of its only major defence against subjugation to the whims of the prime minister and cabinet' (2009: 10). On the other hand, Cameron argued that prorogation served as a kind of 'time out' for all political parties, forcing each of them to reassess their stances and policies, and ultimately reinforcing their accountability to the House of Commons (2009: para. 2.14–16).

During the controversy the House of Commons adopted a motion stating that the prime minister must not advise the governor-general to prorogue Parliament for longer than seven days without the passage of a supporting resolution by the House of Commons (Tremblay 2010). This stimulated arguments for formalizing the relevant conventions into law or the adoption of a Cabinet Manual (Aucoin, Jarvis, and Turnbull, 2011: 108; Harland 2011; Russell and Milne 2011; and see also Chapter 13 in this volume). Some even suggested that prorogation decisions could be subject to judicial review (Sossin 2010; Walters 2011). However, as Newman has pointed out, this suggestion is difficult to square with what the Canadian Supreme Court has repeatedly said about the legal unenforceability of constitutional conventions (Newman 2010; Dodek 2011), a view supported by leading Canadian commentators (e.g., Heard 1991: 3; Hogg 2006: § 1.10(a)). Indeed, some used the occasion to reiterate criticisms that had been levelled against the Canadian Supreme Court for entering the political thicket in the *Patriation Reference* in the first place (Dodek 2011, citing McWhinney 1982: 79, 88; Forsey 1984: 37). On this view, the court should not have 'allowed itself to be manipulated into a purely political role' (Hogg 1982: 320, 324), because the line between recognising and enforcing conventions is so 'artificial and untenable' (Dodek 2011: 127) that the Court is unavoidably drawn into matters that are better left to political resolution and public debate (Strayer 1988: 231).

Responsible government in Australia

As in Canada, there are no Australian cases in which the specific content of a convention has been enforced as such. Moreover, while there are several cases where the existence of conventions has been regarded as a relevant and important consideration in the court's reasoning, because the High Court of Australia does not have advisory jurisdiction, it has not been asked to opine on the existence and content of a convention in the overtly political manner that has occurred in Canada. Rather, in

Australia, conventions have come into judicial reasoning in the course of resolving a legal question that had arisen for determination (*eg*, *Copyright Owners Reproduction Society Ltd* v. *EMI (Australia) Pty Ltd* (1958) 100 CLR 597; *Victorian Stevedoring & General Contracting Company Pty Ltd* v. *Dignan* (1931) 46 CLR 73; *FAI Insurances Ltd* v. *Winneke* (1982) 151 CLR 342; *Commonwealth* v. *Northern Land Council* (1991) 30 FCR 1; *Egan* v. *Willis* (1998) 195 CLR 424; *Egan* v. *Chadwick* (1999) 46 NSWLR 563).

One the most significant examples of the High Court's approach to conventions is to be found in the line of decisions known as *Freedom of Political Communication* cases. In the most authoritative of these, *Lange* v. *ABC* ((1997) 189 CLR 520), the High Court of Australia unanimously concluded that the Australian Constitution, by virtue of its provision for a system of representative democracy, necessarily implies the existence of a constitutionally enforceable guarantee of freedom of communication in relation to political matters. The main thrust of the reasoning in the case was based on particular features of the text and structure of the Australian Constitution (Aroney 1998). According to the Court, the system of representative democracy that operates under the constitution consists of two distinguishable structural principles: 'representative government' and 'responsible government'. Representative government consists of the system of constitutional rules which requires that the legislative powers of the federal government are vested in a bicameral parliament that is directly chosen through voting in regular elections. Several specific provisions of the Constitution combine to require the operation of such a system as a matter of enforceable constitutional law. On the other hand, according to the Court, the principle of responsible government rests upon a combination of both specific rules contained in the written constitution and the familiar Westminster conventions of parliamentary responsible government practised and recognised generally by Australian political actors. These principles constituted the twin foundations for the inference that the Constitution necessarily implies the existence of a legally enforceable freedom of political communication. The doctrine of responsible government played a crucial role in the Court's reasoning because it supported the extension of the implied freedom to communications, not only concerning the conduct of elected members of parliament, but also about the performance of ministers of state in the exercise of their executive powers and responsibilities.

But while *Lange* relied upon the conventions of responsible government as an essential step in its reasoning, the case did not involve the direct enforcement of a particular conventional duty. Nor did it rely upon responsible government as an isolated 'system of conventions' but rather as part of the entire system of government established by the Constitution as a whole. The existence of the written constitution, as setting out a coherent 'plan' of government, thus determined the essential structure of the reasoning. No question arose as to a possible inconsistency between a particular constitutional rule of law and a particular constitutional convention; both elements were construed as part of a coherent constitutional scheme. If the case had involved an alleged contradiction between a rule contained in the written constitution and a conventional rule, the Court would have been placed in a situation similar to that which confronted the Canadian Supreme Court in the *Patriation Reference*. But even in such a case, given the way in which the Court distinguished between representative and responsible government, it seems the most likely from the reasoning of the Australian High Court that a distinction between law and convention would for these purposes have been maintained.

In *Egan* v. *Willis*, for example, the High Court relied upon the Westminster conventions of collective and individual ministerial responsibility to parliament to support the conclusion that the upper house of the New South Wales Parliament, just as much as the lower house, has an inherent power to hold government ministers to account by requiring them to answer questions and to produce documents, backed up by a capacity to impose sanctions for breach of such requirements such as by temporary expulsion of a member from parliament. However, in coming to this conclusion, the Court rigorously maintained a distinction between 'convention and parliamentary practice' on one hand and rules having 'legal or constitutional status' on the other, and emphasised that responsible government is an evolving set of practices, not legally enforceable rules.

Despite the prevailing assumption in Australia that there is a firm distinction between law and convention in this sense, there have been occasional suggestions that some conventions might be legally enforceable. Much of the debate in Australia has revolved around the controversial events of 1975, when Governor-General John Kerr dismissed Prime Minister Gough Whitlam on the basis that he was not able to secure the passage of the annual supply bills through the Senate even though he clearly had the confidence of the House of Representatives. (For more detail, see Chapter 11). In the aftermath of the dismissal, a small number of commentators suggested, albeit very tentatively, that the dismissal might have been justiciable. In the face of formidable legal hurdles of various kinds, however, no such case was brought, and the preponderance of discussion focused on the question of whether the governor-general had acted in conformity with convention and whether the relevant conventions could or should be codified, either by constitutional amendment, statutory enactment or some form of authoritative or public declaration as to their existence and content (Sampford 1987; Sampford and Wood 1987; Bowden and MacDonald 2012: 391–4). The prevailing understanding, in other words, was that there remained a firm distinction between judicially enforceable law and politically enforced convention, and the key questions were whether the relevant conventions had been breached and whether they should somehow be codified into law. In a recent article, however, Geoffrey Lindell has suggested that the *Freedom of Speech* cases suggest that the High Court could possibly be convinced to enforce the conventions of parliamentary responsible government in a sufficiently clear case. In particular, he argues that if events similar to those of 1975 were to occur again it would be open to the Court to declare that the prime minister cannot lawfully be dismissed unless he is first warned of the possibility (1995, 2004, 2014; see also Winterton 1983: 13–26, 71–84; Zines 2008: 339–40).

Lindell's argument is as follows. First, he establishes that a prime minister who has been or is about to be dismissed would be able to invoke the original jurisdiction of the High Court to deal with the matter. Second, he recognises that the crucial issue is not one of jurisdiction in the technical sense, but whether the legal power of the governor-general to dismiss ministers under s. 64 of the Constitution is subject to any legally effective constraints based in convention. Here, Lindell considers two possible lines of argument. The first concerns Australian cases that have recognised that the exercise of vice-regal powers is potentially subject to judicial review and cases in the United Kingdom that have held that the prerogative nature of a power is not of itself a bar to judicial review. Lindell notes, however, that Australian law 'lags behind' UK law in this last respect and that in a very recent decision the New South Wales Court of Appeal refused to accept that the exercise of the power of the governor to appoint and dismiss ministers might be constrained by the rules of procedural fairness (*Stewart* v. *Ronalds* (2009) 76 NSWLR 99). Bearing in mind that Australian judges are likely to continue to believe that the exercise of the discretionary powers of a vice-regal representative should not be subject to judicial review, Lindell proposes a narrower form of judicial review that would require a governor-general or state governor to 'warn' a prime minister about an impending decision to dismiss, rather than a judicial assessment of whether the decision to dismiss accorded with principles of procedural fairness.[3]

However, Lindell does not appear to consider this line of argument to be particularly strong, and he ultimately seems to abandon it in favour of a second argument, based on the system of responsible government which the *Freedom of Speech* cases recognised is established by the text and structure of the Australian Constitution. Now, there can be no doubt, as Lindell points out, that the framers of the Constitution anticipated that a system of parliamentary responsible government of some sort would operate, nor that the conventions of responsible government played a crucial role in the reasoning of the Court in the *Freedom of Speech* cases. But this is not quite the same thing as the Court enforcing the specific content of the conventions as a matter of law. The distinction between 'acknowledgement' and 'enforcement' has not (yet) been breached in Australian law, and this remains a fundamental problem for Lindell's argument. Indeed, noting that the thrust of the Court's reasoning in *Lange* was concerned with the text and structure of the Constitution as a systematic whole rather than the specific content of particular conventions, at a critical point Lindell reframes his argument so that it relies upon certain specific implications that might be drawn from particular legal provisions of the Constitution, namely those that require that there must be an executive council which advises the governor-general (s. 62) and that ministers must be members of parliament (s. 64). Lindell's argument in favour of the enforcement of unwritten conventions thus metamorphoses into an argument based on implications of the text and structure of the Constitution.

The essential difficulty with this argument is that it does not seem to accord sufficient weight to the text and structure of the Constitution. While ss. 62 and 64 are certainly key provisions upon which the system of parliamentary responsible government is founded, the framers of the Constitution plainly believed that there is a sharp distinction to be drawn between law and convention and that the Constitution must reflect this distinction. Thus, the Australian Constitution lays out a complex plan of government involving elements of both hard constitutional law and flexible constitutional convention. The intention and effect of the Constitution are thus to establish certain rules that are legally binding and in

3 Lindell relies here on a consensus among some commentators that the governor-general had acted wrongly in not warning the prime minister before dismissing him.

principle enforceable by the courts. As a matter of law, for example, the Constitution makes clear that the executive council and ministers of state hold office at the 'pleasure' of the governor-general (ss. 62 and 64). The framers likewise intended to leave certain other matters to political practice and evolving constitutional convention, such as the extent of the powers of the Senate over money bills (s. 57), recognising that it is through control over such bills that the parliament exercises effective influence over the executive, enabling it to compel the governor-general to appoint a prime minister who has the support of parliament. Partly because they were divided over the powers of the Senate, they deliberately left the Constitution open to political evolution as far as the practical operation of responsible government was concerned. Indeed, they gave the Senate power to refuse supply knowing that this would enable it to bring down a government if it wished (Aroney 2009: ch. 7–8). In this context nothing in the text and structure of the Constitution suggests that the specific conventions of parliamentary responsible government should be judicially enforceable as hard constitutional law.

What all this indicates is that in the context of a written constitution, arguments over the enforceability of constitutional conventions turn neither on narrow technical arguments about the availability of judicial review, nor upon general theoretical arguments about the relationship between law and convention in the abstract, but ultimately upon arguments founded upon the text and structure of the Constitution itself and the objectively ascertainable intentions that lie behind it. This is necessarily different where there is no written constitution. In the United Kingdom, where the formal powers of the Queen and the parliament are particularly formidable as a matter of strict law, there seems to be a greater sense of concern to ensure that these powers are properly constrained by both convention and law. For this reason also, there appears to be much more talk in the United Kingdom about the deliberate construction of conventions and about their enforcement by the courts. While commentators in Canada and Australia are similarly motivated to see their legal systems and political practices develop in desirable directions, the mode and tone of argument is shaped, and moderated, by the existence of a written constitution.

Conclusions

Conventions come in many kinds; they operate in different contexts; and they are understood from various theoretical perspectives. Lawyers are interested in the question of the distinction between law and convention because it bears on the very nature of 'law' and is relevant to the determination of what kinds of considerations are relevant in legal argument and what kinds of obligations and expectations are going to be enforced by the courts. Background theories of law are clearly relevant, whether they are positivist ones that define law by reference to some 'formal sign' or 'rule of recognition' (Munro 1975: 232–3), historical ones that define law by reference to evolved social practices and expectations (Sirota 2011) or normative ones that define law by reference to its underlying moral principles and values (Allan 2013). But while these theories shape our conclusions as to the nature of, and distinction between, law and convention, the theories are not entirely determinative, at least in the sense that 'inclusive' legal positivists can certainly be open to the theoretical possibility of judicial crystallisation of convention into enforceable law (Maley 1985; Waldron 2006).

And yet, a concrete example of a convention crystallised into law and enforced as such remains elusive as ever. The courts seem resistant to the enforcement of the specific content of constitutional conventions, and strong assertions of the distinction between convention and law have been especially prominent in Canada and Australia. Indeed, in this respect constitutional context seems especially important, as in both Canada and Australia questions about the nature and enforceability of conventions are shaped by the existence of a written constitution which establishes and defines the powers of the governor-general and the parliament, both of which are seen as possessing strictly derivative and limited powers of governance. In such contexts, conventions tend to be understood in relation to the comprehensive 'plan' of government authoritatively established by the constitution and enforced by the courts. Constitutional lawyers and judges in these countries, used to tracing constitutional law to the terms of their respective written constitutions, are habituated to think that constitutional law is one thing while constitutional convention is another. If they do argue in favour of the legal enforceability of conventions, they usually do so in terms of the written constitution and its underlying principles. However, constitutional reform in these countries tends rather to be focussed on attempts (albeit often unsuccessful attempts) at formal constitutional amendment or legislative codification as a means of addressing failures in the system as it operates in practice.

The same is not quite so in New Zealand and especially in the United Kingdom, where the strictly legal powers of Queen, governor-general and parliament are relatively 'raw' and 'unbridled'. Many of the limits on the legal powers of the Queen are in the nature of constitutional conventions that have come about through the use by the parliament of its legal powers and privileges, especially its ability to control supply. In this context, one more frequently encounters in British discussion the term '*constitutional* convention' rather than just 'convention', reflecting, it seems, a desire to underscore the constitutional status of conventions in a way that avoids any need to specify whether they are legal or conventional in nature. One also frequently encounters deliberate attempts to influence the development of conventions through arguments of constitutional morality and efforts to create conventions by political agreement and official resolution. The context also gives rise to more strongly articulated arguments that the line between law and convention is a dubious one and that the courts not only *can* but *should* enforce constitutional conventions.

In all Westminster democracies there are concerns about executive dominance over parliament, and constitutional crises predictably give rise to attempts to shore up the constitutional order, such as by authoritatively recounting the existence and application of conventions in cabinet manuals, codifying them into binding law, or calling for their recognition and enforcement by the courts. But in these debates, constitutional context makes a difference, especially the existence of a written constitution which lays out a relatively comprehensive plan for a system of government. This is because a written constitution encourages the mind to think first in relation to the judicially enforceable law of the constitution, and only secondly and separately about the vitally important conventions that regulate the exercise of legal powers in legislation and executive action.

Acknowledgement

Thanks are due to Nicholas Barber and Grant Huscroft for commenting on an earlier version of this chapter, and to Samantha Henderson for her capable research assistance.

References

Allan, Trevor 1986. 'Law, Convention, Prerogative: Reflections Prompted by the Canadian Constitutional Case'. 45(2) *Cambridge Law Journal* 305.

Allan, Trevor 1993. *Law, Liberty, and Justice: The Legal Foundations of British Constitutionalism.* Oxford: Clarendon Press.

Allan, Trevor 2013. 'Constitutional Convention: Practice and Principle', in *The Sovereignty of Law: Freedom, Constitution and Common Law*. Oxford University Press.

Aroney, Nicholas 1998. *Freedom of Speech in the Constitution*. Sydney: Centre for Independent Studies.

Aroney, Nicholas 2009. *The Constitution of a Federal Commonwealth: The Making and Meaning of the Australian Constitution*. Cambridge University Press.

Aroney, Nicholas, Prasser, Scott and Nethercote, J.R. (eds.) 2008. *Restraining Elective Dictatorship: The Upper House Solution*? Perth: University of Western Australia Press.

Aroney, Nicholas and Thomas, Steve 2012. 'A House Divided: Does MMP Make an Upper House Unnecessary for New Zealand?' [2012] *New Zealand Law Review* 403.

Aucoin, Peter, Jarvis, Mark and Turnbull, Lori 2011. *Democratizing the Constitution: Reforming Responsible Government*. Toronto: Edmond Montgomery.

Baker, John 2009. 'Our Unwritten Constitution'. 167 *Proceedings of the British Academy* 91.

Barber, Nick 2009. 'Laws and Constitutional Conventions'. 125 *Law Quarterly Review* 294.

Berman, Harold 1994. 'Origins of Historical Jurisprudence'. 103 *The Yale Law Journal* 1651.

Blick, Andrew 2012. 'The Cabinet Manual and the Codification of Conventions'. 67(1) *Parliamentary Affairs* 1.

Boston, Jonathan and Bullock, David 2009. 'Experiments in Executive Government under MMP in New Zealand: Contrasting Approaches to Multi-Party Governance'. 1 *New Zealand Journal of Public and International Law* 39.

Bowden, James and MacDonald, Nicholas 2012. 'Writing the Unwritten; the Officialization of Constitutional Convention in Canada, the United Kingdom, New Zealand and Australia'. 6 *Journal of Parliamentary and Political Law* 365.

Cabinet of the National Assembly for Wales and the Northern Ireland Executive Committee 2013. *Memorandum of Understanding and Supplementary Agreements between the United Kingdom Government Scottish Ministers*, Cm 5240.

Cameron, David 2009. 'Ultimately, the System Worked', in Peter Russell and Lorne Sossin (eds.), *Parliamentary Democracy in Crisis*. University of Toronto Press.

Commonwealth of Australia, Parliament of the Australian Commonwealth, The Senate 2008. *Explanatory Memorandum, Defence Amendment (Parliamentary Approval of Overseas Service) Bill 2008 [No. 2]*, C2008B00218.

Commonwealth of Australia, Parliamentary Library Background Note 2010. *Parliamentary Involvement in Declaring War and Deploying Forces Overseas*.

Cooray, Mark 1979. *Conventions, the Australian Constitution and the Future.* Sydney: Legal Books.

Dicey, Albert Venn 1973. *Introduction to the Study of the Law of the Constitution*, 10th edn. London: Macmillan.

Dodek, Adam 2011. 'Courting Constitutional Danger: Constitutional Conventions and the Legacy of the Patriation Reference'. 54 *Supreme Court Law Review* 117.

Elliott, Mark 2002. 'Parliamentary Sovereignty and the New Constitutional Order: Legislative Freedom, Political Reality and Convention' 22 *Legal Studies* 340.

Elliott, Mark 2003. 'Embracing "Constitutional" Legislation: Towards Fundamental Law?' 54 *Northern Ireland Legal Quarterly* 25.

Feldman, David 2013. 'Constitutional Conventions', in Matt Qvortrup (ed.), *The British Constitution: Continuity, Change and the Influence of Europe – A Festschrift for Vernon Bogdanor.* Oxford: Hart Publishing.

Foreign Affairs, Defence and Trade Legislation Committee 2010. *Defence Amendment (Parliamentary Approval of Overseas Service) Bill 2008 [No. 2].*

Forsey, Eugene 1984. 'The Courts and the Conventions of the Constitution'. 33 *University of New Brunswick Law Journal* 11.

Gardner, John 2011. 'Can There Be a Written Constitution?' in Leslie Green and Brian Leiter (eds.), *Oxford Studies in Philosophy of Law, Volume 1.* Oxford University Press.

Government of Canada, Parliamentary Information and Research Service 2006. *International Deployment of Canadian Forces: Parliament's Role*, PRB 00-06E.

Hailsham, Lord 1976. 'Elective Dictatorship'. *The Listener* 496.

Harland, Fraser 2011. 'Constitutional Convention and Cabinet Manuals'. 34 *Parliamentary Review* 25.

Hart, Herbert Lionel Adolphus 1961. *The Concept of Law.* Oxford: Clarendon Press.

Heard, Andrew 1991. *Canadian Constitutional Conventions: The Marriage of Law and Politics.* Toronto: Oxford University Press.

Heard, Andrew 2009. 'The Governor General's Decision to Prorogue Parliament: A Chronology & Assessment'. 18 *Constitutional Forum Constitutionnel* 1.

Heard, Andrew 2012. 'Constitutional Conventions: The Heart of the Living Constitution'. 6 *Journal of Parliamentary and Public Law* 319.

Hogg, Peter 1982. 'Comments on Legislation and Judicial Decisions: Constitutional Law – Amendment of the British North America Act – Role of the Provinces'. 60 *Canadian Bar Review* 307.

Hogg, Peter 2006. *Constitutional Law of Canada*, 5th edn. Toronto: Carswell.

Horwill, Herbert 1925. *The Usages of the American Constitution.* Oxford University Press, Humphrey Milford.

Hough, Barry 2000. 'Conventions and Democracy'. 29 *Anglo American Law Review* 368.

Hume, David [1739–40] 2000. 'Of the origin of justice and property', in David Fate Norton and Mary Norton, (eds.), *A Treatise of Human Nature*. Oxford University Press.

Jaconelli, Joseph 2005. 'Do Constitutional Conventions Bind?' 64 *Cambridge Law Journal* 149.

Jennings, Ivor 1959. *The Law and the Constitution*, 5th edn. University of London Press.

Jones, David and Iyer, T.K.K. 1989. 'The Nature of Political Conventions in a Written Constitutional Order: A Comparative Perspective'. 2 *Governance: An International Journal of Policy, Administration, and Institutions* 405.

Joseph, Philip 2009. 'MMP and the Constitution'. 7 *New Zealand Journal of Public and International Law* 111.

Kitteridge, Rebecca 2006. *The Cabinet Manual: Evolution with Time*, 8th Annual Public Law Forum.

Lagassé, Philippe 2013. *Policy Paper: How Should Canada's Parliament Decide Military Deployments? Lessons from the United Kingdom*. Calgary: Canadian Defence and Foreign Affairs Institute.

Lindell, Geoffrey 1995. 'Responsible Government', in Paul Finn (ed.), *Essays on Law and Government, Volume 1: Principles and Values*. Sydney: Law Book Co.

Lindell, Geoffrey 2004. *Responsible Government and the Australian Constitution – Conventions Transformed into Law?*, Australian National University Centre for International and Public Law: Law and Policy Paper 24. Annandale: Federation Press.

Lindell, Geoffrey 2014. 'Judicial Review and the Dismissal of an Elected Government in 1975: Then and Now?', 38 *Australian Bar Review* 118.

Lord Hailsham 1976. 'Elective Dictatorship'. *The Listener* 496.

Maley, William 1985. 'Laws and Conventions Revisited'. 48(2) *The Modern Law Review* 121.

Marshall, Geoffrey 1984. *Constitutional Conventions: The Rules and Forms of Political Accountability*, 1st edn. Oxford: Clarendon Press.

Marshall, Geoffrey 1985. 'What Are Constitutional Conventions?' 38 *Parliamentary Affairs* 33.

McHarg, Aileen 2008. 'Reforming the United Kingdom Constitution: Law, Convention, Soft Law'. 71 *Modern Law Review* 853.

McLeay, Elizabeth 1999. 'What Is the Constitutional Status of the New Zealand Cabinet Office Manual?', 10 *Public Law Review* 11.

McWhinney, Edward 1982. *Canada and the Constitution 1979–1982*. University of Toronto Press.

Munro, Colin 1975. 'Laws and Conventions Distinguished'. 91 *Law Quarterly Review* 218.

Neale, Thomas 2009. 'Presidential Terms and Tenure: Perspectives and Proposals for Change'. *Congressional Research Service Report for Congress*, R40864.

Newman, Warren 2010. 'Of Dissolution, Prorogation, and Constitutional Law, Principle and Convention: Maintaining Fundamental Distinctions during a Parliamentary Crisis' 27 *National Journal of Constitutional Law* 217.

New Zealand Cabinet Office 2008. *Cabinet Manual.* Available at: http://cabinet manual.cabinetoffice.govt.nz.

New Zealand Government, Constitutional Advisory Panel 2013. *New Zealand's Constitution: A Report on a Conversation.* Wellington: New Zealand Government.

Palmer, Geoffrey 1979. *Unbridled Power? An Interpretation of New Zealand's Constitution and Government.* Oxford University Press.

Palmer, Geoffrey 2005. 'The New Zealand Constitution in 2005', in Jack Hodder (ed.), *New Zealand's Constitutional Arrangements: Where Are We Heading?* Wellington: New Zealand Law Society.

Palmer, Matthew 2007. 'New Zealand Constitutional Culture' 22 *New Zealand Universities Law Review* 565.

Paulsen, Michael, Calabresi, Steven, McConnell, Michael and Bray, Samuel 2010. *The Constitution of the United States.* New York: Thomson Reuters/Foundation Press.

Phillips, Owen Hood, 1996. 'Constitutional Conventions: Dicey's Predecessors'. 29(2) *Modern Law Review* 137.

Russell, Peter and Milne, Cheryl 2011. *Adjusting to a New Era of Parliamentary Government: Report of a Workshop on Constitutional Conventions.* Toronto: David Asper Centre for Constitutional Rights.

Sampford, Charles 1987. '"Recognise and Declare": An Australian Experiment in Codifying Conventions' 7 *Oxford Journal of Legal Studies* 369.

Sampford, Charles and Wood, David 1987. 'Codification of Constitutional Conventions in Australia' [1987] *Public Law* 231.

Sawer, Geoffrey 1977. *Federation under Strain.* Melbourne University Press.

Sirota, Léonid 2011. 'Towards a Jurisprudence of Constitutional Conventions' 11 *Oxford University Commonwealth Law Journal* 29.

Sossin, Lorne 2010. 'The Unfinished Project of Roncarelli v. Duplessis: Justiciability, Discretion, and the Limits of the Rule of Law' 55 *McGill Law Journal* 661.

Strayer, Barry 1988. *The Canadian Constitution and the Courts: The Function and Scope of Judicial Review*, 3rd edn. Toronto: Butterworths.

Tremblay, Guy 2010. 'Limiting the Government's Power to Prorogue Parliament' 33 *Canadian Parliamentary Review* 16.

United Kingdom Cabinet Office 2011. *The Cabinet Manual: A Guide to Laws, Conventions and Rules on the Operation of Government*, 1st edn. Available at: www.gov.uk/government/publications/cabinet-manual.

United Kingdom House of Commons Political and Constitutional Reform Committee 2013. *Parliament's Role in Conflict Decisions: An Update*, Eighth Report of Session 2013–14, HC 649.

United Kingdom House of Commons Political and Constitutional Reform Committee 2014. *Parliament's Role in Conflict Decisions: A Way Forward*, Twelfth Report of Session 2013–14, HC 892.

United Kingdom House of Lords *Debates (Hansard)* 1998, Vol 592.

United Kingdom House of Lords Select Committee on the Constitution 2006. *Waging War: Parliament's Role and Responsibility*, House of Lords 15th Report of Session 2005–06, HL 236-I.

United Kingdom House of Lords Select Committee on the Constitution 2013. *Constitutional Arrangements for the Use of Armed Force*, Second Report of Session 2013–14, HL 46.

United Kingdom Ministry of Justice 2007. *The Governance of Britain*, Cm 7170.

United Kingdom Ministry of Justice 2007. *The Governance of Britain: War Powers and Treaties: Limiting Executive Powers*, Cm 7239.

United Kingdom Ministry of Justice 2008. *The Governance of Britain – Constitutional Renewal*, Cm 7342-I-III.

United Kingdom Political and Constitutional Reform Committee 2011. *Parliament's Role in Conflict Decisions*, Eighth Report of Session 2010–12, HC 923.

United Kingdom Public Administration Select Committee 2004. *Taming the Prerogative: Strengthening Ministerial Accountability to Parliament*, Fourth Report of Session 2003–4, HC 422.

Waldron, Jeremy 2006. 'Constitutional Norms as Legal Norms' 75 *Fordham Law Review* 1697.

Walters, Mark 2008. 'Written Constitutions and Unwritten Constitutionalism', in Grant Huscroft (ed.), *Expounding the Constitution: Essays in Constitutional Theory*. Cambridge University Press.

Walters, Mark 2011. 'The Law behind the Conventions of the Constitution: Reassessing the Prorogation Debate' 5 *Journal of Parliamentary and Political Law* 127.

Wheare, Kenneth 1962. *Modern Constitutions* [rev. ed.]. London: Oxford University Press.

White, Nigel 2013. 'Written Evidence', PCD, 10 October 2013. Available at: http://data.parliament.uk/writtenevidence/WrittenEvidence.svc/EvidenceHtml/2838.

Winterton, George 1983. *Parliament, the Executive and the Governor-General: A Constitutional Analysis*. Melbourne University Press.

Zines, Leslie 1991. *Constitutional Change in the Commonwealth*. Cambridge University Press.

Zines, Leslie 2008. *The High Court and the Constitution*, 5th edn. Sydney: Federation Press.

3

Executive conventions

BRIAN GALLIGAN

This chapter explores the fundamental conventions of constitutional monarchy that limit the powers of the head of state, Queen and vice-regal representatives, governors-general, lieutenant governors and governors, and constitute the institutions of parliamentary responsible government. There is broad agreement on the largely formal and limited role of the head of state: for example to be consulted, but to act on advice. The adage that the Queen can do no wrong depends on the Queen's acting on the advice of the prime minister, the real political leader who has the support of the popular house of parliament and takes responsibility for the decision. The well-established conventions governing the head of state developed over time to reflect the shifts in real power that underpinned the enduring monarchic façade.

The UK Parliament limited the powers of the monarchy, and with democratisation the House of Commons bested the lords. The prime minister who takes responsibility for executive decisions is the political leader controlling the popular house of parliament.

Conventions constitute the fundamental institutions and practices of executive government in the constitutional systems of the United Kingdom, Canada, Australia and New Zealand. All four countries are constitutional monarchies in which the executive, to the extent that it is formally spelt out in constitutional and other basic texts, is couched in formal and absolutist monarchic terms. This is clearly stated in the constitutions of Canada and Australia, the two countries with written constitutions. Section III of Canada's Constitution Act 1867 and Chapter II of Australia's Commonwealth constitution both vest executive power in the Queen to be exercised by the governor-general (and lieutenant governors in Canada's provinces). Both constitutions specify there will be advisory councils – Privy Council for Canada, and Federal Executive Council for Australia – 'chosen and summoned' by the governor-general. In both countries these institutions are forums for transmitting government decisions and legislative bills for vice-regal approval. There is no mention in the constitutional text of the 'real' or substantial executive, prime minister and cabinet, nor the rules for determining who forms that executive and how it functions. All of this is part of the conventional executive governed by constitutional conventions.

The general rule is that the Crown, Queen, governor-general, lieutenant governors and governors act on the advice of the real executive, except when exercising the few discretionary 'reserve powers'. The reserve powers are exceptional instances when the head of state acts on her or his own discretion. It is generally agreed that there are four major reserve powers: appointing a prime minister when it is not clear, or contested, as to who has the confidence of the lower house of parliament; dismissing a prime minister in exceptional circumstances; refusing a prime minister's advice to dissolve parliament – too soon after an election, or when a prime minister loses the confidence of the house but refuses to tender resignation; and dissolving parliament. Exceptional cases are becoming less exceptional, however. There has been a fraying of the two-party paradigm that characterised most Westminster systems for the best part of a century; the adoption of proportional voting systems in some countries has stimulated the rise of minority parties; and voters tend to be less 'rusted on' in their allegiance to major parties. As minority and multi-party governments have become more common in Westminster systems as Scott Brenton explains in Chapter 6, the conventions that govern the processes of appointing governments and terminating parliaments have come more to the fore. This has sparked moves to codify conventions, as discussed by Peter Russell in Chapter 13. But so far at least, as this chapter will show, the executive conventions of parliamentary responsible government have proved robust and mainly reliable.

The reserve powers are there to ensure the working of the Westminster executive system in non-routine and hard cases. The successful resolution of hard cases requires fine judgment and an outcome that is accepted as a legitimate application or extension of an agreed convention. If the four areas of reserve powers are generally agreed, there is less agreement over the precise limits of such reserve powers in particular cases. A notable instance is that of Australian Governor-General Kerr's dismissal of Labor Prime Minister Whitlam in 1975 when Whitlam had majority support in the House of Representatives but could not get supply passed by a hostile Senate. This dismissal was highly contentious and raised ongoing questions about conventions in the Australian system. Accepting or declining to accept the advice of a prime minister to dissolve parliament is one scenario that puts the head of state on the spot politically. Granting or not granting a prorogation request that suspends all parliamentary business from an embattled prime minister threatened by a vote of no confidence is another. Canada had a notable case of this in 2008, and other jurisdictions might expect similar contestations during periods of minority and multi-party government.

Executive conventions define the 'efficient' or real parts of the executive, and how they relate to the formal monarchic parts. Bagehot in *The English Constitution* ([1867] 1936) cast the latter as a populist screen for the former. Besides the theatre of monarchic pomp and personality, the formal or written articulations of the monarchic office tend to be couched in absolutist terms even in written constitutions such as in the Canadian and Australian constitutions. These overblown formulations are not to be read literally or as law, however, but according to the conventions of responsible government. Executive conventions in effect define the offices of formal monarchic head of state and the prime minister and cabinet and govern their relationship. They constitute the basic rules of responsible government – how governments are formed and whether they continue in office, and the limited discretionary reserve powers of the head of state. This chapter is concerned with the core executive conventions of parliamentary responsible government in Westminster systems, and how they have operated in routine and crisis situations. In Chapter 4 Patrick Weller discusses more specific conventions applying to the functioning of cabinet, and in Chapter 5 Jennifer Menzies and Anne Tiernan consider caretaker conventions.

Since A.V. Dicey's classic account that has been influential in framing discussion for more than a century, the discussion of conventions has focused on executive conventions as rules for governing the exercise of the monarch's prerogative. That prerogative was defined as every kind of action that could be legally taken by the Crown, or the residue of executive power not controlled by Acts of Parliament. According to this account, the King once had the sovereign power to make decisions in his own right, legislating by royal proclamations or decrees or authorising some other body such as a council or parliament to legislate provided it conformed with his will. That sovereign power passed to parliament, with the residual remaining formally with the Crown but now governed by conventions. Dicey acknowledged the fact that 'political sovereignty' based on the will of the electorate or nation underpinned both the supremacy of the elected House of Commons and the rule that gives the appointment and control of the government mainly to the House of Commons (Dicey [1885] 1973: 431). However, Dicey's focus was mainly a legal one that treated conventions as 'understandings' or 'habits' from a pre-legal or political world with which he was not much concerned. Our purpose in this chapter is to focus on executive conventions as primary institutions of Westminster constitutional systems that structure the executive and are based on broad political and social support (Hardin 2013).

The political view of executive conventions

Responsible government executives of the Westminster kind retain the dual features that Dicey from a legal perspective and Bagehot from a political perspective identified: formal monarchy with real executive of prime minister and cabinet. Such a constitutional system works because the latter control the former and deliver democratic government that is both effective and has the support of political elites and electors or the people at large. The real executive of prime minister and cabinet govern the country, leading the ruling party or coalition that dominates the legislature, and are chosen through the processes of representative democracy in the various countries. The formal monarchy is retained because there is broad support for its largely symbolic role and because changing it is too difficult. Popular support for the monarchy fluctuates, and is comprised of those who admire the Queen and royal family and those who support the office of a non-political head of state. Changing the system that works tolerably well most of the time has a high threshold, as the Australian experience of 1999 showed. Although strong majorities favoured a republican head of state at the time, republicans were divided over whether the president should be directly elected by the people or chosen by the prime minister in consultation with the leader of the opposition and endorsed by parliament. The direct-election or 'real' republicans joined with the monarchists in voting down the model of an appointed head of state by fifty-five to forty-five per cent.

A political account of constitutional conventions needs to explain their character and status, and why they are observed. It is not sufficient to say, as constitutional lawyers following Dicey are wont to do, that conventions are not laws and define them negatively as 'mere conventions' or customs. Not being laws or codified in constitutional texts, conventions lack crisp definition. Furthermore, they are not subject to Court adjudication that might give authoritative rulings in contested cases. That does not make them inferior; rather they are core parts of the political constitution. As set out in Chapter 1, both legal and conventional parts of constitutions have the same political basis but take different institutional forms. Political consensus gives law and courts the constitutional role and authority that they enjoy. The same political consensus gives conventions their constitutional form and authority. The example of the Canadian Senate might help to illustrate the point. According to the text of the Canadian Constitution Act 1867 the Senate is a powerful legislature with senators appointed for life. This belies its relatively weak status in practice, rarely having an input into legislation and no say in determining the executive, as Campbell Sharman explains in Chapter 8. In other words, conventions trump the written text.

To focus our discussion of executive conventions it is as well to identify the core ones. There are two: one identifying who governs and the other ensuring that they actually govern. The first is that the real executive or government, the prime minister and cabinet, is formed by those who have majority support in the popular house of parliament. The second is that the formal executive, Queen or vice-regal representative, acts on the advice of the real executive. Both need some qualification. As already pointed out, the head of state retains limited 'reserve powers' to act independently in certain special circumstances. Nor is the first convention without controversy, as the 1975 Australian crisis showed. In that instance the governor-general sacked Prime Minister Whitlam who had majority support in the House of Representatives but could not get supply passed by an opposition-controlled Senate. The reserve powers and the 1975 crisis will be discussed further on in the chapter – they are exceptions that prove, albeit by modifying, the general rule.

These dual core conventions ensure a democratic regime in which the people are sovereign, or more specifically that the electors through the system of representative democracy have the determining say in governing. The first convention has the executive drawn from the popularly elected house of parliament, which at least in the UK and Canadian cases are the elected ones. For Australia with an elected Senate the situation is less clear, with the Australian constitutional founders opting to combine a responsible government executive with a bicameral legislature including an American-style Senate directly elected by the people of the states and having virtually the same legislative power as the House of Representatives. Some warned that the hybrid system would not work, and Sir Samuel Griffith, leader of the first constitutional convention and subsequently the first chief justice of the High Court, thought that Australia should develop an executive form more suited to the bicameral legislature they were creating. The majority view was to retain both traditional responsible government and a powerful Senate, and except for 1975 this unlikely combination has worked reasonably well. For New Zealand with its unicameral parliament, there are no legislature complications for the core convention of majority support in the popular house of parliament.

The second convention that the Queen or vice-regal representatives act on the advice of the government ensures democratic rule by the government elected by the people. This is hardly an issue in modern times when democracy is pervasive and taken for granted. It is necessary, however, because the monarchy is retained as the formal head of state and once was sovereign in its own right. In a passage not usually noted, Dicey himself gives a brief account of 'political' sovereignty to explain the basis of conventions that controlled the executive – the prime minister and cabinet effectively ruling, and the primacy of the House of Commons where they were based. The 'ultimate object' of conventions was 'to secure that Parliament, or the Cabinet which is indirectly appointed by Parliament, shall in the long run give effect to the will of that power which in modern England is the true political sovereign or the State — the majority of the electors or (to use popular though not quite accurate language) the nation.' (Dicey [1885] 1973: 430)

Hard cases

It is sometimes said that hard cases make bad law. They do show, however, the contested character of law, and that judges in split decisions can have differing views and supporting reasons. There may be no clear answer or common reasoning, but a final decision by a court majority that decides the outcome. Hard conventional cases are similarly contested, but lack definitive rules to determine final outcomes. By probing hard cases in contested situations, we can see how conventions play out in political practice.

Australia 1975

Australia's 1975 constitutional crisis tested the basic convention that the government of the day, prime minister and cabinet, is responsible to the popular house of parliament, the House of Representatives in Australia's case, and entitled to remain the government while it retains that confidence or majority support in that House. As alluded to earlier, the Australian founders were quite aware that they were combining traditional British responsible government in which they were well practised as colonial parliamentarians with a powerful American-style Senate that was directly elected by the people in state constituencies and given virtually equal powers to the House of Representatives. Although some had reservations about such a hybrid, the majority wanted both in the Commonwealth Constitution adopted in 1901. They provided no fail-safe mechanism for dealing with possible deadlocks between the two chambers of the legislature that might also paralyse the government, trusting that good political sense among experienced political leaders would ensure the system worked. And it did until the 1975 crisis. The issues of 1975 are discussed in Chapter 11, so we need only highlight those aspects that shed light on the character of executive conventions, and how they fared in a crisis situation.

The bare bones are these. A prime minister with majority support in the House of Representatives but unable to get supply passed by an opposition-controlled Senate was dismissed by the governor-general without warning. Prime Minister Whitlam had gone to government house to propose a half Senate election to break the deadlock. Governor-General Kerr had decided in advance that he would dismiss Whitlam if he did not resign or advise a general election, so he dismissed Whitlam. Liberal opposition leader Fraser, waiting in an adjacent room, was commissioned to form a government provided he would undertake to get supply passed and advise an election, both of which he did. In the ensuing election Fraser won a resounding victory. Kerr became a controversial figure whose public appearances were dogged by protests; he subsequently left office and Australia.

The resolution of the 1975 crisis depended on the relative professionalism of the actors despite their sharp disagreement on core conventions, as well as the confluence of some key events. The most significant of these was the ensuing general election that endorsed the new prime minister with strong popular support and a large majority in parliament. Another was Whitlam's acceptance of his sacking – he did not return to the House to withdraw the supply bills or carry motions of confidence in his government, but instead retired to the Lodge for a steak lunch. Meanwhile the Senate passed the supply bills. The Labor Speaker of the House then authorised the supply bills to go forward to the governor-general for signing – he did not, as some have suggested he might, lock them away in his safe. Hence the crisis was ended with the supply bills being passed and a general election held. The electoral endorsement of Fraser was no imprimatur for altering the basic convention of responsible government to include also having the confidence of the Senate for passing supply, or at best only an indirect one. Voters were more focused on turfing out an unpopular government than with the niceties of how the election was triggered.

The key conventional issues in 1975 were twofold. The first was whether the reserve powers extended to resolving a parliamentary deadlock between the House of Representatives and the Senate by dismissing a prime minister who could not get supply through the Senate but refused to advise an election for the House of Representatives. Related to this, but even more fundamental, was the core convention of responsible government. The generally accepted view prior to 1975 was that the prime minister and government held office while ever they had support of the House of Representatives. Whitlam and his supporters relied, unquestioningly, on this core convention. The counter Liberal coalition strategy depended on revising the meaning of responsible government to responsibility to parliament. Given that the Senate had power to pass or not pass supply, a government would need to have sufficient Senate support to pass supply if it were to govern. If it did not, it would have to resign or be dismissed. This was an unprecedented innovation in the understanding of responsible government, but one that has some plausibility for a bicameral legislature like that of Australia. Making the tenure of the prime minister and government responsible to parliament and dependent on Senate support was a bold innovation, opportunistically effective when coupled with the innovation of expansive vice-regal power. Neither side respected the founders' constitutional design of combining partly incompatible institutions without a fail-safe circuit breaker and trusting the operation to the politicians' good sense and compromise. The founders never envisaged that the governor-general might come in as the circuit breaker.

There remains sharp disagreement in Australia over the governor-general's actions in 1975, and whether that office has, or should have, any legitimate discretionary powers at all. Some, like Sir David Smith, a loyal secretary to five governor-generals and personally knighted by the Queen, remain strong defenders of Kerr's dismissal of Whitlam and champions of vice-regal reserve powers (Smith 2005). A recent biography vindicates Whitlam and questions whether the governor-general has any reserve powers to act against the advice of an elected prime minister

(Hocking 2012: 307). In response to Hocking's outing of the 'third man' – Sir Anthony Mason who advised Kerr informally during the crisis – senior Labor figures affirmed the view that the governor-general must act on advice, and that 1975 was a breach of conventions (Galligan and Brenton 2013).

How are these matters to be resolved? The answer is by contested practice and sufficient consensus, albeit partial or qualified, that enable politics to go on. An example of the latter was the post-1975 constitutional change put to the people by the Fraser government and carried by referendum requiring that vacating senators be replaced with senators from the same party. State governments appoint replacement senators and prior to the Whitlam government followed this practice. Two anti-Labor state governments of Queensland and New South Wales broke this tradition and appointed non-Labor Senators to give the Liberal opposition control of the Senate in 1975. After the passing of the constitutional amendment this cannot happen again. A further example is minority parties that often control the Senate pledging never to block supply. However, if the government is unpopular and the opposition controls the Senate and is bent on forcing an election it expects to win, then using the Senate's power to block supply may seem an attractive ploy. There would be no point, however, unless the governor-general were to follow the Kerr precedent and dismiss the prime minister, and the fallout from 1975 has made that less likely. Nevertheless, despite protestations to the contrary, the Australian governor-general continues to have limited reserve powers.

Who should advise the governor-general on their exercise is also contentious. The Chief Justice Sir Garfield Barwick publicly advised Kerr in 1975, endorsing his interpretation of conventions and his action in dismissing Whitlam. Sir Anthony Mason, then a justice of the High Court and subsequently Chief Justice, also advised Kerr as a personal friend. Barwick's public advice drew him into the political controversy, while Mason's informal advice sparked criticism when belatedly disclosed. The matter remains open and contentious, with public backlash a likely constraint in the future.

Most significant of all, these disputes over executive conventions in 1975 have not changed the subsequent practices of Australian government. Over four decades since then, governments have been formed by the party having majority support in the House of Representatives, including Julia Gillard's minority Labor government (2009–13). During this period governments have rarely controlled the Senate, the exception being the Howard Liberal coalition for a brief period (2004–7). There has been no occasion for the governor-general to exercise reserve powers, or even dream of dismissing a prime minister. What this shows is that the normal conventions will usually operate, and that aberrations like 1975 are unlikely. The core convention of responsible government, although not without some dispute, is still stated by authoritative bodies such as the 1988 Constitutional Commission in traditional form:

> the ministers are individually and collectively answerable to the parliament and can retain office only while they have the 'confidence' of the lower House, that is, the House of Representatives in the case of the Commonwealth and the legislative Assembly or House of Assembly in the case of the States.
>
> (Constitutional Commission 1988: 84)

Canada 2008

The Canadian prorogation crisis of 2008 was a hard case that tested the two key executive conventions concerning who is entitled to govern and whether the governor-general must act on advice. Only six weeks out from an inconclusive election in 2008, Prime Minister Stephen Harper who led a minority Conservative government advised Governor-General Michäelle Jean to prorogue parliament for two months. That would suspend all business including a pending vote of confidence by opposition parties that his government would almost certainly lose. The governor-general agreed; parliament was prorogued; and despite acrimonious debate the Harper government continued in office and won a majority at the next election in 2011. In Chapter 13 Peter Russell discusses the case, and opposing views are explained, so we need only highlight the key issues here.

This case tested the basic convention of responsible government that the prime minister and government have the support or confidence of the House of Commons. In a minority government situation where this is not always clear, the litmus test is a vote of confidence by the House. In this case there was no confidence motion, but there was an announcement of intention by the opposition parties and a petition to the governor-general signed by a majority, confirming their support for an impending no confidence vote. Harper avoided the vote of confidence that he would almost certainly have lost by advising the prorogation of parliament that the governor-general accepted. Although this novel use of prorogation was unprecedented, the two-month cooling-off period proved effective: the Harper Conservative government survived and parliament carried on in the new year. Harper's trump card was that his government had not lost a confidence motion in the House of Commons. His additional defence relied on two main political reasons: that the opposition parties had not received electoral endorsement for their coalition at the recent election; and the Bloc Quebecois that was needed for a majority was pledged to the dismemberment of Canada.

Opponents rejected Harper's case and emphasised that it was entirely improper for parliament to be suspended in this way. The government would not survive a vote of confidence and that should have taken its course, and a new government formed by the Liberal party leader Stephan Dion who headed the recently formed coalition. This alternative course depended crucially on the governor-general rejecting the advice of the prime minister. That would likely have precipitated an angry confrontation not seen in Canada since the King–Byng crisis of 1926. In that instance Governor-General Lord Byng refused a dissolution to Prime Minster Mackenzie King who wanted a new election rather than facing a no confidence vote in the House. The Conservative government that replaced King's Liberals lasted only a few months before it lost a no-confidence motion, and King won the ensuing election.

There is no consensus among Canadians on the key conventional matters at issue in 1926 and 2008. As Russell recounts, all participants at a special symposium of senior constitutional scholars and officials in 2011 agreed on the confidence convention, that the right to govern depends on maintaining the confidence of the House of Commons. There was no agreement on the governor-general's response to requests for an early election, but acknowledgement that a large number of factors would need to be taken into account. All participants agreed that the governor-general had a reserve power to decline a prime minister's advice to prorogue Parliament. However, a motion carried in the House of Commons in 2010 by the non-government parties, that a request to prorogue for more than a week should be supported by a majority in the House of Commons, was opposed by the minority Conservative government, now a majority Conservative government.

Despite the ongoing controversy over the key conventions and their application among political elites and scholars (reviewed by Knopff and Snow 2013) and the Russell initiative for greater codification of conventions, Canadian politics has continued on in its accustomed ways. That has also been the case in Australia since 1975. Conventional concerns in the two countries differ because of the different crises faced and the ways in which they were resolved. As it stands the Canadian precedent of 2008 confirms that a vote of confidence in the House decides who governs; and that the governor-general follows the advice of the prime minister in granting prorogation of parliament. The 1975 Australian precedent had the governor-general dismissing a prime minister who had the confidence of the House but could not get supply passed by an opposition-controlled Senate. Both remain deeply contested, suggesting they were as much aberrations as precedents.

Keeping reserve powers in reserve

Constitutional crises and hard cases such as the ones mentioned earlier are the rare exception. For the most part, executive conventions operate in a consensual way and produce outcomes that are generally acceptable. During the four decades from 1945 to 1986, there were only a handful of 'episodes' for the four countries under consideration. Episodes are defined by Anthony Low as occurring 'when a constitutional head in the Commonwealth has been involved in decision-making or when a constitutional head's position has been an issue' (Low 1987). Besides 1975, Low listed four instances for Australia – two when a prime minister died in office in 1945 and 1967, and two when 'double dissolution' requests were contentious in 1951 and 1974. The first two cases entailed the swearing in of interim prime ministers until party processes produced a successor; the latter two entailed the governor-general's accepting the prime minister's advice despite political controversy as to whether a double dissolution and election of both houses of parliament were necessary. Low has only one episode for Canada, in 1967 when a special vote of confidence followed defeat of the government's budget. The United Kingdom had only two episodes that involved commissioning a new Conservative prime minister in 1957 and 1963 when incumbents resigned from office because of ill health. Following the 1963 episode, during which there was much internal party jostling, the Conservative party adopted rules for choosing a successor. Overall we can conclude that all of these episodes except 1975 were played out without crisis or lasting controversy.

Missing from Low's list is New Zealand, which had no episodes during this forty-year period. As Grant Duncan points out in Chapter 12 this was during the long period of two-party contests and the formation of majority governments. New Zealand merits further consideration because of its record before and after Low's period in resolving matters by political means without vice-regal intervention. As Duncan documents, this has been the case for more than one hundred years, including since the introduction of mixed member proportional (MMP) voting in 1996 that makes it unlikely for a single party to win a majority in the House. The reserve powers of the governor-general have been kept in reserve, with political leaders sorting out who is to form government in contested and unclear situations, although not always without some authoritative vie-regal prompting as in 1911.

In 1911 the then Governor-General Lord Islington parried the request from the incumbent Premier Sir Joseph Ward to prorogue parliament for six months rather than face a vote of confidence. Ward was in a precarious position after a close election and sought to prorogue parliament for six months to avoid a confidence vote. However, Lord Islington responded by pointing out that his acting on the advice of the Premier was dependent on his having the confidence of the House. Since this was in doubt it was necessary for Ward to face the parliament. Ward agreed and survived a no-confidence motion in early 1912, only to lose a second confidence vote later in the year, with a pursuant change in government in routine fashion.

In all the other instances of the formation of minority and coalition governments and changes to the party composition of governments mid-term, New Zealand conventional politics has functioned under surveillance of the vice-regal radar but without triggering the reserve powers. Since 1996 and the introduction of MMP and multi-party governments, the New Zealand tradition of political settlement without vice-regal intervention has continued – but again with some vice-regal prompting. Sir Michael Hardy Boys made various public statements clarifying conventions after the 1996 election when there was no clear winner and protracted political negotiations. He reiterated well-established practices: that the incumbent government remain in office in caretaker mode, and that negotiations among political leaders continue until an agreement was reached on who should form the new government, the test being who would likely have the confidence of the House. The governor-general would then commission the new government and its legitimacy be tested when parliament met. This eventually occurred, and so the 1996 formation of government followed established conventional practices. Similarly, a messy party realignment and change in government was again achieved in 1998 through political means. Of the three Westminster clones, New Zealand surely takes the prize for being the most conventional parliamentary system and the one closest to that of the United Kingdom.

The United Kingdom is somewhat different because of the superior status of the Queen that helps ensure her distance from the political machinations over government formation. The Queen plays a more exalted role in the life of the country than a governor-general of a Commonwealth country. As Vernon Bogdanor explained, she attracts 'sentiments quite different from those evoked by the more utilitarian and less historic institution of the Governor-Generalship', and 'through the magic of monarchy' holds a more central position in the consciousness of the nation (Bogdanor 1991: 11). The Queen's royal position makes her involvement less likely in settling disputes between deadlocked parties by sacking a prime minister as in the Australian case, or saving a government from defeat by granting a prorogation as in the Canadian case.

The aftermath of the 2010 election provided something of a test case when Gordon Brown's Labour government lost its majority and, after some intensive negotiations, the Conservatives formed a coalition agreement with the Liberal Democrats. This is the UK case of 'controversies and stresses' analysed by Menzies and Tiernan in Chapter 5. As they relate, Brown initially decided not to resign while the parties negotiated. However, officials at Buckingham Palace were concerned to ensure that the Queen not be drawn into the fray by having to choose the new prime minister, and there was tabloid criticism of Brown's being 'a squatter in Downing Street'. Brown resigned four days after the election but the day before the Conservative/Liberal Democratic coalition agreement was finalised. This course of events raised two issues: Brown's continuing in office after losing the election; then resigning before the alternative coalition party agreement was confirmed. Both issues arose because of an inconclusive election. Arguably, Brown ought to have stayed in office in caretaker mode until the coalition majority were clear, and then resigned while also advising the Queen to appoint the Conservative and coalition leader Cameron in his place. Nevertheless, the transition proceeded according to the basic executive convention that the leader who can command a majority in the House is appointed prime minister and forms the government. Moreover, although an inconclusive election was a novel occurrence in recent UK politics, the Queen was kept out of the fray with her reserve powers in reserve.

Nor is the Queen likely to become embroiled in other countries' crises. This was apparent in 1975 when the Queen was not contactable by Australian leaders, and her officials made it clear that Australians should resolve their own constitutional disputes. Although officially representing the monarch, the governor-general is part of the constitutional system of the particular Commonwealth country concerned. Consequently, as Marshall and Moodie point out:

> It follows that his involvement in controversy concerns himself alone, and not necessarily the place of the Crown. The temporary and appointive nature of his office, moreover, means that the real or apparent partisanship of any one incumbent need imperil nothing more than his own tenure.
>
> (Marshall and Moodie 1967: 45)

The 1975 Australian crisis might well be blamed on the particular vice-regal incumbent, with the antidote being more careful selection of wise and prudent people to fill the office.

Conventional proprieties

The New Zealand record shows that political negotiations can sort out who should govern in difficult cases of minority or coalition government, or when governments change through party disintegration during a parliamentary term. There are other less dramatic instances where the niceties of executive conventions are affirmed or might be contested. A notable Australian case concerned a newly appointed prime minister having to meet the House of Representatives. Such a meeting ensures that the prime minister has the confidence of the House, thereby vindicating the governor-general's decision in appointing that person. Normally this is routine after an election. There was some doubt, however, when Kevin Rudd replaced Julia Gillard as Australian Labor prime minister just prior to the 2013 election.

Having lost the leadership ballot in a meeting of the Labor parliamentary caucus on 26 June 2013, due to her poor showing in the opinion polls, Gillard advised Governor-General Quentin Bryce to 'send for Mr Rudd and ask him to accept appointment to the office of Prime Minister' (Letter of 26 June 2013, quoted in Galligan and Brenton 2013). This seemed straightforward, but the political situation was somewhat more complicated. Gillard had relied on agreements she had made with key independents to both form government in 2010 and maintain a majority in the House of Representatives. It was unclear whether they would continue to support the Labor government if Rudd were reinstated, or if they would support an opposition no-confidence motion if one were put. Rudd was a controversial figure who had previously lost the prime ministership to Gillard because of his erratic leadership. Parliament was about to shut down for the winter recess with an election to follow.

According to convention, the governor-general would be expected to accept the outgoing prime minister's advice. The complication here was that it was not clear Rudd would be able to meet the basic conventional rule of responsible government that the prime minister have the confidence or support of a majority of the House of Representatives. The governor-general needed that assurance: for Rudd to 'announce his appointment at the first possible opportunity to the House of Representatives in order to give the House the opportunity for whatever, if any, action it chooses to take' (Letter of 26 June 2013, quoted Galligan and Brenton 2013: 19). The acting solicitor general whose advice she sought had a different view: that it was open to the governor-general to seek an assurance from Rudd to meet the House, but he could not be required to do so: 'I confirm that I do not think that the Governor-General can require such an assurance or make the appointment conditional on such an assurance' (Letter of 26 June 2013, quoted Galligan and Brenton 2013: 19). The matter was not tested because Rudd promptly confirmed his intention to announce his appointment to the House of Representatives when the House convened later that day. He was duly commissioned mid-morning and met the House in the afternoon. There was no motion of confidence, and parliamentary business proceeded with the new prime minister in place. As it turned out, Rudd's second term in the office was short-lived, with Labor being badly defeated at the ensuing election. While it is hard to fault the governor-general's procedural propriety in handling the transition, the case shows there can be disagreement over some of the detailed requirements of conventions at the highest level, with the governor-general in this instance having the final say.

Another Australian instance from 1983 also shows the vice-regal power to insist on proper process. Liberal coalition Prime Minister Malcolm Fraser had made a sudden decision to call a double-dissolution election (entailing elections for the entire Senate as well as the House of Representatives) to capitalise on instability in the opposition Labor party that was meeting in Brisbane to elect a new leader (Hawke replacing Hayden). Fraser went to Government House at 12:15 and had scheduled a press conference to announce the election only three-quarters of an hour later, intending to catch the Labor party off balance. However,

Governor-General Sir Ninian Stephen was about to receive the Polish ambassador and his wife for lunch, and advised Fraser that he would not be able to deal with his request until after lunch. On subsequently reviewing the request, Stephen was not satisfied that Fraser had made a sufficient case for a double dissolution of both houses of parliament. Fraser was required to submit a second letter confirming that a double dissolution was 'critical to the workings of the Government and of the parliament'. That took another four hours but ensured the prime minister's request was properly documented (Galligan 1991: 74–5). Fraser's hasty ploy was spoiled, although that was incidental to his losing the ensuing election to the popular new Labor leader, Bob Hawke.

Clarifying reserve powers and responsible government

The reserve powers of the monarchic head of state are the only vestiges of real power that remain in what was once a powerful office, and their functioning depends on conventions that limit and tie their exercise to conventional principles. The head of state can act independently of the prime minister in a limited number of special circumstances, but such action is geared to ensuring the system of parliamentary responsible government carries on. For notable authors of the past such as H.V. Evatt, there was danger in leaving the reserve powers undefined. Evatt marshalled past instances to make a case for 'the desirability of some authoritative definition of the Crown's reserve powers, preferably in Statute form' (Evatt 1936: 7). Evatt was writing about the King and his dominion governors when, as K.H. Bailey pointed out in this volume's introduction, the formulation of constitutional conventions in the Dominions had 'naturally been materially hampered and delayed by the persistence into our own times of something of the Crown Colony outlook' (Evatt 1936: xxxvi). Those times have well passed, but the challenge of precisely articulating the reserve powers continues.

Recent attempts to specify the reserve powers have been prominent in Australia in the aftermath of 1975 (Sampford 1987), and in the republic referendum of 1999. Despite considerable effort in assessing the 1975 constitutional crisis and multiple proposals for defining and refining conventions and practices through a series of constitutional conventions (Advisory Committee on Executive Government 1987), there were no outcomes other than the ones noted earlier. These were a constitutional amendment to ensure state governments appointed replacement senators for those who died or resigned office from the same party as the vacating Senator. This change ensures that the Senate party composition cannot be changed by state governments, but does not address the core issue of the Senate using its legislative power to block supply. In addition the political ructions of the time provide some prudential deterrent against political actors pushing the system to crisis resolution when there is no fail-safe remedy. The enduring deep divisions between the main political parties and legal and political experts have precluded any consensus on changing the status quo. This was evident in the treatment of the office of head of state during the failed republic referendum. The example shows the difficulty of explaining the reserve powers, and the muddle that resulted.

The republican proposal put to the people in 1999 was touted as a 'minimalist' one that changed very little except substituting an appointed president for the Queen and governor-general. To say the least this was an anomalous proposal that would give a republican head of state the same formal absolutist powers as a monarch. Much of the open-ended formulation of the executive chapter was retained, but now vested in the president, and with more specific reference to the prime minister and reserve powers. This was the first time that the prime minister and reserve powers would be mentioned in the constitutional text. The proposed amendment stipulated:

> The President shall act on the advice of the Executive Council, the Prime Minister or another Minister of State; but the President may exercise a power that was a reserve power of the Governor-General in accordance with the constitutional conventions relating to the exercise of that power. (Constitutional Alteration (Establishment of Republic) Bill 1999, s. 59)

Explaining this novel proposal, the official Explanatory Statement said that the proposed section 59 required the president to exercise 'his or her ordinary powers' on the advice of the government of the day 'in accordance with the principle of responsible government which governs the exercise of nearly all of the Governor-General's powers'. The only exception related to the reserve powers, previously possessed by the governor-general, which would be passed on to the president. The Statement explained:

> There were probably only four reserve powers:
>
> 1. to appoint the prime minister
> 2. to dismiss the prime minister
> 3. to refuse to dissolve the Parliament; and
> 4. to force a dissolution of the Parliament (Constitutional Alteration (Establishment of Republic) Explanatory Statement 1999, s. 5.13)

Such bald articulation is misleading because as they stand these are not reserve powers. In each of the four instances limiting qualification have to be added: to appoint the prime minister when it is unclear who might have the confidence of the House of Representatives; or to dismiss a prime minister who loses the support of the House in a no-confidence motion and refuses to resign; and to refuse or force dissolution of parliament only if the prime minister's advice is unreasonable, for example soon after an election when an alternative government is possible. These are the real reserve powers that the official Statement fails to mention. The Statement seeks to retrieve some restrictions by specifying that 'in exercising a reserve power, the Governor-General ordinarily acts in accordance with established and generally accepted rules of practice known as "conventions"'. The Statement then notes that there could be circumstances 'where there are no generally agreed conventions to control the exercise of the Governor-General's reserve powers' and cites 1975 when the governor-general dismissed the prime minister. Nevertheless, it claims that the proposed s. 59 'would continue the reserve powers and apply existing constitutional conventions to the exercise by the President of those powers', while allowing for the development and evolution of conventions governing the reserve powers (Constitutional Alteration (Establishment of Republic) Explanatory Statement 1999, s.s. 5.14–5.16).

The problem with this attempt to describe the reserve powers is that it classifies as reserve powers the ordinary exercise of the office, with the governor-general's acting on the advice of the prime minister, as well as the exercise of the office in disputed circumstances such as 1975. This mixes up the ordinary with the hard cases; the ordinary when the reserve powers are not in play, and hard cases like 1975 when there is fierce dispute as to whether the power properly exists. It misses the usual but small list of reserve powers when the governor-general acts on her or his discretion against the advice of the prime minister at the time when that advice is without good reasons. The failure of the republic referendum ensured that this muddle was never tested in practice. Nor would it be sorted out by judicial decisions, with a future High Court being enticed into determining matters arising from the stipulation that 'the President may exercise a power that was a reserve power of the Governor-General in accordance with the constitutional conventions relating to the exercise of that power'.

Perhaps this is why constitutional lawyers have revisited the scope for judicial resolution of responsible government conventions. In a recent article, Geoffrey Lindell (2014) explores whether the governor-general's 'legal power' to dismiss ministers at will under the absolutist language of the executive chapter, s. 64 of the Constitution that Kerr appealed to in 1975, is subject to any legally effective constraints based on convention. This was mooted by some in 1975 but never tested. Lindell suggests that now judicial precedents are somewhat more promising. Lindell has a procedural argument that the Court might find that the governor-general has a duty to warn a prime minister of a likely dismissal. Such warning was a key recommendation of Sir Anthony Mason in his informal advice to Sir John Kerr. Mason was prepared to have his advice supporting the dismissal made public by Kerr, providing his advice that the governor-general must warn the prime minister was also made public. Kerr refused, so Mason's role was not made public at the time and only revealed recently (Hocking 2012).

In Chapter 2, Nicholas Aroney critically assesses Lindell's further argument for the High Court's deciding responsible government conventions. To say the least, deciding a dispute involving the vice-regal reserve power and responsible government conventions would be different from instances in the past, such as the *Freedom of Speech* cases of the 1990s when the Court acknowledged representative and responsible government as structures of representative democracy that the Constitution's 'direct election' sections implied. Judicial intervention seems highly unlikely in crisis situations like 1975, but more likely with a republican president if the constitutional text specifies that the president may exercise reserve powers in accordance with constitutional conventions. Intimating or partly articulating executive conventions in a written constitutional text that otherwise uses a formal language of absolutist monarchism is fraught with danger. If Australians sense this, they have not been successful in working out a plausible alternative.

References

Advisory Committee on Executive Government. 1887. Report. Queensland Government.

Bagehot, Walter [1867] 1963. *The English Constitution*. London: Collins/Fontana.

Bogdanor, Vernon. 1991. 'The United Kingdom', in Butler, David and Low, D.A. (eds.), *Sovereigns and Surrogates: Constitutional Heads of State in the Commonwealth*. London: Macmillan, 10–40.

Constitution Alteration (Establishment of Republic) Explanatory Statement. 1999. House of Representatives, Parliament of the Commonwealth of Australia.

Constitutional Commission 1988. *Final Report of the Constitutional Commission*, Volume I. Canberra: Australian Government Publishing Service.

Dicey, A.V. [1885] 1973. *Introduction to the Study of the Law of the Constitution*, 10th edn. Oxford University Press.

Evatt, H.V. 1936. *The King and His Dominion Governors*. Oxford University Press.

Galligan, Brian 1991. 'Australia', in Butler, David and Low, D.A. (eds.), *Sovereigns and Surrogates: Constitutional Heads of State in the Commonwealth*. London: Macmillan, 61–107.

Galligan, Brian and Brenton, Scott 2013. The Political Theory of Constitutional Conventions. Paper presented to the Australian Political Studies Association Conference. Hobart, 2013.

Hardin, Russell 2013. 'Why a Constitution?', in Galligan, Denis and Versteeg, Mila (eds.), *Social and Political Foundations of Constitutions*. Cambridge University Press, 51–72.

Hocking, Jenny 2012. *Gough Whitlam: His Time: The Biography*, Volume II. Melbourne University Publishing/Miegunyah Press.

Knopff, Rainer and Snow, Dave 2013. '"Harper's New Rules" for Government Formation Fact or Fiction?', *Canadian Parliamentary Review* 36: 18–27.

Lindell, Geoffrey 2014. 'Judicial Review and the Dismissal of an Elected Government in 1975: Then and Now?', *Australian Bar Review* 38: 118.

Low, D.A. 1987. *'A List of Episodes, Appendix III', Report of the Advisory Committee to the Constitutional Commission*. Canberra: AGPS, 83–4.

Marshall, Geoffrey and Moodie, Graeme C. 1967. *Some Problems of the Constitution*. London: Hutchinson.

Sampford, C.J.G. 1987. '"Recognise and Declare": An Australian Experiment in Codifying Conventions', *Oxford Journal of Legal Studies* 7: 369.

Smith, Sir David 2005. *Head of State: The Governor-General, the Monarchy, the Republic and the Dismissal*. Sydney: Macleay Press.

4

Cabinet government

PATRICK WELLER

In 1984 Prime Minister Bob Hawke was presented a challenge: how to maintain fundamental political conventions while solving a pressing political crisis. One of his cabinet ministers, Stewart West, objected to a cabinet decision on the mining and export of uranium. To protect his left-wing credentials he wanted to resign from cabinet but remain as a minister, so that he could oppose the decision in the Labour caucus. But Hawke had declared, on becoming prime minister, that all ministers would be bound by collective responsibility in all forums, including the caucus; that was no more than a standard interpretation of the convention. He asked the secretary of the Department of the Prime Minister and Cabinet, Geoff Yeend, for assistance.

Yeend worked with his colleagues to develop a definition of collective responsibility that allowed the minister to make his opposition known in caucus without his having to resign from the government. A revised version of the *Cabinet Handbook* (1983) blandly declared:

2.1 The convention of the collective responsibility of Ministers for Government decisions is central to the Cabinet system of government. Cabinet Minutes reflect collective conclusions and are binding on Cabinet Ministers as Government policy both outside the Party and within. This applies also to non-Cabinet Ministers co-opted to attend Cabinet meetings, in respect of matters dealt with while they are present.

2.2 Minutes of the Ministry are binding on all Ministers, similarly, both outside the Party and within, in respect of issues handled by the Ministry.

2.3 All Ministers are expected to give their support in public debate to decisions of the Government; non-Cabinet Ministers, however, are not prevented from debating in Caucus decisions in areas apart from their portfolios. Caucus decisions are binding on all Ministers.

The additional last interpretation in the clause thus released some ministers from collective responsibility within the party. A minister had to be present in cabinet before he was bound by the decision on caucus. In effect the change allowed West to resign from cabinet, but not from the ministry! Such an interpretation undermined traditional understandings of the convention, but no one cared. It was a device that accommodated internal difficulties, and then required neat drafting to bring the description of the convention in line with the practice.

The incident illustrates two fundamental facets of cabinet government. First, the great traditional conventions: individual ministerial and collective responsibilities exist, but they are flexible and open to interpretation. Their interpretation is contingent on circumstance and prime ministerial interpretation. Second, the rules of cabinet, whether set out in cabinet handbooks or manuals, are in a sense a formulation of the existing practices; they spell out how the traditional conventions will be applied for the time being, and they are as often designed to reflect as much as to lead practice and are vehicles through which prime ministers adjust their management of government. In this instance, the clause was set out as though nothing had changed, as though the Handbook were merely stating the obvious, accepted and long-standing practice. But of course it was not; it allowed a flexibility that had not previously existed for the Hawke government, but which had existed in the Whitlam government where ministers were allowed to re-fight in caucus battles they had lost in cabinet.

The new version of the Handbook points to a fundamental element of cabinet government. Cabinet government is based on convention, not law. Its significance and longevity is a tribute not to its formal power but to its ability to react to circumstance and to adjust procedures and practices to meet changing demands.

The conventional nature of cabinet should be no surprise, given its origins. It emerged slowly as the monarch ceased to turn up to meetings of his key council and as ministers became more answerable to the parliament than to the King. They agreed to agree in order to prevent the King from pursuing a policy of divide and rule (Mackintosh 1962). Gradually the monarch's executive council became, in Bagehot's (1963) terms, a formal and dignified, but not a working, part of the constitution. Cabinet evolved and gathered authority precisely because there were no rigid rules that could be readily bypassed or gamed. It should be no surprise that it continues to evolve.

Indeed when the Australian Constitution was written, cabinet was noticeable for its absence. The colonial governments all had systems of cabinet government that they took as a given when they devised the constitution, but they preferred to describe the formal 'dignified' structures of monarch/governor and executive council, rather than try to define a way that cabinet should work. Prime ministers were absent from the constitution too, left to devise their own means of procedure.

This chapter deals primarily with the development of cabinet conventions in Australia and the United Kingdom. It could have readily looked at Canada and New Zealand because the conventions and practices have mutated there in similar ways, whether in the face of demands for transparency, for greater control or, more often, in reaction to political necessity. There are differences; they will be illustrated later by citing the other definitions of collective responsibility. The conclusions, however, would be similar.

Cabinet conventions

Cabinet conventions can be classified at two levels:

- The broad constitutional conventions of ministerial and collective behaviour that notionally define the expectations of ministers in relation to the cabinet, the government and the parliament.
- The rules and routines that in effect put those conventions into practice; they describe the way that cabinet is run, papers are considered and decisions made. These can be found in the cabinet handbooks, manuals, guidelines and codes of conduct that have been issued in the recent decades.

I argue that in neither case are the conventions fixed and uncontested. There is no absolute agreement on how the conventions should be applied in all cases. There is no set of rules for cabinet procedure that provide rigid structures that cannot be changed. Rather, at both levels of convention the prime ministers are the principal authorities that determine what the conventions mean, whether and how they should be applied, and when even normal procedures can be relaxed or ignored because it is convenient to do so.

In making decisions about the application of the conventions and rules, prime ministers must calculate how much can be altered. Ignoring and adjusting the conventions are not cost-free. How they apply the conventions and shape the rules, in what way they determine to enforce the rules of cabinet, when they decide to consult with which colleagues, all have important consequences for the running of government and the cordial relations with ministerial colleagues. The implementation of governing by rules is regarded as the foundation for good government.

The broad conventions

The core element of collective responsibility is easy to assert. Ministers may argue for or against a proposal in the privacy of the Cabinet Room, but once a decision has been made, they are required to support it in public, or at least acquiesce and say nothing. That convention is based on the assumption that they had an opportunity to put their case, that they lost the argument with their colleagues and that therefore they support the cabinet decision in public. The principle then goes further. Ministers must support cabinet decisions even if they were not present when the decision was made. Some cabinet committees are given the authority to make decisions on behalf of government; they have the same standing as those of cabinet. Ministers are equally bound to them, even if they were not involved in the debate and decision.

In all cases prime ministers can make exceptions, usually for solid political reasons. Hawke's convenient reinterpretation of the doctrine has been noted. Harold Wilson relaxed the collective responsibility rules for the referendum on membership of the European Community. When the coalition government as formed in the United Kingdom in 2010 the Cabinet Office quietly released its new description of cabinet rules: 'All government ministers are bound by the collective decisions of Cabinet and Cabinet Committees, save when it is explicitly set aside' (United Kingdom Cabinet Office 2010).

So collective responsibility still applies, except where it does not! Here was another case of allowing political necessity and constitutional convention to find some practical common ground. Some concession had to be made to the coalition partners to make the cabinet process palatable. Prime Minister Cameron devised a cabinet system that took account of the expectations of his coalition partners and gave them an apparent share of influence. This was reflected in the constitution of the cabinet committees. Each cabinet committee has a chair from one party and a deputy chair from the other, and each has 'the right to remit an issue to the Coalition Committee if it affects the operation of the coalition and cannot be resolved by the originating committee' (United Kingdom Cabinet Office 2010). The four leaders, two from each party, made up the Coalition Committee. Even though the Coalition Committee was in form a cabinet committee, in practice it was a committee for politics.

These arrangements were an indication of the pressures on normal practice created by coalition government.

Whether the actual processes worked the way they were originally planned is less important here than the insight they allow into the flexibility of cabinet conventions. It was after all a coalition; that was unusual in Britain and required novel forms of decision making to ensure that both partners felt they had a reasonable opportunity to put their case. The new arrangements were presented in terms that implied business as usual, as though, in terms of practice and constitutionality, nothing had changed. But they played havoc with what had been regarded as normal views of cabinet government and stressed yet again that collective responsibility is ultimately a flexible doctrine that can be adjusted to fit political circumstances, but in a way that still allows some meaning and underpins a coherent government. Leaders have to find a balance.

Ministerial responsibility too has its ambiguities. Ministers are answerable for the actions of their departments and their officials. If departments mess up, they need to explain and fix. They are not, never were and never should be required to resign only because a department has mismanaged a program. But once the problems are public and known, it is seen as reasonable that ministers should ensure that they are fixed. The oft-demanded idea that ministers should resign is no more than a distraction. Ministers will only contemplate resignation if their fingerprints are all over the area under attack, if they have given instructions that led to the circumstances, if they planned and oversaw its delivery.

If the fingerprints are the minimum condition, they do not by themselves constitute adequate cause. Resignation is normally a decision of the prime minister. Normally resignations are remembered for far longer than the cases where there was a crisis that did not lead to a departure. Prime ministers will calculate how long a crisis will continue and whether they want to keep the minister, as much as they will consider any intrinsic evidence.

Ministerial responsibility should be distinguished from ministerial probity. Many ministers are forced to resign because they misused travel accounts, gave advantage to friends and relatives, had conflicts of interest in share holdings that they forgot to mention, abused staff, lied to the prime minister or parliament or sundry other personal errors. We expect high standards of probity from ministers. Because they are clearly personally involved, there is little chance to slough off these errors or to blame someone else. Prime ministers again must use their judgement and decide whether they wish to tough it out. It may well depend on their opinion of the minister as much as the sin committed. These all-too-common cases are not constitutional issue of ministerial responsibility; they are just decent behaviour and standards. They still tend to get muddled.

The essence of these traditional constitutional conventions is their potential ambiguity or flexibility; their application is contingent on time, situation and the prime minister. When they seem to have been breached, the question is whether and what sanctions should be applied. The final judge and executioner will be the prime ministers. The prime ministers will receive plenty of advice, from academics, journalists and judges, and of course the opposition, about how and when the standards should be upheld.

But ambiguity does not mean these conventions are devoid of meaning or have no influence on ministers or cabinets. Practitioners are constantly aware of the potential impact of these grand constitutional conventions because they realise the political costs that are incurred by those who do not meet reasonable standards. Ministers who kept diaries and recorded the arguments in cabinet meetings often annoyed their colleagues who wanted to have a private debate and present a picture of public cohesion. That is stripped away by the records of division that diaries reveal. When Australian minister Neal Blewett, dedicated his *Cabinet Diary* (1999): 'to my cabinet colleagues in the hope that they will understand if not forgive', he hit a chord. They were not pleased. There is a good political reason for a government to appear united.

The ministers are conscious too that they will be judged in public for their competence; as a consequence they take questions in parliament seriously too. They are aware that they can lose standing with their colleagues and backbenchers if they cannot perform well, whatever system of parliamentary questions is used. They relax when question time is over. Responsibility for their departments is not a myth but something real and pressing. So even if they can never explain with precision what will happen if these grand constitutional principles are abused, even if they do not know precisely what may be required in every circumstance, they are aware that the conventions are present, they matter and that the potential consequences are very real.

The conventions must remain ambiguous because it is impossible to write rules for all circumstances. Sometimes the interpretations will be very general indeed. Every country can have their own interpretation; it may well differ from decade to decade. I have considered those in Australia and the United Kingdom; it is worth a detour to look at other practices.

Canada is now the most direct. The rules are set out in *Accountable Government: A Guide for Ministers and Ministers of State* (Privy Council Office 2011). There is an introduction by Prime Minister Stephen Harper explaining the need for speaking with one voice. The rules themselves are blunt. There is no velvet glove, no doubt where power lies.

> 'I.1 Individual Ministerial Responsibility
>
> Ministers are accountable to the Prime Minister: they are appointed by the Governor General on the advice of the Prime Minister and the Prime Minister may ask for their resignation at any time.
>
> Ministers are also accountable to Parliament. . .
>
> I.2 Collective Ministerial Responsibility
>
> All members of the Ministry are collectively responsible for carrying out the government's policies as established by the Cabinet. They are therefore expected to work in close consultation with their ministerial colleagues. This principle is the foundation of a key constitutional convention known as Cabinet solidarity.
>
> Policies presented to parliament and to the public must be the agreed policies of Cabinet. Ministers and Ministers of State cannot disassociate themselves from or repudiate the decisions of Cabinet or their Ministry colleagues unless they resign from the Ministry' (Privy Council Office 2011: 1–2).

So, ministers, take care.

New Zealand's Department of the Prime Minister and Cabinet (DPM&C) is gentler in its description, in part because many of its governments have been coalitions, and like the United Kingdom the practices have to take account of junior partners.

> 5.23 Acceptance of ministerial office means accepting collective responsibility. Issues are debated vigorously within the confidential setting of Cabinet meetings, although consensus is usually reached and votes are rarely taken. Once Cabinet makes a decision, Ministers must support it, regardless of their personal views and whether or not they were at the meeting concerned.
>
> 5.24 In a coalition government, Ministers are expected to show careful judgment when referring to party policy that differs from government policy. Subject to paragraphs 5.24–5.27 a Minister's support and responsibility for the collective government position must always be clear (DPM&C 2008: 65).

Paragraphs 24–26 talk about the agreement to disagree, but it is a permission given to coalition *parties*, not to individual ministers (DPM&C 2008: 65–6). Paragraph 5.27 explains that ministers in supporting parties outside cabinet are bound only in relation to their particular portfolios (DPM&C 2008: 66). There are therefore a number of gradations of collective responsibility, from cabinet ministers, to non-cabinet ministers from different parties, to ministers from supporting parties. No wonder the UK Cabinet Office looked to New Zealand for precedents when they had to devise rules of a coalition government. The value of the New Zealand formulation is illustrated by the fact that the cabinet manual has not been amended since 2008. Indeed the introduction is still under the signature of long-gone Prime Minister Helen Clark. The new government, it seems, saw no need to update them, or even re-issue them under the new prime minister's name.

However, here is the most flexible interpretation I have ever found.

The Irish manual, *Government Procedure Instructions* (1983), provides a wonderfully elusive description of expectations:

> 18. The doctrine of collective responsibility requires that each Minister should inform his colleagues in Government of proposals he or a Minister of State at his Department intends to announce and, if necessary, seek their agreement. This applies, in particular, to proposals for legislation which can be initiated only after formal approval by Government. Ministers are responsible for implementing decisions.

And the Irish rules go on to explain ministerial responsibility:

> 23. It is the responsibility of the Minister concerned to ensure that Government decisions, whether formal or informal, are implemented at the earliest practicable date.

So then collective responsibility means ministers telling their colleagues what they propose to do, and ministerial responsibility means implementing government decisions. The concept of informal decisions, presumably what ministers chose to think they had been authorised to do, but without a formal record, would provide some ministers with great scope for initiative!

The rules of cabinet procedure

The challenge for leaders is how to make these conventions work. Over the recent decades a series of rulebooks have been developed, in part by bureaucracies, in part by prime ministers, to spell out the expectations of how ministers should act. These rulebooks are, in a real sense, the exposition of the constitutions in working form. Two examples of their gradual development can illustrate how rulebooks put flesh on the skeletal conventions and how they raised questions about how cabinets should work.

The Australian experience

Initially prime ministers kept their own notes of meetings and left ministers to tell their departments what cabinet had decided. In the 1914–18 war this process did not always work well, but it left Prime Minister Billy Hughes free to determine what he wanted to do too. Only with the highly organised Prime Minister Stanley Bruce did the system change. In 1927 there was the first formal step to create a cabinet secretariat and a set of rules. On 28 November cabinet appointed Sir Neville Howse, a minister, to carry out the duties of secretary to cabinet. Ministers were circulated with a letter describing how cabinet should work and what the expectations on them were.

Officials in the prime minister's department had prepared a draft. The prime minister then went through the document amending it where necessary and initialling each paragraph when he was satisfied. This first set of rules, like every other one as the procedures developed, were part of the prime minister's prerogatives to determine when and how the cabinet should be run.

The variations between the draft from officials and Bruce's final wording illustrate how the official desire for order clashed with the political need for cohesion and flexibility. Bruce added a clause to allow ministers to tell the secretary if they wanted to 'absent themselves from a cabinet meeting'. Officials wanted due notice for all submissions. Bruce decided to waive these demands 'in matters of extreme urgency' but required that ministers advise the secretary if they wanted to bring up an item without notice (*see* Weller 2007).

Officials wanted tight Treasury control, proposing that: 'The Secretary will not place questions on the list of waiting subjects until they have been discussed in their financial aspects between the Department concerned and the Treasury'. Bruce softened the stance: 'It would greatly facilitate Cabinet business if, before submitting questions for Cabinet decision, they have been discussed in their financial aspects between the department concerned and the Treasury.'

The prime minister approved the agenda for each meeting. The secretary summoned ministers and kept records that 'should be as short as possible and apart from the decision itself will be limited to such explanation as is indispensable to render the decision intelligible'. The secretary would communicate the decisions to ministers. 'The duty of the Secretary will end after he has communicated the decision to the Minister.' The secretariat had no responsibility to follow up the decisions.

The draft from officials emphasised that '[n]o mention will be made of the views of individual Ministers and the principle of the collective responsibility must be carefully maintained', but also suggested that, '[i]n exceptional cases, by decision of Cabinet, a statement by a Minister may be reproduced and annexed to the minutes of decisions after the approval by the Prime Minister'. Bruce excised the second proposal; there were to be no alternative or individual views after cabinet made a decision.

The official draft and the version approved by the prime minister illustrate the inevitable tension that existed in determining the workings of cabinet. Officials want, indeed need, a good record of what is considered and decided as a necessary basis for implementing the decisions of government. It is useful to know what cabinet decided! Ministers need a forum where they can have a healthy debate, secure in the knowledge that the differences of opinion expressed there will not leak into the media. So any formal records that identified division is unwelcome. Bruce's amendments reflected this tension. It also illustrated that, whatever drafts the officials may develop, the prime minister decided what will be acceptable, and in what way it will be enforced.

The first version of the rules was short. Gradually over the years additions were made as problems developed and officials responded by amending the rules to prevent a repetition. In 1941 for the first time the secretary of the DPM&C attended cabinet to maintain a record of decisions. The last minister-secretary had proved hopeless, so that departments could not discover what had been decided in cabinet. In wartime this was a problem (for history, see Weller 2007).

In the 1950s Menzies welcomed each new cabinet with a lecture on the need to listen to their departmental secretaries and follow the cabinet rules. Bit by bit, detail was added, on the items that should be brought to cabinet, on format and presentation of submissions. The *Cabinet Handbook*, as it became titled, grew in coverage and detail. It included definitions of collective responsibility and cabinet confidentiality, required the forecasting of cabinet business, established a ten-day rule for the provision of submissions, set out the format that should be followed, allocated responsibility for implementation and established the rules for access to the cabinet documents of previous governments. In all, by 1980 there were 152 paragraphs.

The Handbook remained confidential; there was no need for the public, or the parliament, to know how the cabinet worked. It was implied that cabinet ministers knew what was required; no one else needed to know. In 1982, in breach of copyright, the *Cabinet Handbook* was published in *Politics*, the journal of the Australasian Political Studies Association. No one cared. When the Handbook was being revised in 1984, officials in PM&C decided that, as an earlier version had been published, they may as well publish the revised edition officially with the Australian Government Printing Service. Since then the cabinet handbooks have been public documents, now available on the PM&C website.

The UK experience

In 1945 Clement Attlee became the first prime minister to circulate rules of procedure to ministers. The document, *Questions of Procedure for Ministers* (QPM), was a consolidation of prime ministerial directives for general guidance' (Baker 2000: 1–3). It was amended by each of Attlee's successors over the next decades. It remained secret. In the late 1980s Peter Hennessy wrote to Number 10 Downing Street asking that the United Kingdom follow the Australian precedent and release the most recent version of QPM; he sent a copy of the Australian *Cabinet Handbook* with the request as evidence of precedent elsewhere. He argued that QPM was the 'nearest thing we have to a written constitution for the proper conduct of cabinet government' (Hennessy 1989). He received a blunt refusal (for the history of QPM, see Baker 2000).

He tried again when John Major became prime minister. This time he had more success. Major agreed in the 1992 election to release the document. He raised the issue in cabinet. It was the only time QPM was discussed by ministers, and the question was whether it should be released, not what procedures ministers should follow. There were some cosmetic changes to the document, making it more positive in places. The core elements were maintained.

The released document was stapled and xeroxed; its somewhat amateur presentation was evidence of its standing as a temporary and working document. QPM became the *Ministerial Code* in 1997. A number of versions have followed. There were also codes for special advisers and civil servants, all now public and available on the Cabinet Office website.

In recent years the government decided to go further. Prime Minister Gordon Brown asked the Cabinet Office to draft a cabinet manual 'to be a source of information on the UK's law, conventions and rules, including those of a constitutional nature, that affect the operations and procedures of government' (United Kingdom Cabinet Office 2010). Seen as particularly important was the chapter that proposed procedures for settling a situation where no government won a clear majority at an election. The titles of the chapters tell the story. They included: Elections and government formation; The Executive – the prime minister, ministers and the structure of government; Collective Cabinet decision-making; The Executive and parliament; The Executive and the law; and Ministers and the civil service. The manual also covered relations with devolved administrations, the European Union and other international organisations.

Prime Minister Cameron wrote in the foreword to a version that was revised and released after the creation of the coalition government that:

> The Cabinet Manual sets out the internal rules and procedures under which the Government operates. For the first time the conventions determining how the Government operates are transparently set out in one place. Codifying and publishing these sheds welcome light on how the Government interacts with other parts of our democratic system (*Cabinet Manual* 2011: iii).

He stated that 'the laws, conventions and rules do not change from one administration to the next'.

Of course there were still special circumstances. All ministers 'were bound by the collective decisions of cabinet, save where it is explicitly set aside' (4.2). Is that a passing rule or a binding constitutional convention? Will it survive a return to majority government?

There were bigger concerns too. Was the manual, or could it become, the first step towards a written constitution? On that there was debate. Committees in both the House of Commons and the House of Lords took evidence and reported on a draft of the manual. The Cabinet Secretary insisted the manual was 'by the executive, about the executive and for the executive' (HC 2010–2011). It was a set of internal rules and guidelines, nothing more.

The problem for members of parliament was that in seeking to codify and record conventions, the manual also had to interpret them. The draft was littered with phrases like 'usually' and 'normally'. But a convention was 'defined as "rules of constitutional practice that are binding in operation but not in law".' There was a clash in the idea that a convention was said to be binding and yet could not be defined with precision.

There is certainly recognition that the manual would create expectations of proper behaviour. The cabinet secretary stated at one point in his evidence: 'The question is what should be the expectations about what PMs should do? Prime Ministers will always be able to do whatever they want in these circumstances. The convention says what they should do' (HC 2010–2011: 23).

Here lies the challenge: determining what they should do while acknowledging that they are not bound to do so. The manual sets out normative understandings of what was proper, even if political calculations might sidetrack them.

The House of Commons discussed whether the manual should be debated in parliament and then endorsed. It agreed with the sentiment of the House of Lords Committee that such a step would give it a false status in its current form as a document by and for the executive. But the committee believed that if the manual were to become part of a shared understanding of the way that the UK's previously un-codified constitution should develop, the parliamentary debate would be appropriate.

The significance of conventions, guidelines and rulebooks

There are a number of conclusions that can be drawn from the above discussion.

First, *all* the cabinet rules, handbooks, guidelines and codes of conduct are essentially the prime ministers' prerogative, to change, alter and interpret. That is true of all the countries mentioned. The prime ministers sign off on the documents. After each election, and particularly when there is a new government, the prime ministers have the opportunity to revise and re-issue the instructions. Even when the prime ministers endorse the rules in a foreword, flexibility remains.

Of course the drafting is done within the bureaucracy, and officials will at times add sentences or sections that cover problem areas that have emerged in the past few years, whether they relate to the procedures and content of submissions or the behaviour of ministers. The ever-expanding content, and the new documents, make up a secret history of past errors and crises. Officials want to make procedures predictable and comprehensive. On the other hand, the prime ministers want to be persuaded that the new rules of procedure are effective and will work to encourage ministers. The need to maintain a balance between political and administrative imperatives will continue. Decisions on the content and format of the rules will be made by prime ministers. The rules are theirs alone. The only occasion when QPM were open for discussion within cabinet was when Major wanted to discuss their publication, not their content.

Prime ministers too decide when and if the rules will be enforced. If there is a ten-day rule to require that ministers have the opportunity to consider issues, prime ministers can decide to dispense with that rule. If items should go first to a committee, prime ministers can still bring them directly to cabinet. If the practice is to circulate decisions to all ministers, prime ministers can decide to limit that circulation. Cabinet committees can be given the authority to make final decisions. Sometimes prime ministers will announce a policy before cabinet has had time to consider it. If they then bring it to cabinet for endorsement, ministers are rather bound to support the prime ministers, as the alternative is to effectively censure and remove them. This hasn't ever happened.

None of these powers are new. Prime ministers used these tactics long before they were incorporated into handbooks and codes. They remain a matter of calculation. What is different is that there are sets of basic rules from which judgements can be made about the wisdom of the judge.

What would happen if they became more than that? That is a very British question. When a committee of the House of Commons reviewed the cabinet manual, the question was raised whether it was the first step in codifying the UK Constitution; by writing the conventions down, the manual created expectations of proper behaviour. There was a concern that 'a cluster of guidelines can grow and harden, first into expectations, then into conventions and ultimately into code if not quite into a fully-fledged constitutional artefact' (Hennessy 2000). If its application was to become broader, should the House of Commons become more formal in its endorsement? The cabinet office insisted not; it was, they said, 'of the executive and for the executive' (HC 2010–2011).

Indeed the questions raised issues about the distinctions between entrenched constitutions, legislative limits on the executive, regulations and codes/guidelines. The House of Commons were concerned that the manual might move up that scale to become formalised, even legislated. Yet that was never an issue in Australia. Given an entrenched constitution it was always clear there that these were indeed rules for the running of government, creating expectations perhaps, but never more. The manual developed and explained rules regarding how ministers should behave but did not provide a legislative basis for their actions. That already existed in the Constitution, but only in the barest of forms. There was in practice little difference between a cabinet within a constitution and one where ideas are unwritten; but there was a greater angst about possible directions. No Australian would suggest, as Peter Hennessy did, that QPM represented elements of the UK Constitution. In countries with a written constitution, there has never been such a concern. Cabinet handbooks are guidelines, useful, creating expectations indeed, but never seen as anything more.

As soon as it becomes more, then the question is raised as to whether it is a document that is open to be justiciable. Can a case be made in a court that the 'proper conventions and procedures' have not been followed? There remains a common conviction that cabinet debates should be private. Insofar as it dealt with cabinet, this made good sense. Cabinet discussion is a debate among colleagues who at least had the future of the government in common. Outside the room they want to appear united; inside they could disagree until they came to a decision. Cabinet developed to meet a need: the opportunity to have a frank and open discussion about difficult problems, where alternative solutions and policy options were possible.

If those protections were removed, if cabinet became more open, ministers would simply remove their discussions somewhere else and would use the formal cabinet meetings to endorse without debate what they had decided already. Cabinet would very quickly become a formal and dignified, rather than a working, part of the constitutions.

That was behind the Australian cabinet decision to protect the cabinet notebooks from courts. The notebooks were the records kept by the official note takers. They were not a verbatim record of the discussions, rather they included as much of the discussions as the individual note taker thought necessary to ensure an accurate decision. Some were fuller than others; all were in part idiosyncratic. When a court sought to subpoena the records cabinet passed legislation that protected them for fifty years. They may in any event have not proved useful, but it was important that individual minister's views were not publicised.

Cabinet is valuable because of its flexibility. Prime ministers can adjust the working and the forums in the way that they see best. They do not have to ask if the procedures are somehow right, but rather whether they work in reaching a properly informed decision.

Are cabinet rules conventions?

The introduction to this volume cited Wheare's (1960) definition of a convention as 'a binding rule, a rule of behaviour accepted as obligatory by those concerned in the working of the Constitution.' Are the rules discussed here binding or accepted? The cabinet manual talks as though UK conventions are binding and clear, even while qualifying them. Therefore the answer must surely be a 'yes, but...'

Collective responsibility may be accepted as a binding rule, but quite what it means and how/whether it will be applied varies from case to case. Ministers take the concept of ministerial responsibility seriously. They know that they have to account for their actions and answer to parliament. But they do not know exactly what is regarded as satisfactory performance and whether, in a time of crisis, they may fall short of that mythical line of competence. Nor can they predict whether prime ministers will stick with them or cut them adrift if they perform poorly or get caught in a scandal.

So too the 'rules' of cabinet are less than binding. Even the most solid of 'conventions' may suddenly be found short. All the handbooks have a clause that limits the access to the cabinet records of previous governments. Access to those records requires the approval of the leader of the party that had held government. That was the 'rule'. But in 2014 the Australian government released some cabinet records of its predecessor to a royal commission without asking approval. There was nothing the former government could do to prevent it.

That decision might have been an extreme. It raises the question whether there are *any* sections of the cabinet handbooks or codes that could not, with the approval of the prime minister, be put into abeyance. If the prime ministers are the author, judge and executioner for the application of the handbooks, then at any time they can chose to ignore a rule. At different times they have bypassed, ignored or interpreted some of them almost out of existence. The cited comment of the UK Cabinet Secretary that prime ministers will do what they want merely stresses that interpretation.

But they still always do so while insisting that their interpretation aligns with the principles of collective or ministerial responsibility. The principle *is* usually largely kept intact as an element of political necessity. To ignore any one rule is surely very different from saying prime ministers can put all the rules into abeyance. Nor would they want to; they are essential elements of cohesive government. If it is difficult to argue that the rules and conventions of cabinet are prescriptive and precise in determining how prime ministers can act, but that is not to suggest they can ignore all the rules at the same time.

Of course some argue that is exactly what has happened on occasion. It comes to a question of what cabinet government constitutes. One view can be termed *constitutional.* Blair, it was argued, practised 'sofa government', because cabinet no longer made the crucial decisions; rather these were determined in committee and through cooperation between the prime minister and committee chairs. Cabinet was for an exchange of information; it was no longer the driving force of government. Canadian conclusions were similar: cabinet government was dead under Chrétien (Savoie 1999).

An alternative political or realist view is that modern pressures have simply changed the demands on prime ministers and on cabinet. Conventions have adjusted to satisfy these new demands. One academic reports an early comment from Blair that 'Ministers have to understand they are the agents of the centre. They have been sent to the departments to carry out a strategy.' His evaluation of Blair's statement is that: 'I cannot imagine many other Prime Ministers saying that' (Kavanagh, evidence to 2010 HL 30: 22).

This realist version wants to describe what is and then make it work better. Blair adviser Jonathan Powell suggests that: 'Rather than arguing about the death of Cabinet government, when it in fact died a long time ago, we should spend more effort reinforcing the cabinet committees and their supporting infrastructure as a key part of government decision making' (cited in HL 2010: 180).

A civil servant, now cabinet secretary, too shrugged off the debate:

> I think it partly depends on whether you mean Cabinet government as a meeting once a week or Cabinet government as a set of principles... Every single decision coming through one meeting a week at which there are 20–25 people is not a test of whether Cabinet government is dead (Heywood in HL 2010: 158).

He suggested that civil servants tried to ensure that 'all the Cabinet departments and Cabinet Ministers with a responsibility have every opportunity to debate, discuss, disagree, agree and we do not announce a policy unless everyone with an interest is signed off and then everyone is bound by the principle of collective responsibility [that is] alive and well in Whitehall' (HL 2010: 158).

If that interpretation is accepted, then it may be possible to argue that cabinet government can be seen as an only partly defined convention, and that under pressure none of the component parts can be regarded as binding. If government is collective government, and the consent of the collectivity of ministers, or at least their acquiescence, has to be obtained, then there are a multiplicity of ways that can be achieved.

Handbooks and manuals are one interpretation, albeit the current one. How seriously they are regarded (and the evidence suggest they are taken more seriously in the United Kingdom than in Australia), then the costs of ignoring them may be greater. But they still can be adjusted for new circumstances.

Prime ministers who do not work with their ministers can create trouble for themselves, not so much on individual policy issues, but in the longer run. New prime ministers, whether following Thatcher, Blair, Chrétien or Rudd, promise that they will re-institute 'proper' cabinet government; they appeal to a broader notion of how government in these systems should be run.

If that is so, then the political conventions of ministerial and collective government fall short of Wheare's binding and obligatory rules, because they are too vague in their application to be binding. The handbooks and codes that instruct ministers and explicate these conventions are less than binding too because prime ministers can interpret them on any occasion in a way that suits their purposes. That does not mean that they do not matter or that ministers somehow feel relieved of the imprecise burden that they impose. Flexibility does not define these ideas out of existence. Rather, they need to be understood within the broader convention that prime ministers work with ministers in changing forums designed to achieve desired outcomes. These forums may include cabinet meetings but are not limited to that. Cabinet government is an ideal, a convention, a process, to achieve the government's outcomes; it cannot be limited to a forum or a weekly meeting.

Perhaps Wheare's formulation is too rigid. Ministers understand the conventions and their flexibility. Most prime ministers are aware that there are limits beyond which it is unwise to push. The expectations created by the conventions of cabinet government are more important than the precise meanings of the grand conventions or the implementation of binding rules of procedure that determine how cabinet government will work.

References

Bagehot, Walter [1867] 1963. *The English Constitution* (with an introduction by R.H.S. Crossman). London: Fontana.

Baker, Amy 2000. *Prime Ministers and the Rule Book*. London: Politico's.

Blewett, Neal 1999. *A Cabinet Diary*. Adelaide: Wakefield Press.

Commonwealth of Australia 1983. *Cabinet Handbook*. Canberra: Australian Government Publishing Service.

Government of Canada Privy Council Office 2011. *Accountable Government: A Guide for Ministers and Ministers of State*. Ottawa: Government of Canada.

Hennessy, Peter 1989. 'Thatcher Declines to Disclose Rules of the Ministerial Game', *The Independent*, 1 May 1989.

Hennessy, Peter 2000. 'Preface, to Baker, Amy 2000'. *Prime Ministers and the Rule Book*. London: Politico's.

Mackintosh, John 1962. *The British Cabinet*. London: Stevens.

New Zealand Department of Prime Minister and Cabinet 2008. *Cabinet Manual*. Wellington: DPM&C.

QPM 1992. *Questions of Procedure for Ministers*. London: Cabinet Office.

Savoie, Donald 1999. *Governing from the Centre*. University of Toronto Press.

United Kingdom Cabinet Office 2010. *The Cabinet Manual – Draft*. Available from: www.gov.uk/government/uploads/system/uploads/attachment_data/file/60645/cabinetdraftmanual.pdf.

United Kingdom Cabinet Office 2011. *Cabinet Manual*. London: Cabinet Office. Available from: www.gov.uk/government/uploads/system/uploads/attachment_data/file/60641/cabinet-manual.pdf.

United Kingdom House of Commons Political and Constitutional Committee 2011. *Constitutional Implications of the Cabinet Manual*, Sixth Report of Session 2010–2011, HC 734.

United Kingdom House of Lords Select Committee on the Constitution 2010. *The Cabinet Office and the Centre of Government, 4th Report Session 2009–2010, HL 30*. London: Stationery Office.

Weller, Patrick 2007. *Cabinet Government in Australia, 1901–2006: Practice, Principles, Performance*. Sydney: University of New South Wales Press.

Wheare, K. C. 1960. *Modern Constitutions*. Oxford University Press.

5

Caretaker conventions

JENNIFER MENZIES AND ANNE TIERNAN

Elections are nervous times for both the incumbent government and the opposition. Modern politics is hard fought, and in such a win/lose environment there is great pressure not to give an edge to political opponents. The Westminster parliamentary model provides for both continuity and restraint during the election and transition period with caretaker conventions. The aim of the conventions is to hold the incumbent government to a 'status quo' until the new government is formed (Laver and Shepsle 1994: 292). Westminster governments share an inheritance on the structure and organisation of government. This is supplemented by a set of beliefs and practices about how these core institutions should be managed. The Westminster convention of responsible government- where the executive and government are held accountable to the parliament - remains a core belief (Rhodes et al. 2009: 3). Although adapted to local circumstances and experience, it is a governing tradition shared by the Australian, Canadian, New Zealand and UK parliamentary systems.

Caretaker conventions are a subset of the convention of accountability of the elected government to parliament. They are intended to moderate the advantages of incumbency by constraining the power of the political executive until a new government is formed (Menzies and Tiernan 2014:13). Like other conventions, they adapt and respond to changing political practice and mores, as well as to community values. Caretaker conventions seek to constrain the behaviour of politicians in the heat of partisan contest. Perceived breaches of the conventions draw controversy and commentary, both informed and ill-informed. As self-nominated custodians of the caretaker conventions, public officials have sought to promulgate the caretaker principles and to protect the impartiality of the public service. Their efforts to do so are apparent in the trend to greater guidance and documentation of the practices that govern administrative behaviour during the caretaker period. These 'guidance' documents, often published and publicly available, are designed to guide both ministerial and bureaucratic decision making during the caretaker period. They are reviewed and updated regularly to incorporate new issues as they arise.

This chapter describes the evolution and application of the caretaker conventions at the national level in four Westminster-style systems – Australia, Canada, New Zealand and the United Kingdom. We analyse their similarities and differences and consider how and why new and different practices have evolved over time. We use case study examples to illustrate how officials seek to resolve the dilemmas they encounter as custodians of the caretaker conventions and to show that a breach of the caretaker conventions is often a catalyst for increased documentation. This is evident in the proliferation of guidance documents that provide increasingly more specific advice on the caretaker principles. We argue the guidance documents serve two purposes. First, they have become an important means by which senior officials seek to preserve institutional memory for future generations of public servants. Second, the guidance documents have become a useful means of 'pushing back' and defending the principle of restraint in an increasingly partisan context. We conclude that public servants' custodianship of the moral and technical elements of caretaker conventions have implications and perhaps too, unintended consequences, for mutual obligation and reciprocity, which remain the identifying characteristics of a constitutional convention.

Characteristics

Constitutional conventions share a number of characteristics. For those countries with a written constitution, the provisions of the constitution comprise the formal rules of government. In areas about which the constitution is silent, political behaviour is guided by 'well established practice, methods, habits, maxims and usages' which were 'inherited from colonial parliaments, which in turn inherited them from Westminster' (Reid 1977: 244). Marshall and Moodie defined constitutional conventions as follows:

> By conventions of the constitution, we mean the binding rules of constitutional behaviour which are considered to be binding by and upon those who operate the constitution, but which are not enforced by the law courts (although the courts may recognise their existence), nor by the presiding officers in the houses of Parliament (Marshall and Moodie 1971: 26).

Caretaker conventions, like all constitutional conventions, are not legally binding (Dicey 1959: 439). Political actors recognise and abide by conventions because 'they are believed to formulate valid rules of obligation' (Marshall, cited in Jaconelli 2005: 151). For a convention to exist, actors must be aware of the obligation to curtail their behaviour and to continue to believe they are bound by the convention (Wheare 1951: 179). Conventions are 'practice-dependent'; they are followed because others have followed them (Marmor 2007: 591). Marshall notes that conventions arise from 'a series of precedents that are agreed to have given rise to a binding rule of behaviour' (Marshall 1984: 8). Alternatively, a convention may derive from some 'acknowledged principle of government which provides a reason or justification for it' with many conventions being negative in form – connoting that political actors should constrain their behaviour or refrain from certain courses of action (Marshall 1984: 9). The caretaker convention shares all of these characteristics: they are not legally binding; political actors acknowledge their existence and feel obliged to take note of the convention, and to curtail their behaviour.

There are two elements of caretaker conventions. The first is to prevent an outgoing government from locking an incoming government into major, new policy, funding commitments or significant appointments. The intention here is to maintain the policy 'status quo' until the next government is sworn in. The second element is to ensure the incumbent government does not gain an unfair electoral advantage by inappropriately drawing on the resources of the public service to support its activities. Applying Heard's classification, caretaker conventions fall into the category of a *semi-convention*, by which he means a set of rules which prescribe a desirable manner of behaviour but may be occasionally disregarded without significant impact, for example triggering a constitutional crisis (Heard 1989: 73).[1]

Conventions are considered inherently political – they originate with political actors developing practices and principles to direct political actors on how to behave in managing the business of government (Heard 1991: 146). This political stewardship is seen as critical to the continuation of a convention. Forsey describes the lifecycle of a convention in political terms: 'first and foremost, they are political; political in their birth, political in their growth and decay, and political in their

[1] Heard identified five types of conventions – fundamental conventions, meso conventions, semi-conventions, infra-conventions and usages (Heard 1991: 145–9).

applications and sanctions' (Forsey, quoted in Heard 1991: 5). To remain relevant, a convention must be passed on to each next generation of politicians, who learn through experience 'how things are done'.

But the literature is silent on how this transmission occurs. Rhodes (2014) highlights the informal and experiential processes of apprenticeship and socialisation by which this often tacit and secret 'craft knowledge' is passed on. Both the nature of modern politics and the politicians it attracts have raised questions about the processes of knowledge-transfer implicit to Forsey's formulation, and more fundamentally about partisans' ability to remember and learn from experience (Rhodes and Tiernan 2014). We argue the role of the public service has been underplayed with respect to the transmission of caretaker conventions and that by default officials have become custodians of certain conventions. The most politically fraught and dangerous time for the public service is during election campaigns and transitions of government. The motivation for public servants to have a tool to push back against political requests and to put boundaries around their activities during an election campaign is high. Officials are held accountable for breaching caretaker conventions in ways politicians are not. The requirement for public servants to be impartial is legalised within codes of conduct and public service acts (Menzies and Tiernan 2014: 15–16).

The bureaucracy has responded by reconstituting the norm of caretaker conventions for each election and taking a role in managing decisions of what does or does not constitute a breach. The danger is this activity weakens political actors' commitment because their 'obedience' is not driven by the 'moral' or 'obligatory' elements intrinsic to a convention but is externally applied.

Origin and documentation

Tracing the origin of a convention is not easy. Many are formulated over time and only written down long after initial application. The convention of ministerial responsibility to parliament can be traced back to the mid-nineteenth century in the United Kingdom when customary practices began to take form and was systematised and articulated (Rhodes et al. 2009: 57–8). With the acceptance of ministerial responsibility grew the acceptance of the need for restraint by the incumbent government during the election campaign.

Australia

In Australia, caretaker conventions were first articulated when Prime Minister Robert Menzies wrote to his ministers in 1951 at the outset of a double dissolution election:

> I should also be glad if you would note that whilst continuing to take whatever action you deem necessary in connection with the ordinary administration of your department, you should not make decisions on matters of policy or those of a contentious nature without first referring the matter to myself (quoted in DPM&C 1987: 40).

By 1961, the established practice was for the prime minister to write to all ministers advising them explicitly of the need to avoid 'major policy decisions or important appointments' in the relevant period (DPM&C 1987). The ball was firmly in the ministers' court, it being their responsibility to behave accordingly. More detailed guidance – particularly on consultations with the opposition – was needed when, after two decades of Coalition government, the 1969 election raised the prospect of a change of government. In the event, three more years would elapse before it became a reality. The 1972 election saw the public service confront a transition for the first time in twenty-three years (Tiernan and Menzies 2007: 16).

The conventions were gradually refined over the years (Codd 1996: 23). The first detailed text of their intent and application was published in 1987 as a special article in the Department of the Prime Minister and Cabinet's (DPM&C) *Annual Report 1986–87*. Noting the relative lack of written material on the conventions, it reflected 'the Department's experience in relation to the conventions and associated practices, arising from its advisory and coordinating role' (DPM&C 1987: 39). This may indicate that the imperative for clarifying caretaker arrangements had shifted from the realm of the political (guidance to ministers about what they could and should do) to the administrative. A major review and consolidation of the existing caretaker arrangements was undertaken by the DPM&C after the 1987 election. Thereafter, a summary of the guidance on caretaker conventions, with an emphasis on cabinet matters, was incorporated into the *Cabinet Handbook*. This is supplemented at each election with the DPM&C's *Guidance on Caretaker Conventions* which now runs to twelve pages (DPM&C 2013).

Canada

In Canada, articulation of the convention first appeared in the *Manual of Office Procedure of the Government of Canada* released by the Privy Council Office (PCO) in 1968. The Manual was a document for senior public servants. It was circulated internally, but was not subsequently reviewed or updated and is not available publicly (Bowden and MacDonald 2012: 374). This early exposure of caretaker conventions has not become the norm for Canada: it is the only jurisdiction surveyed that does not make its caretaker guidance publicly available.

However, the PCO does maintain a detailed guidance that is updated after every election, as discussed in Chapter 13. The guidance is reviewed at the last cabinet meeting held before the election and is then issued to both ministers and deputy ministers (departmental heads) as a cabinet in confidence document (Senior Canadian Official, 2014, personal communication). The 2008 guidance was released through a freedom of information request and in the scope of issues covered closely resembles the Australian and New Zealand equivalents.[2] The lack of a published guidance means the opposition's role in maintaining the reciprocity of the convention is diminished. Despite this, since the 1993 Pearson airport dispute, there have been low levels of controversy around the application of the caretaker convention. This lack of publication seems to have given Canadian officials greater authority in putting boundaries around government activity during the caretaker period. The role of Clerk of the PCO has been enhanced: 'the caretaker convention entrusts the Clerk with the authority to ensure no significant decisions are made that might bind a future government' (Public Policy Forum 2012: 6). The entrusting of the responsibility to the Clerk implies it is public officials who take on the moral custodianship of the conventions, rather than politicians in government and opposition.

However, recently Canadian public officials have had constraints put around their activity during an election campaign. Like other Westminster jurisdictions, Canadian officials have been able to brief the opposition on issues of transition to help them prepare for a possible change of government. Both Prime Ministers Stephen Harper and Paul Martin have refused requests for these sessions to take place (Zussman 2013:

[2] The senior official from the Privy Council Office interviewed for this chapter (2014) stated this version is now outdated. Canada goes to the polls in October 2015, so a new guidance document will be in development. We have used the 2008 guidance document as a reference point to compare the scope of the Canadian guidance with the other jurisdictions surveyed.

111). Prime Minister Harper has also curtailed the activities of public servants during an election, discouraging them from giving speeches, conference presentations and explaining policies and programs at public events (Zussman 2013: 107). This constraint on the public service continuing the normal business of government during an election has added complexity to the Canadian caretaker period, which is not alleviated by publicly available guidelines setting out proper processes.

New Zealand

In New Zealand, caretaker conventions are documented in the *Cabinet Manual*, first produced as an internal document to government in 1979, and subsequently published in 1996 as a response to the uncertainty arising from the introduction of a mixed-member proportional (MMP) electoral system in New Zealand (Boston et al. 1998: 637). The adoption of the MMP electoral system has had a profound impact on New Zealand's caretaker arrangements with the expectation that longer transition times would become the norm in forming government in New Zealand. Boston notes that this development 'supplied the necessary political incentive for a more careful formulation of the conventions governing caretaker administrations', and a new formulation was developed to give guidance to the period after the election but before the swearing in of the new government (Boston et al. 1998: 637). Caretaker conventions have 'two arms', each of which has its own constitutional principles. The first arm applies when it is not clear who will form the next government, and the second applies when it is clear who will form government, but they have not yet taken office. The Cabinet Manual is updated every five years to reflect change in legislation or cabinet decisions (Kitteridge 2006).

The United Kingdom

The articulation of caretaker conventions did not emerge until post-World War II when Winston Churchill was commissioned, before the 1945 election, to lead a two-month caretaker government in response to Labour leader Clement Atlee leaving the National government (Killey 2009: 238). Despite this early articulation, it has been argued the UK caretaker convention remained underdeveloped for some time (Hazell and Riddell 2010: 1). The Cabinet Office produced internal guidance that was issued as the *Head of Department's Personal Handbook*. This was superseded by the publication of the two-volume *Civil Service Guidance* in 2010, which was again a document internal to the civil service (Cabinet Office 2010).

However, amidst speculation the 2010 general election could deliver a 'hung parliament', the Prime Minister, Gordon Brown, announced that he had 'asked the Cabinet Secretary to lead work to consolidate the existing, unwritten, piecemeal conventions that govern much of the way central government operates under our existing constitution, into a single written document' (Brown 2010). Cabinet Secretary Sir Gus O'Donnell provided a copy of the draft chapter covering elections and government formation to the House of Commons Justice Committee, which held an evidence session to canvas 'how constitutional principle, provision and practice apply after general elections' (House of Commons Justice Committee 2010: 3). O'Donnell and several of his predecessor cabinet secretaries gave evidence about the application of caretaker principles, along with academic and other constitutional experts.

After the 2010 election, guidance was supplemented in 2011 with the release of the first edition of the *Cabinet Manual.* Prime Minister David Cameron hailed publication of the manual as a codification of the conventions under which the government operated (Cameron 2011: iii). The Manual described its role as a 'guide for those working in government' and was developed in response to the hung parliament that followed the 2010 election (O'Donnell 2011: v). Though the manual has a section on elections and government formation, the real detail on how to manage during the caretaker period is provided in the *General Election Guidance*, released by the Cabinet Office before the election. The Guidance presents detailed advice for civil servants on a range of government activities and how they should deal with them. At thirty-nine pages, it is the most detailed of the guidance documents surveyed for this chapter (Cabinet Office 2015).

Caretaker principles

Our survey of the four jurisdictions reveals a high degree of consistency. The principles underpinning caretaker conventions are accepted by all four jurisdictions, and there are strong similarities in ways they are articulated. There is consensus that caretaker conventions are based on two principles:

1. with the dissolution of the House, there is no popular chamber to which the Executive government can be responsible; and
2. every general election brings with it the possibility of a change of government (DPM&C 1987: 39).

> From these two principles, a number of sub-principles emerge. They include:
>
> - not binding or limiting the freedom of an incoming government;
> - that the incumbent government should exercise restraint in its decision-making;
> - the routine business of government continues;
> - if urgent matters arise which require a decision, the opposition should be consulted;
> - final decisions concerning the conventions sit with the prime minister;
> - the resources of the public service should not be used for electoral advantage;
> - public servants should remain impartial.

Such consistency is unsurprising, considering all four jurisdictions have evolved from a common set of beliefs that constitute the Westminster model. It may also reflect learning and policy transfer amongst senior officials from the Westminster network, who meet regularly to share experience and ideas. These beliefs have developed their own governmental traditions, as they were adapted to local circumstances, imperatives and arrangements over time (see Rhodes et al. 2009: 5–9; Wanna 2014). This, along with efforts to address dilemmas confronted by political actors at different points, may account for divergent practices. Still, there is striking similarity in the beliefs and practices that surround the caretaker principles in our four countries as they have come to be formalised in written guidance documents.

When do the conventions apply? The emerging issue of long transitions

There is divergence between Australia and other jurisdictions about what is considered the caretaker period. In Australia, the caretaker conventions apply from the dissolution of parliament and conclude when the election result is known with either the confirmation of the continuation of the incumbent government or the commissioning of a new government (DPM&C 2013). For Canada, New Zealand and the United Kingdom, there is a subtle distinction between the election period, from the dissolution of parliament until election day, and the post-election transition under a 'caretaker' government until the new government is sworn in (NZDMP&C 2008; Cabinet Office 2015; Senior Canadian Official 2014).[3] In the first phase, it is acknowledged the government retains full legal authority to govern during the campaign but must exercise restraint (Government of Canada 2008: 1; Cabinet Office 2015: 3). For example in New Zealand, restraints have tended to be applied from approximately three months before the general election is due or, if the period between the announcement of the election and polling day is less than three months, from the announcement of the election (DPM&C 2008: 76–7). Until recently in the United Kingdom, restrictions on government activity during the pre-election period were commonly referred to as the election 'purdah'. Anticipation in the lead up to,[4] and the experience of, the 2010 election,[5] prompted reconsideration of the use of the term 'purdah'. The current Cabinet Manual does not refer to purdah or caretaker, instead using the phrase 'restrictions on government activity'.

In the post-election-day phase, if there is a change of government, the focus is on ensuring the outgoing government cannot bind the new government to major policy or financial decisions. For the purpose of this chapter we define the caretaker period as from the dissolution of parliament until the new government is commissioned.

In the past, the focus of caretaker conventions was on the period from the calling of the election until the result was known. With relatively short election periods and the dominance of single-party majority governments, transitions were usually swift and government formation was easily achieved. This changed for New Zealand with the introduction of the MMP electoral system from the 1990s which led to lengthy periods of government formation – as happened in 1996, for example, when the caretaker period lasted for nine weeks. In response, the New Zealand

[3] Though the caretaker period technically begins with the dissolution of the parliament, the public service usually begins to apply the election guidance from the date the election was announced (Cabinet Office 2015: 3).

[4] The House of Commons Justice Committee published a report into the constitutional processes following a general election in 16 March 2010, before the election. The report recommended the use of the term 'caretaker' in formal guidance over 'purdah', as it found that 'purdah' traditionally referred to restrictions on government announcements, as opposed to more general restrictions as per caretaker conventions in other jurisdictions.

[5] The House of Commons Political and Constitutional Reform Committee published its report into the lessons for the process of government formation from the 2010 general election.

caretaker conventions have a substantial section to guide officials on decision making during that interregnum (Cabinet Office 2011: 1).

For Australia and the United Kingdom, hung parliaments, and the long transition periods that accompany their formation, have been rare in the post–World War II period. The focus for the operation of caretaker conventions was on the period until election results were known, usually on election day, or soon after. The need to develop specific guidelines regarding the period after elections emerged as an issue for both Australia and the United Kingdom after their 2010 national elections. Both faced the challenges of a long transition because for the first time in more than forty and thirty years respectively, voters delivered neither political party a majority in the lower house (see House of Commons Political and Constitutional Reform Committee 2011; Costar 2012). Canada too began a cycle of hung parliaments from 2004, and this added complexity to what was traditionally a long transition period from election day to the first sitting of the new parliament (Franks 2011: 23).[6]

To manage these unusual circumstances in Australia, the DPM&C quickly developed and distributed *Guidelines for Post-election Consultations with Independent Members* (2010). These guidelines advised that senior officials could hold discussions with independent members after agreement from the prime minister and after giving notice of the meeting to the leader of the opposition. They also outlined the restrictions on public service advice and the need to offer only factual information or advice on technical and procedural aspects of administration and policy administration (DPM&C 2010).

It was noted earlier that, in the United Kingdom, officials, politicians and analysts were concerned about the possibility of a hung parliament and a lengthy transition period well before the May 2010 general election. A draft cabinet manual was in development, but no authoritative advice was available to either the civil service or the general public on the role of the incumbent government during the five days it took for Conservative leader David Cameron to negotiate to form a Coalition government with the Liberal Democrats. To respond to the uncertainty created by the lack of precedent, and under pressure from Buckingham Palace, the cabinet secretary published his advice offering a framework for negotiation on forming a Coalition government in the event of a hung parliament

[6] In Canada, the average time between the dissolution of parliament and the first sitting of the new parliament is 144 days. When there is a change of government, the average transition time from election day to the first sitting is 91 days (Franks 2011: 21–3).

(House of Commons Political and Constitutional Reform Committee 2011: Ev 49). Like Australia, the advice allowed for the leaders of political parties to seek the support of the civil service on constitutional issues, machinery of government and the costing of policies (DPM&C 2010). In the event, there was little take-up of the civil service's assistance. The political parties handled negotiations directly (House of Commons Political and Constitutional Reform Committee 2011: 14–15).

In Canada, the uncertainty around hung parliaments resulted in an ongoing debate about the lack of clear, publicly available guidelines on the process of government formation and the extended caretaker period that this entails (Russell 2009; Bowden and MacDonald 2012; Public Policy Forum 2012; Cappe 2013). As Peter Russell explains in Chapter 13, critics have called for the development and publication of a Canadian cabinet manual, based on the UK and New Zealand models, to reduce confusion about the principles and conventions which apply to government formation and to bring Canada into line with other Commonwealth countries (Public Policy Forum 2012: 3).

Controversies and stresses

Conflict over perceived breaches of caretaker conventions during an election period can be sharp and bitter. The stakes are high and concerns about breaches during the campaign frequently lead to long post-mortems, particularly when there is a change of government and the outrage experienced in opposition remains undiminished in government. The following four case studies describe such a turning point in the jurisdictions surveyed; they also serve to highlight that it is public service officials who are required to give evidence to any post-election enquiry, not their former political masters.

Australia: 'By Boat, No Visa'

During the 2013 Australian federal election, the Labor government, headed by Prime Minister Kevin Rudd decided to continue the $30-million 'By Boat, No Visa' advertising campaign after the caretaker period commenced. The advertisements, run in mainstream media, including television, radio and newspapers, both in Australia and overseas, were designed to deter asylum seekers from arriving in Australia by boat. The issue had been controversial in Australia for a number of years with both sides of politics seeking to show they were 'tough' on people smugglers. In line with the *Guidance on Caretaker Conventions*, all advertising campaigns were reviewed at the beginning of the caretaker period by the Departments of Finance and Deregulation and Prime Minister and Cabinet. Bipartisan agreement was then sought for campaigns that were to continue. In the case of the 'By Boat, No Visa' campaign, opposition leader Tony Abbott wrote to Prime Minister Rudd advising the opposition did not support the continuation of these ads in Australia and that he believed they 'were being used for partisan political purposes' (Abbott 2013).

When the government decided to continue airing the advertisements, the opposition leader then followed up with a letter to the secretary of the DPM&C, Ian Watt, asking him to enforce the conventions. The secretary replied:

> responsibility for observing the conventions ultimately rests with decision makers, be they agency heads or, in the cases where they are involved, with Ministers and/or the Prime Minister. Decision makers, including Ministers, are not prevented from making decisions, as the conventions are not legally binding. The Department does not have the power to enforce the observance of the conventions (Watt 2013).

In defending this decision, Immigration Minister Tony Burke said the caretaker conventions provided for consultation and that had occurred (Ross 2013). The independent auditor-general, Ian McPhee, was also involved in the controversy when a complaint about the continuation of the ads was made to him. His response was 'the caretaker conventions give the government latitude when it comes to advertising campaigns, and noted in any case the conventions were not legally binding' (Morozow 2013). As Ian Watt pointed out in his letter to Tony Abbott, the respective secretaries were directed by their ministers to continue the campaign. He said 'both Secretaries have complied with the directions, as they are required to under the *Public Service Act*' (Watt 2013). Watt's letter makes clear the basis on which the advertising campaign would continue – at the lawful direction of ministers, which by law and convention, officials are bound to follow. His response can be read as an effort to safeguard public service neutrality amidst a bitter and rapidly escalating partisan battle.

Following the election of the Liberal coalition government, the secretary of the Department of Finance, David Tune, was asked about the continuation of the advertising at the Senate Estimates hearings. He described his involvement:

> The issue was on this occasion we were in the caretaker period and there are conventions around actions by public servants in that period of time, which I take seriously as a secretary and my department takes seriously. There was a contrary view. As a result of that the direction occurred (Senate Estimates Hearing 2014: 43).

The secretary went on to say he could not recall another instance where a senior official was directed by a minister to continue an advertising campaign during an election.

Canada: Pearson airport

The Pearson airport controversy during the 1993 election coalesced around the signing of a contract to privatise the Pearson airport. If signed, it would bind future governments to a fifty-seven-year lease (Parliament of Canada 1995). Prime Minister Kim Campbell approved the contract for the privatisation of the Pearson airport after the dissolution of the parliament. The airport privatisation had been the centre of substantial debate for a number of years. Concerns were expressed about the tender process and the Mulroney government's apparent preference for a proposal submitted by the company Paxport. These concerns came from both within government and outside. The Treasury Board Secretariat issued several memoranda outlining its concerns about the process including the non-compliance of Paxport with the request for proposal (RFP). This official advice was supported by a Deloitte and Touche report that Paxport did not have the capacity to finance the project (Parliament of Canada 1995). There was also political opposition, with leader of the opposition Jean Chrétien expressing his concerns in parliament.

In the run up to the election, public servants from the Privy Council Office and other departments faced intense pressure to finalise complex negotiations for the signing of the lease before the election. Officials spoke of 'the political pressure that was applied' and of the prime minister's active interest in the project (Parliament of Canada 1995: 19). Parliament was dissolved on 8 September 1993 with the election date set for 25 October. In February that year, Kim Campbell, who replaced Brian Mulroney as prime minister, said she maintained the government's commitment to finalising the airport deal.

The challenges for public servants dealing with the Pearson airport contract during an election campaign were many. The signing of the contract was an obvious breach of the caretaker conventions. The

Guidelines on the Conduct of Ministers, Secretaries of State, Exempt Staff and Public Servants During an Election assert the government should restrict policy and expenditure decisions to activities that are routine, non-controversial, urgent, reversible by a new government or agreed to by the opposition (Government of Canada 2008: 1). The signing of the contract breached all of these criteria. Yet officials were powerless to prevent this action and, when directed by the prime minister, were obliged to properly implement her instructions. Conventions were designed to regulate political behaviour, yet it was the officials who were compelled to appear before the Special Senate Committee on the Pearson Airport Agreements to explain their role in the signing of the contracts. The sanctions on politicians for breaching the caretaker conventions are moral and political. Public unease regarding signing of the contract likely contributed to the significant defeat the Progressive Conservative party faced at the election.[7]

New Zealand: currency crisis

The July 1984 general election delivered a landslide victory to Labour, and ended the term of the National government led by Prime Minister Sir Robert Muldoon. It was expected to take about ten days for the return of the writs. During the campaign, currency speculators, expecting Labour would devalue the currency, made a run on the New Zealand dollar leading to a foreign exchange crisis (Boston et al. 1998: 635). Controversy arose, however, when outgoing Prime Minister Muldoon refused to act on advice from the New Zealand Reserve Bank that the dollar should be devalued because of the run on the nation's foreign currency reserves.[8] As a currency crisis loomed, the defeated Muldoon refused to meet with officials over the weekend, despite their concerns that opening of the foreign exchange markets would trigger a financial crisis.

7 The Conservative party was annihilated at the election and lost all but two of its previous 156 seats.

8 In his biography of Muldoon, Barry Gustafson (2000, 384–96) explains Muldoon's rationale for rejecting this advice. He had been in dispute with the Secretary to the Treasury and the Reserve Bank Governor over the matter for several months. Muldoon suspected that they were using the opportunity provided by the pre-election run on the New Zealand currency to re-prosecute advice he had previously rejected.

The governor of the Reserve Bank also briefed the prime minister elect David Lange on the need for urgent action to devalue the currency. Lange supported devaluation and suggested 'Muldoon should either implement the incoming government's instructions or resign and let another member of the National Cabinet take over as caretaker prime minister for a week until Labour took office' (Gustafson 2000: 392). After much wrangling, Muldoon relented under pressure from his cabinet colleagues,[9] but the situation raised questions about the authority and responsibilities of a defeated government during the period leading up to its formal replacement by an incoming administration.

The experience was a catalyst for more explicit guidance about the actions of outgoing governments during the caretaker period. In 1986, an Officials Committee on Constitutional Reform was established. Its recommendations on the constraints on an outgoing government during the caretaker period were accepted by both parties (Boston et al. 1998: 635). The convention, formalised by its subsequent incorporation into the Cabinet Manual, states:

The outgoing government should:

> act on the advice of the incoming government on any matter of such constitutional, economic or other significance that it cannot be delayed until the new government formally takes office – even if the outgoing government disagrees with the course of action proposed (NZDPM&C 2008: 79).

The currency crisis led to an explicit articulation of the constraints of an outgoing government and a further explanation of the caretaker principle that already existed. During the crisis, Reserve Bank and DPM&C officials were consulting with both parties in order to reach a decision of devaluation. After the election, it was a bureaucratic process that led to the articulation of the caretaker convention and the subsequent increase in guidance in the Cabinet Manual.

The United Kingdom: Transition of Government 2010

The likelihood of a hung parliament had been widely anticipated. Indeed, for eighteen months prior to the May 2010 election, analysts including notably the Institute for Government had been promoting debate about

[9] Who were prepared to advise the governor-general that Muldoon no longer enjoyed their confidence and should hand over to his deputy.

constitutional conventions and other issues relevant to transitions of government and the formation of minority governments. Despite their work and acknowledged efforts by the Cabinet Office to share the details of proposed arrangements, concerns emerged about:

- the legitimacy of the prime minister continuing to hold office;
- the role of the civil service in negotiations over the formation of a minority government;
- how to ensure the Monarch did not become mired in controversy over the formation of a new government.

As noted, for the first time since 1974, the May 2010 general election delivered neither of the parties a majority in the House of Commons. Labour had lost its majority. Controversy arose when Prime Minister Gordon Brown initially decided not to resign, but to remain in office while both parties negotiated with the Lib-Dems. The Coalition won 306 seats to the government's 258 (House of Commons Political and Constitutional Reform Committee 2011: 6); it quickly became apparent the Conservative party was more likely to secure support from the Liberal Democrats to form government (Laws 2010; Adonis 2013). In typically sensational style, the tabloid newspapers accused the prime minister of being 'a squatter in Downing Street' (see, for example, *Daily Mail*, 10 May 2010).

With media and public pressure on Brown mounting, officials at Buckingham Palace reportedly became concerned to ensure the Queen not be put in a position where she would have to choose between the parties to ensure a stable government could be formed. Brown pre-empted this outcome, tendering his resignation on the evening of 11 May 2010 – four days after the election. His decision, taken when it became clear he could not retain government, but before details of a coalition agreement between the Conservatives and Liberal Democrats were announced the following day, was described as precipitous, including by senior Labour colleagues. Brown was criticised for abrogating his constitutional 'obligation' to ensure the Monarch would not potentially be left without an adviser.

Criticism of Brown must be understood against the backdrop of public and media hostility towards a deeply unpopular leader (see, for example, Heppell 2013). A House of Commons committee later concluded: 'Gordon Brown resigned at a constitutionally appropriate time. He did not have a constitutional obligation to remain in office for longer, nor to resign sooner' (House of Commons Political and Constitutional Reform Committee 2011: 11).

But uncertainty over what constituted appropriate practice in the period after an election also reveals a lack of understanding about caretaker principles in the United Kingdom – a polity that lacking a written constitution, has a long tradition of resisting documenting (or at least making public) its practices. It remains to be seen whether publication of the Cabinet Manual in 2011 will provide greater clarity around caretaker conventions in future.

The risk for public servants

Each of the case studies above highlights both the similarities and differences in the respective Westminster traditions and political cultures. For instance, in Australia, recent elections have been characterised by on-going caretaker controversies and accusations that the incumbent government has abused the benefits of incumbency (Menzies and Tiernan 2014). Yet, in both Canada and New Zealand, after the controversies described, it seems both jurisdictions settled into a pattern of little or no controversy during the caretaker period. Elections in the United Kingdom seem similarly not to be riven by caretaker conflict; it was uncertainty about how to operate in the event of a hung parliament in 2010 that brought the practices under the spotlight.

Yet despite the differences in levels of controversy, officials from all four jurisdictions appear to be engaging in more defensive behaviour during the caretaker period. Rhodes et al. (2009: 182–5) document a trend to codification of public service beliefs and practices. In all four jurisdictions this has been a response to the challenges of managerialism and reforms to make the public service more responsive. Writing down the conventions makes the rules and conventions explicit. It preserves institutional memory. Guidance documents:

> tell how a good public servant should behave and react. They also tell ministers what they can expect. They provide not only a standard of behaviour but also protection from the behaviour of others (Rhodes et al. 2009: 182).

It is difficult to distinguish substantive concerns from the partisan and personality issues that have dominated election campaigns in Australia, Canada and the United Kingdom. In Australia and Canada, more frequent complaints about caretaker breaches reflect the intense partisanship that characterises modern politics. The most egregious breaches of the conventions have tended to come from governments that, facing electoral oblivion, calculate they have little to lose by continuing advertising campaigns or seeing through a policy commitment, as in the Pearson airport case.

However, for all jurisdictions, whatever the frequency and nature of reported controversies, the risk for public servants is the same. As noted, the key characteristic of a convention is that it is not legally binding and is based on evolving practice rather than legislation. Politicians who have breached conventions are subject to 'political' and 'moral' sanctions (Dicey 1959: 444; Marshall 1984: 17). So though not legally binding on politicians, a different standard applies for public servants. The introduction of statutory public sector codes of conduct mean public servants have legal obligations for non-partisan behaviour (Menzies and Tiernan 2014: 15–16). For example, the UK *Civil Service Code* is set out in the *Constitutional Reform and Governance Act 2010*, which includes the exhortation to not 'act in a way that is determined by party political considerations, or use official resources for party political purposes' (UK Government 2010). The same applies to the Australian Public Service with its stated value of impartiality; the New Zealand *Standards of Integrity and Conduct* which identifies the need to 'maintain the political neutrality required to enable us to work with current and future governments'; and the need to maintain the non-partisanship of the public service as outlined in the Canadian *Public Service Employment Act* (Australian Public Service Commission 2014; Canada Public Service Commission 2014; New Zealand State Services Commission 2014). For officials, breaching these standards includes penalties as severe as dismissal. This double standard of accountability means ministers have very little to lose in pushing the boundaries. The pressure and stress sits with the bureaucracy during an election campaign. It calls for high levels of judgement and caution (Menzies and Tiernan 2014: 76–7).

The aftermath of major caretaker controversies also falls on the shoulders of public servants caught up in the issue. In all four of the case studies described above, there was a post-election enquiry into the breach where public officials were required to give evidence on their knowledge and behaviour during the election period. Little wonder then that in all four jurisdictions, officials have sought to document and specify the expectations of conduct and behaviour during the caretaker period through manuals and guidance documents.

Preserving institutional memory or pushing back?

Caretaker guidance documents have evolved to give detail and substance to the application of the caretaker principles. They are 'practitioners' handbooks' intended to assist decision makers to exercise discretion and judgement in applying the convention (Bowden and MacDonald 2012: 373). They do not seek to be the authoritative word as 'constitutional conventions exist independently' of the guidance (Kitteridge 2006). Nor do they represent a covert attempt to introduce written constitutions in jurisdictions that don't currently have them (House of Commons Constitutional and Political Reform Committee 2011: 26). What cabinet manuals and caretaker guidance documents seek to do is provide detailed advice on issues such as how to manage communication campaigns and websites, protocols for briefing the opposition, the management of appointments, handling cabinet documents and the relationship with ministers' offices.

The guidance documents aim to help officials to moderate the advantages of incumbency, ensure the policy status quo is maintained, manage contentious issues and ensure the impartiality of the public service cannot be challenged. Officials have become custodians of the caretaker conventions, but decision making about their observance still rests with the prime minister. We contend that written guidance on the caretaker conventions serves two functions:

1. it is an effort by officials to preserve the institutional memory of caretaker periods for future generations of civil servants;
2. it is also a useful means of 'pushing back' against demands from ministers and their staff on matters that may contravene the spirit and intention of the caretaker principles and/or compromise the impartiality of the public service.

The preservation of institutional memory and practice cuts across some of the key characteristics of a constitutional convention. Instead of politicians being aware of their obligations to the convention, it becomes the public service that brings these obligations to their notice. The custodianship by public officials also diminishes the flexibility politicians have in updating conventions. If the rule is felt to be 'outdated' or 'inconvenient', politicians by agreement can change a convention (Marshall 1984: chapt XIII p 4 of 5). With caretaker conventions, the philosophy and practice tends to be 'locked in' by public officials, who with each successive election present more and more detailed guidances to cabinet for approval.

Conclusion

Conventions are considered 'morally' and 'politically' binding (Marshall 1984: 17). Unlike laws, conventions can be opaque and nebulous because they do not have the authoritative interpretation that legal precedent gives to the law (Marshall 2003: 39). During election campaigns, public officials have established themselves as the authoritative interpreters of the caretaker convention by presenting to politicians detailed and curated guidelines on how to 'behave' during an election campaign. By doing this, they have shifted the onus of obligation to abide by conventions from the ministry to the public service.

It has been said that 'obedience is yielded to the conventions because of the consequences that would plainly ensue if they were disregarded' (Hood Phillips et al. 2001: 143). For incumbent governments, particularly ones on the way out, the consequences for breaches tend to accrue after the election when blame can be apportioned through the post-mortem of a parliamentary enquiry. In the case studies of breaches explored in this chapter, public officials at the time pointed out their concerns to their political masters and were then directed to undertake a course of action they disagreed with. After the election, they were then in a position to 'plug the hole' by adding additional material to the guidance on how to handle that particular situation. When bureaucrats fail to prevent questionable activity, public opinion can also be a sanction against untoward behaviour. However, the rapid news cycle and the complexity and confusion around media reporting of breaches do not make it easy to form an opinion on the rights and wrongs of a case.

Caretaker conventions provide a case study in the de-politicisation of conventions through the rising custodianship by the public service. The characteristics of conventions include reciprocity and obedience by both sides of parliament. The bureaucratic takeover circumvents the bi-partisan management of conventions and erodes the concept of mutuality. The idea of a convention being a reciprocal obligation is diminished when public service custodianship replaces the political stewardship that is meant to be critical to the continuation of a convention (Forsey cited in Heard 1991: 5). The example of caretaker conventions calls into question the focus on the 'political' characteristics of a convention and opens up a further discussion on who 'owns' caretaker conventions.

References

Abbott, Tony 2013. *Communication – 06 August*. Available at: www.dpmc.gov.au/media/docs/2013-08-06-Letter-to-Mr-Abbott.pdf.

Adonis, Andrew 2013. *5 Days in May: The Coalition and Beyond*. London: Biteback Publishing.

Australian Public Service Commission 2014. *APS Values*. Available at: www.apsc.gov.au.

Boston, Jonathan, Levine, Stephen, McLeay, Elizabeth, Roberts, Nigel, and Schmidt, Hannah 1998. 'Caretaker government and the evolution of caretaker conventions in New Zealand'. *Victoria University of Wellington Law Review*. 28 (4): 629–48.

Bowden, James W. J. and MacDonald, Nicholas A. 2012. 'Writing the unwritten: the officialization of constitutional convention in Canada, the United Kingdom, New Zealand and Australia'. *Journal of Parliamentary and Political Law*. 6 (2): 366–400.

Brown, Gordon 2010. 'Towards a new politics'. Speech to the Institute for Public Policy Research, 10 February. Available at: www.ippr.org/events/the-new-politics-with-gordon-brown.

Cameron, David 2011. 'Foreword by the Prime Minister'. *The Cabinet Manual: A Guide to Laws, Conventions and Rules on the Operation of Government*, 1st ed. Available at: www.gov.uk/government/uploads/system/cabinet-manual.pdf.

Canada Public Service Commission 2014. *Public Service Employment Act*. Available at: www.psc-cfp.gc.ca/centres/legislation-eng.htm.

Cappe, Mel 2013. 'The Caretaker Convention: Part II'. *The Inside Agenda Blog*, 5 March. Available at: www.theagenda.tvo.org/blog/agenda-blogs/guest-post-caretaker-convention-part-ii.

Codd, Michael 1996. 'National elections: Caretaker conventions and arrangements for transition', Australian Institute of Administrative Law (AIAL) Forum No. 10.

Commonwealth of Australia, Department of the Prime Minister and Cabinet (DPM&C) 1987. 'Caretaker conventions and other pre-election practices', *Annual Report 1986–87*, AGPS, Canberra.

Commonwealth of Australia, Department of the Prime Minister and Cabinet (DPM&C) 2010. *Guidelines for Post-election Consultations with Independent Members*, AGPS, Canberra.

Commonwealth of Australia, Department of the Prime Minister and Cabinet (DPM&C) 2013. *Guidance on Caretaker Conventions*, Department of the Prime Minister and Cabinet, Canberra.

Commonwealth of Australia Senate Estimates Committee 2014. *Finance and Public Legislation Senate Committee*, 29 May. Available at: parlinfo.aph.gov.au/parlInfo/download/committees/estimate/c9605ee6-62b3-4b19-

96454f8e3bf236ea/toc_pdf/Finance%20and%20Public%20Administration %20Legislation%20Committee_2014_05_29_2519.pdf;fileType=application %2Fpdf#search=%22committees/estimate/c9605ee6-62b3-4b19-9645-4f8e3 bf236ea/0000%22.

Costar, Brian 2012. 'Seventeen days to power: Making a minority government'. In Simms, Marian and Wanna, John (eds.), *Julia 2010: The Caretaker Election*. Canberra: ANU Press.

Dicey, A.V. 1959. *Introduction to the Study of the Law of the Constitution*, 10th ed. Basingstoke: Macmillan Education Ltd.

Franks, C.E.S (Ned.) 2011. 'Observations: Parliaments, 1945–2008: Dissolution, Elections, First Sittings, Etc.' in Public Policy Forum *Towards Guidelines on Government Formation: Facilitating Openness and Efficiency in Canada's Governance*. Final Report April 2012. Available at: www.ppforum.ca/sites/default/files/Towards%20Guidelines%20on%20Government%20Formation-Eng%20May%2031-21.pdf.

Government of Canada 2008. *Guidelines on the Conduct of Ministers, Secretaries of State, Exempt Staff and Public Servants during an Election*. Document released under Access to Information Act. Available at: http://jameswjbowden.files.wordpress.com/2011/07/guidelines-cartaker-convention1.pdf.

Gustafson, Barry 2000. *His Way: A Biography of Robert Muldoon*. Auckland University Press.

Hazell, Robert and Riddell, Peter 2010. *A Draft Caretaker convention for the UK Modelled on that in Australia and New Zealand*. Supplementary Memorandum to Justice Committee. Available at: www.ucl.ac.uk/constitution-unit/research-archive/CaretakerConvention.

Heard, Andrew 1989. 'Recognizing the variety among constitutional conventions'. *Canadian Journal of Political Science*. 22 (1): 63–81.

Heard, Andrew 1991. *Canadian Constitutional Conventions: The Marriage of Law and Politics*. Toronto: Oxford University Press.

Heppell, Timothy 2013. 'The fall of the Brown government, 2010', in Heppell, Timothy and Theakston, Kevin (eds.), *How Labour Governments Fall*. Basingstoke: Palgrave Macmillan.

Hood Phillips, Owen, Jackson, Paul and Leopold, Patricia 2001. *Constitutional and Administrative Law*, 8th ed. London: Sweet & Maxwell.

House of Commons Justice Committee 2010. 'Constitutional processes following a general election'. *Fifth Report of Session 2009–10*. HC 396. Available at: www.publications.parliament.uk/pa/cm200910/cmselect/cmjust/396/396.pdf.

House of Commons Political and Constitutional Reform Committee 2011. 'Lessons from the process of Government formation after the 2010 General Election'. *Fourth Report of Session 2010–11*. HC 528, 28 January.

Jaconelli, Joseph 2005. 'Do constitutional conventions bind?' *Cambridge Law Review* 64 (1): 149–76.

Killey, Ian 2009. *Constitutional Conventions in Australia: An Introduction to the Unwritten Rules of Australia's Constitutions*. Melbourne: Australian Scholarly Publishing.

Kitteridge, Rebecca 2006. 'The Cabinet Manual: Evolution with time'. Presented at 8th Annual Public Law Forum, 20–21 March.

Laver, Michael and Shepsle, Kenneth A. 2004. 'Cabinet government in theoretical perspective', in Laver, Michael and Shepsle, Kenneth A. (eds.), *Cabinet Ministers and Parliamentary Government*. Cambridge University Press.

Laws, David 2010. *22 Days in May*, 2nd ed. London: Biteback Publishing.

Marmor, Andrei 2007. 'Deep conventions'. *Philosophy and Phenomenological Research* LXXIV (3): 586–610.

Marshall, Geoffrey 1984. *Constitutional Conventions: The Rules and Forms of Political Accountability*. Oxford Scholarship Online. DOI:10.1093/acprof:oso/9780198762027.001.0001.

Marshall, Geoffrey 2003. 'The constitution: Its theory and interpretation', in Bogdanor, V. (ed.), *The British Constitution in the Twentieth Century*. Oxford University Press.

Marshall, Geoffrey and Moodie, Graeme C. 1971. *Some Problems of the Constitution*. London: Hutchinson.

Menzies, Jennifer and Tiernan, Anne 2014. *Caretaker Conventions in Australasia*, 2nd ed. Canberra: ANU Press.

Morozow, Anna 2013. 'Asylum seeker policy ads fine to run during election campaign', Auditor-General rules, *ABC News*, 15 August.

New Zealand Cabinet Office 2011. 'Constitutional procedures after the election'. *Circular* (11) 05.

New Zealand Department of the Prime Minister and Cabinet 2008. *Cabinet Manuel*. Wellington: NZPM&C.

New Zealand State Services Commission 2014. *Standards of Integrity and Conduct*. Available at: www.ssc.govt.nz.

O'Donnell, Gus 2011. 'Preface by the Cabinet Secretary'. *The Cabinet Manual: A Guide to Laws, Conventions and Rules on the Operation of Government*, 1st ed. Available at: www.gov.uk/government/uploads/system/cabinet-manual.pdf.

Parliament of Canada 1995. 'Special Senate Committee on the Pearson Airport Agreements'. *Minority Report*. Available at: www.parl.gc.ca/Content/SEN/Committee/351/pear/rep/p-ii-e.htm.

Public Policy Forum 2012. 'Towards guidelines on Government formation: Facilitating Openness and Efficiency in Canada's Governance'. *Final Report*. Available at: www.ppforum.ca/sites/default/files/Towards%20Guidelines%20on%20Government%20Formation-Eng%20May%2031-21.pdf.

Reid, Gordon 1977. 'Commentaries', in Evans, Gareth (ed.), *Labor and the Constitution: Essays and Commentaries on Constitutional Controversies of the Whitlam Years in Australian Government*. Melbourne: Heinemann.

Rhodes, R.A.W. 2014. *'Recovering the 'craft' of public administration in network governance'.* Plenary address to the International Political Science Association World Congress. Montreal, 19–24 July.

Rhodes, R.A.W. and Tiernan, Anne 2014. *Lessons in Governing: A Profile of Prime Ministers' Chiefs of Staff.* Carlton: Melbourne University Press.

Rhodes, R.A.W., Wanna, John and Weller, Patrick 2009. *Comparing Westminster.* Oxford University Press.

Ross, Monique 2013. 'Government accused of violating caretaker conventions over asylum seeker ad blitz'. *ABC News,* 10 August.

Russell, Peter H. 2009. 'The need for agreement on fundamental conventions of parliamentary democracy'. *National Journal of Constitutional Law* 27 (Constitutional Update 2009): 205–15.

Tiernan, Anne and Menzies, Jennifer 2007. *Caretaker Conventions in Australasia: Minding the Shop for Government.* Canberra: ANU e-press.

United Kingdom Cabinet Office 2010. *Directory of Civil Service Guidance,* Vol. 2. Available at: www.gov.uk/government/civil-service-conduct-and-guidance.

United Kingdom Cabinet Office 2015. *General Election Guidance.* Available at: www.gov.uk/government/uploads/system/uploads/attachment_data/file/420139/General_Election_Guidance_2015_2_.pdf.

United Kingdom Government 2010. *Statutory Guidance: The Civil Service Code.* Available at: www.gov.uk/government/civil-service-conduct-and-guidance.

Wanna, John 2014. 'Australia's future as a "Westminster Democracy" – threats to combat, stark choices to make'. *Australian Journal of Public Administration.* 73 (1): 19–28.

Watt, Ian 2013. *Communication – 09 August 2013.* Available at: www.dpmc.gov.au/media/index.cfm#secretary.

Wheare, Kenneth 1951. *Modern Constitutions.* Oxford University Press.

Zussman, David 2013. *Off and Running: The Prospects and Pitfalls of Government Transitions in Canada.* University of Toronto Press.

6

Minority and multi-party government

SCOTT BRENTON

As Campbell Sharman will discuss in Chapter 8, the existence of an autonomous upper house upsets the majoritarian tradition of Westminster parliamentary democracy. Minority and multi-party governments in the lower house further and fundamentally test the tenets of the Westminster political system. In one of the landmark texts in the field of comparative politics, *Patterns of Democracy* (1999, 2012), Arend Lijphart delineates between two models of democracy: Westminster and consensus. Traditional Westminster systems are generally majoritarian (adversarial) dominated by two major parties, with minimal incentive to form cross-party alliances if party discipline is maintained (Paun 2011: 440–1). The advent of multi-party and minority government is described as 'one of the most significant developments among Westminster democracies', particularly in the United Kingdom and Australia where it is not a consequence of proportional representation (Curtin and Miller 2011: 3). For a brief period in 2011, all four key Westminster parliaments lacked single-party majorities.

This chapter charts the transition towards the consensus model, which has been driven by voters and new political parties, but has also been facilitated by the major political parties. Conventions have been adapted in such a way as to preserve the dominant position of the major political parties. Firstly, it elucidates the 'Westminster Model of Democracy' and considers how Westminster systems have embraced elements of consensus democracy in the face of electoral threats. Secondly, it examines two sets of conventions covered in other chapters – cabinet government and parliamentary conventions – that have been challenged by new political actors seeking power. Finally, it will show how conventions remain stable yet adaptable, which is the third foundational question of this volume.

Westminster majoritarian model of democracy

The similarities between the Westminster system and majoritarian democracy are such that the terms can be used almost interchangeably (Lijphart 2012). The best example of this was New Zealand prior to a change in their electoral system in 1996, with their political system once described as being 'more Westminster than Westminster'. Lijphart (2012: 10–16) identifies five defining characteristics of the traditional Westminster majoritarian system in relation to the executive and parties, which in recent times have weakened in all four countries.

1. *Concentration of executive power in one-party or bare-majority cabinets.* Lijphart observes how the UK political system has produced two principal parties of equivalent strength, which results in narrow one-party majorities. In the post-war period there have been only two minority Labour cabinets in the 1970s, and from 1977 a short-lived 'Lab-Lib Pact' existed whereby the Liberals supported the government on matters of confidence in exchange for enhanced consultation. Yet after the 2010 election, a coalition government was formed between the Conservatives and Liberal Democrats, with a formal agreement and shared cabinet posts. In the devolved parliaments of Scotland and Wales, the mixed-member proportional (MMP) representation electoral systems have resulted in several minority and coalition governments since 1999. The year 2011 was the first time that each had majority governments.

As can be seen in Table 6.1, in the post-war period most cabinets have been comprised by ministers from one party. While at first glance Australia appears to be an exception, the 'coalition' between the Liberals and the rural National party is so strong that for all intents and purposes they can be treated more like factions of the same party. At a national level they have been in coalition for all but two brief periods, which were while they were in opposition, the last time in 1987. They generally do not challenge each other's sitting members at elections, and they run joint-tickets (electoral lists) for the Senate in many states. At a sub-national level, they have now merged in the state of Queensland and the Northern Territory. The federal coalition agreement rests on a brief, private letter signed by the two parliamentary party leaders, and from 1949 to 1987 was only signified by a handshake (Costar 2011). The main issues have been around allocating ministerial portfolios in proportion to seats held (and sometimes the portfolio area). The Nationals' leader becomes the deputy prime minister. They have also generally held the portfolios of transport and regional services, trade, and agriculture.

Table 6.1. *Composition of cabinets and legislative dominance since 1946*

	Australia		Canada		New Zealand		United Kingdom	
Year	Cabinet	No. of MPs	Cabinet	No. of MPs	Cabinet	No. of MPs	Cabinet	No. of MPs
1946	Labor	**43**/75			Labour	**42**/80		
1949	Lib./CP	**74**/123	Lib.	**190**/262	Nat.	**46**/80		
1950							Labour	**315**/625
1951	Lib./CP	**69**/123			Nat.	**50**/80	Con.	**321**/625
1953			Lib.	**171**/265				
1954	Lib./CP	**64**/123			Nat.	**45**/80		
1955	Lib./CP	**75**/124					Con.	**345**/630
1957			P.C.	112/265	Labour	**41**/39		
1958	Lib./CP	**77**/124	P.C.	**208**/265				
1959							Con.	**365**/630
1960					Nat.	**46**/80		
1961	Lib./CP	62/124*						
1962			P.C.	116/265				
1963	Lib./CP	**72**/124	Lib.	129/265	Nat.	**45**/80		
1964							Labour	**317**/630
1966	Lib./CP	**82**/124	Lib.	131/265	Nat.	**44**/80	Labour	**363**/630
1968			Lib.	**155**/264				
1969	Lib./CP	**66**/125			Nat.	**45**/84		
1970							Con.	**330**/630
1972	Labor	**67**/125	Lib.	109/264	Labour	**55**/87		
1974	Labor	**66**/127	Lib.	**155**/264			Labour	301/635
								319/635

Table 6.1. (*cont.*)

	Australia		Canada		New Zealand		United Kingdom	
Year	Cabinet	No. of MPs	Cabinet	No. of MPs	Cabinet	No. of MPs	Cabinet	No. of MPs
1975	Lib./NCP	**91**/127			Nat.	**55**/87		
1977	Lib./NCP	**86**/124						
1978					Nat.	**51**/92		
1979			P.C.	136/282			Con.	**339**/635
1980	Lib./NCP	**74**/125	Lib.	**147**/282				
1981					Nat.	**47**/92		
1983	Labor	**75**/125					Con.	**397**/650
1984	Labor	**82**/148	P.C.	**211**/282	Labour	**56**/95		
1987	Labor	**86**/148			Labour	**57**/97	Con.	**376**/650
1988			P.C.	**169**/295				
1990	Labor	**78**/148			Nat.	**67**/97		
1992							Con.	**336**/651
1993	Labor	**80**/147	Lib.	**177**/295	Nat.	**50**/99		
1996	Lib./Nat.	**94**/148			Nat./NZF	**61**/120		
1997			Lib.	**155**/301			Labour	**419**/659
1998	Lib./Nat.	**80**/148						
1999					Labour/Alliance	59/120		
2000			Lib.	**173**/301				
2001	Lib./Nat.	**82**/150					Labour	**413**/659
2002					Labour/Progressive	54/120		
2004	Lib./Nat.	**87**/150	Lib.	135/308				
2005					Labour/Progressive	51/120	Labour	**356**/646

Table 6.1. (*cont.*)

	Australia		**Canada**		**New Zealand**		**United Kingdom**	
Year	Cabinet	No. of MPs	Cabinet	No. of MPs	Cabinet	No. of MPs	Cabinet	No. of MPs
2006			Con.	124/308				
2007	Labor	**83**/150						
2008			Con.	143/308	Nat.-led	58/122		
2010	Labor	72/150					Con./LD	**364**/650
2011			Con.	**166**/308	Nat.-led	59/121		
2013	Lib./Nat.	**90**/150						
2014					Nat.-led	**60**/121		
2015							Con.	**331**/650

Sources: *Parliamentary Handbook of the Commonwealth of Australia*, 2011; Parliament of Canada's PARLINFO; Electoral Commission New Zealand; The office website of the New Zealand Government; New Zealand Parliament; BBC News 2010.

Key: Lib – Liberal; CP – Country Party; NCP – National Country Party; Nat. – National Party; P.C. – Progressive Conservatives; Con. – Conservatives; LD – Liberal Democrats.

Bolded numbers indicate parliamentary majorities.

*Includes two territory members who did not have full voting rights.

Policy issues have generally not been a feature of Australian coalition agreements, unlike in other countries.

At a sub-national level, minority governments became more common in the 1990s and 2000s, with independents and minor parties holding the balance of power in the lower houses of every jurisdiction at some point. The national parliament finally followed this trend in 2010 when Labor formed a minority government with the support of the Greens and independents. Labor signed separate agreements whereby they committed to a range of policy initiatives, parliamentary reform and privileged consultation in exchange for supply and qualified confidence. The qualification was that each Green and independent signatory was free to move or second a no-confidence motion but had to oppose any no-confidence motion moved and seconded by others.

Canada has the longest history of minority government, with eleven minority governments formed after elections since confederation and a further two formed in between elections. Yet coalition government has been more elusive (only one since confederation) despite the comparatively larger number of significant parties in the lower house. As Andrew Banfield discusses in Chapter 10, where a single party has not secured a majority in the lower house, the *custom* is that the party with a plurality of seats is given an opportunity to form a government. In doing so, the party must be confident that opposition parties will not pass a vote of no confidence, which is a negative rule of government formation. Yet opposition parties have rarely united in this way, so single-party minority governments have not been uncommon. These minority governments have at times relied on informal, ad hoc, shifting or loose 'alliances' with other parties to ensure their survival.

Minority government has been less common at the sub-national level: the province of Alberta has never had a minority or coalition government, while the provinces of British Columbia, New Brunswick, Newfoundland and Labrador, and Prince Edward Island have had single-party majority governments in recent decades. In the other provinces, there have been single-party minority governments, but rarely with any kind of formal agreement. After the 1985 Ontario election, the second-placed Liberals reached an 'Accord' with the third-placed New Democratic Party on confidence and supply for two years by agreeing to a series of legislative proposals. After the 1999 Saskatchewan election, the New Democratic Party formed a coalition government along conventional lines with the small Liberal Party.

As Grant Duncan discusses in Chapter 12, majority Labour or National governments with clear electoral mandates were the norm in New Zealand politics from 1935 until the introduction of a new proportionally representative electoral system in 1996. Unlike many other countries, there are no constitutional rules in relation to who manages or leads inter-party negotiations, what the process is and how a government is confirmed by the legislature (Boston 2011). Thus, a 'free-style bargaining' environment has developed, and in turn, different variations and experimentations have occurred (Boston 2001, 2007). After the 1996 election, a more traditional and straightforward coalition was formed between the right-of-centre National Party and the small populist/nationalist New Zealand First Party, which together held enough seats for a bare parliamentary majority. The written coalition agreement explicitly referred to the need for consensus. For example, Part B acknowledged that: 'The experience of similar democracies to New Zealand with coalition governments is that policy is developed by consensus it being recognised that co-operation is critical to the long term stability of coalition government'.[1] Part C stipulated that: 'Development of policy is achieved through consensus and good sense'. Duncan details the breakdown of the coalition and the confusion over the operation of conventions in Chapter 12.

After the 1999 election, left-of-centre parties Labour and the Alliance formed a minority coalition government, relying on the Greens for confidence and supply in exchange for enhanced consultation but without a formal agreement. After the following two elections, Labour again formed minority coalition governments, this time with the small left-wing Progressive Party. In that coalition's first term, an agreement with the centrist United Future party provided a parliamentary majority on issues of confidence and supply, in exchange for a commitment to a policy programme related to families, along with enhanced consultation. By the coalition's second term, United Future negotiated a 'ministerial position outside cabinet' for its leader, in addition to a broader set of policy commitments and more consultation. Still short of a majority, a similar agreement was negotiated with New Zealand First, as both it and United Future were hostile towards Greens' participation in government. Instead, Labour and the Greens negotiated a separate agreement whereby some policy concessions were made: two Greens became

[1] Coalition Agreement between New Zealand First and the New Zealand National Party, 11 December 1996.

'Government Spokespeople' in exchange for abstaining on confidence and supply votes to guarantee the government a working majority after the appointment of the speaker.

The most recent elections have seen National form minority governments under a similar arrangement. The ACT, United Future and Māori parties accepted ministerial positions outside cabinet and received policy commitments and close consultation by pledging confidence and supply. Interestingly, National only needed the support of one minor party after each election for a parliamentary majority but opted to include more parties. After the 2008 election they also signed a memorandum of understanding with the Green Party to identify policy areas where they could potentially cooperate. Boston (2009) first identified seven forms of multi-party governance arrangements in New Zealand following MMP, to which Boston and Bullock (2010) added an eighth. My own typology of governing arrangements in Australia (2013) is overlaid to present ten types of minority and multi-party executive arrangements in Westminster democracies in Table 6.2.

2. *Cabinet dominance.* During periods of majority government, the cabinet dominates the parliament due to strong party discipline. This is no longer the case in New Zealand, and after a series of experiments with and evolutions of multi-party governance arrangements, cabinet power has been curtailed. Significantly, the National government has opted to give minor parties influence even when they do not require their votes, recognising the longer-term advantages for them in pursuing more consensus-style arrangements. This is discussed further in the next section, as conventions have come to the fore.

Maintaining dominant cabinets has long been more of a challenge in Canada, where the threats and actual instances of no-confidence votes are not uncommon. Again conventions around what constitutes no confidence have become the subject of debate. For example, there has even been the bizarre situation of the minority Liberal government losing a vote over an amendment to the Income Tax Act, before successfully moving a subsequent vote to clarify that such a defeat of a 'money' bill did not constitute a no-confidence vote as conventionally understood.

Cabinet dominance in Australia is partially tempered by a powerful upper house where the government usually lacks a majority. Yet public displays of party unity can mask fractious internal dynamics where cabinet is often challenged. Again, Australia provides the starkest example of this, with the most recent Labor governments changing prime

Table 6.2. *Minority and multi-party executive arrangements in Westminster democracies*

Type	Arrangement	Recent examples
Cabinet coalition – high unity/ minimal dissent	Agreement between parties to form govt where each is represented in cabinet with collective responsibility upheld	Aust.: Liberal-National (1996–2007; 2013–); *also in many states at various times.* Aust. (WA): Liberal-Ind. (2008–13) Can. (SK): NDP-Liberal (1999–2001) NZ: National-NZF (1996–8)
Cabinet coalition – high unity but several specified areas of disagreement	Agreement between parties to form govt where each is represented in cabinet with provision to disagree on specified matters negotiated in advance of coalition's formation	Aust. (ACT): Liberal-Ind. (1998–2001); Labor-Green (2012–) NZ: National-United Future (1996) UK: Conservative-Lib. Dem. (2010–15)
Cabinet coalition/partnership/ multi-party cabinet – provision for 'agree to disagree'	Agreement between parties to form govt where each is represented in cabinet with provision to 'agree to disagree' through agreed process	Aust. (SA): Labor-National-Ind. (2002–10); Labor-Ind. (2014–) Aust. (Tas.): Labor-Greens (2010–14) Aust. (WA): Liberal-National (2008–) NZ: Labour-Alliance (1999–2002); Labour-Progressives (2002–08)
Executive (non-cabinet) coalition – 'enhanced' confidence and supply	Agreement between parties where minor party secures ministry outside cabinet and is only bound by collective responsibility in areas of direct portfolio responsibility	NZ: Labour-NZF (2005–08); Labour-United Future (2005–08); National-ACT Party (2008–); National-Māori (2008–); National-United Future (2008–)
Ordinary confidence and supply	Agreement with minor party/parties/ independents to support major party on matters of confidence and supply in exchange for certain concessions	Aust. (ACT): Labor with Greens (2008–12) NZ: Labour with Greens (1999–2002); Labour with United Future (2002–05)

Table 6.2. (*cont.*)

Type	Arrangement	Recent examples
'Enhanced' cooperation	Agreement where minor party cooperates with major party on various policy and procedural matters (inc. not opposing govt on confidence & supply) in exchange for rights & resources incl. speaking for govt on specific issues.	NZ: Labour with Greens (2005–08)
Conditional cooperation	Agreement where major party cooperates with minor party/independents on various policy and procedural matters in exchange for supply and commitment not to support no-confidence motions from other parties	Aust.: Labor with Greens Independents (2010–13) Can. (ON): Liberals with NDP (1985–7)
Ordinary cooperation	Agreement where minor party cooperates with major party on various policy and procedural matters (incl. not opposing govt on confidence & supply) in exchange for certain concessions	NZ: Labour with Greens (2002–05)
Minority government without formal agreement	Major party governs with tacit support of minor party/parties	Aust. (ACT): Labor with Democrat & Green (2001–04) Aust. (Tas.): Liberals with Greens (1996–8) Can.: *various times*
Memorandum of understanding	Agreement to work together to develop policy in areas of common interest	NZ.: National with Greens (2009–11)

Key: Ind. – Independent; Lib. Dem. – Liberal Democrat; NDP – New Democratic Party; NZF – New Zealand First; ACT – Australian Capital Territory; ON – Ontario; SA – South Australia; SK – Saskatchewan; Tas. – Tasmania; WA – Western Australia.

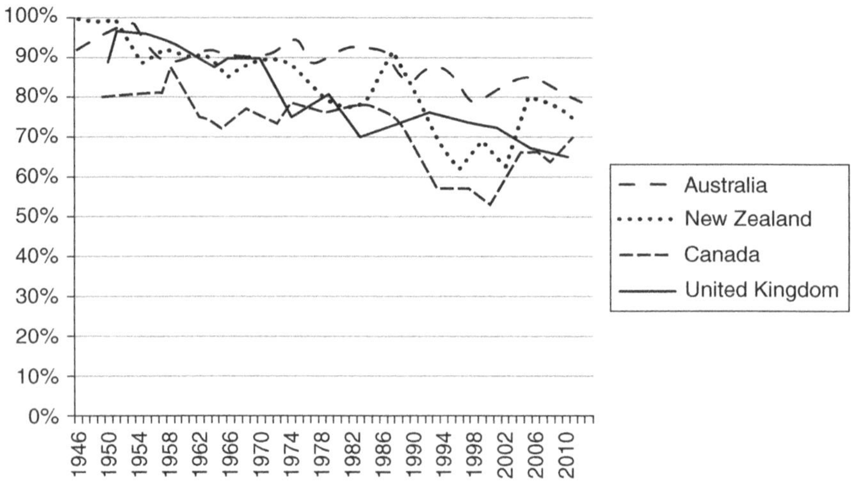

Figure 6.1: Proportion of the vote of the two major parties

ministers twice and frequent cabinet and caucus leaks with the aim of destabilising leaders and their supporters.

3. *Two-party system.* The two-party system is in decline in all four countries, as can be seen in Figure 6.1. In Australia, until the 1987 election, the major parties received over eighty-five per cent of the primary vote, and often more than ninety-five per cent. At the 2013 election the combined vote had fallen under eighty per cent for the first time, and three minor parties held seats in the lower house, in addition to independents.

In New Zealand, almost one hundred per cent of the vote was once shared between the two major parties, which were often the only parties represented in the parliament. In the first election using the new electoral system in 1996, their combined share of the vote was only sixty-two per cent. At the 2014 election their share was seventy-two per cent, but the number of represented parties had increased to seven.

The Canadian major party vote shares have also been erratic, yet the shares of over eighty per cent in the late 1940s and the 1950s have never been repeated. In the 1960s, 1970s and 1980s, the shares were around seventy-five per cent, falling to fifty-seven per cent in the 1990s and just fifty-three per cent at the 2000 election. Throughout the 2000s the shares had increased to around sixty-five per cent, and at the 2011 election, the figure was seventy per cent. The number of parliamentary parties has remained fairly static at four to five, but the present-day Conservative Party has experienced several incarnations. Its predecessor, the Progressive Conservatives, only won two seats at the 1993 election.

In the United Kingdom, the earlier elections saw the two major parties sharing about ninety to ninety-five per cent of the vote, before falling to seventy-five per cent in 1974 and below seventy per cent for the first time at the 2005 election. At the 2015 election the major parties received sixty-seven per cent of the vote, with three parties contesting government.

4. *Majoritarian and disproportional systems of elections.* While the devolved parliaments adopted more proportional electoral systems, Westminster has retained plurality voting using single-member districts. As part of the Conservative–Liberal Democrat Coalition Agreement, there was a referendum to change to an Alternative Vote system, as used to elect the Australian lower house. The proposal was resoundingly defeated, but proposals to democratise the House of Lords using proportional representation remain on the agenda for electoral reform.

Australia's system of preferential voting for lower house seats still gives the major parties a disproportionate share of the seats, but increasingly minor parties and independents are making it to the final count and even winning seats. Symbolically, the independent Australian Electoral Commission now refers to final count once all preferences have been distributed as the 'Two Candidate Preferred' rather than the traditional 'Two Party Preferred' vote. In the Senate, proportional representation by single transferable vote makes government majorities difficult to achieve. Aside from a brief period from 2005 to 2008, minor parties and independents have held the 'balance of power' in the Senate since 1981.

New Zealand has changed to a more proportional electoral system, while Canada has retained the UK model, along with similar calls for electoral reform.

5. *Interest group pluralism.* On this criterion, all four countries have largely retained a pluralist interest group system, where interest groups compete in an uncoordinated manner. However, the traditional roles for unions, and in some respects farmer groups, have changed, while there has been a rise of postmaterialist interest groups, particularly environmental groups. Postmaterialist issues have often been at the centre of the policy platforms of third-party challengers, and many power-sharing agreements have included such issues.

The Westminster majoritarian model of democracy still exists in some form in all four countries but has had to adapt as minorities have challenged the status quo. The next section more closely examines the recent instances of minority and multi-party government to identify the most contentious conventions.

Multi-party governance arrangements

In Westminster-derived parliamentary democracies government formation has few formal rules, with no formal investiture vote required or clear protocol for who has first right to form a government, so the incumbent government occupies a privileged position, remaining in office until faced with a loss of confidence (Strøm, Budge and Laver 1994: 311; Paun 2011: 447). The head of state does not initiate government formation, in terms of designating a *formateur* or *informateur*. Where the incumbent government retains their majority, they continue to govern; if they lose their majority and the opposition gains a majority, the incumbent leader resigns and advises that the opposition leader be invited to form a government. Where both the government and the opposition fail to win a majority, conventions can be tested.

The two major choices are either a coalition that binds partners to a joint policy platform negotiated during the government formation phase or a pure single-party minority government that requires ongoing negotiation, but international experience shows several variations of these arrangements (Paun and Hazell 2010: 215–16; Paun 2011: 448–9). Collective cabinet responsibility is seen to favour policy-compact coalitions (Strøm, Budge and Laver 1994). There are risks for minor parties and independents in entering coalition-type partnerships explaining a preference for minority government formation (Curtin and Miller 2011: 8).

Collective cabinet responsibility has been challenged by multiparty governance arrangements, but actually has remained largely intact with the emergence of what is commonly known internationally as the 'New Zealand' model. In this model collective responsibility is loosened and support parties can gain ministerial roles while maintaining the right to dissent on certain issues (Paun 2011: 450). Yet like so many presumed New Zealand innovations, the experimentation with conventions began in Australia (although New Zealand went much further).

The first stage of the 'Australian' model began in the early 1990s and continued into the 2000s. Unlike minority governments in Canada, the major parties negotiated with minor parties and independents and attempted to reach agreements – ideally in writing – where guarantees of confidence and supply were exchanged for commitments on political and/or policy reforms.

Independents have had written undertakings with minority Labor governments in Queensland, Victoria, South Australia, the Northern Territory, and a minority Liberal government in New South Wales. Every written agreement has the stated aims of stable government and accountability. For the government, the main issue was ensuring supply and confidence, while placing conditions under which a motion of no confidence could be supported; generally it could only be moved by the independent member (rather than the opposition) and only due to corruption, mismanagement or similar wrongdoing. In most agreements the government also pledged to run full term or to introduce fixed terms, which is a lasting consequence of many of these agreements in many states. In New South Wales, Victoria, and at the Commonwealth level, most of the independents negotiated and signed the agreements as a group. Earlier agreements with independents had focused more on parliamentary and other accountability reforms, along with promises to be consulted, committee positions, and extra staffing and resources.

The first significant deviation from the traditional Westminster practice of collective cabinet solidarity occurred in the small jurisdiction of the Australian Capital Territory (ACT) in 1998. This is unsurprising given the proportional representation electoral system, history of non-majority governments, and other non-traditional Westminster features such as the absence of a vice-regal post and necessity of an investiture vote.

Prior to the appointment of independent Michael Moore to Chief Minister Kate Carnell's Liberal cabinet, the government commissioned Professor Philip Petit to investigate the basis upon which a non-government member could become a minister. In his report, *Review of Governance of the Australian Capital Territory*, Petit identified three conditions for such an appointment: Moore had to give prior notice of the issues on which he reserved the right to dissent in public and in the legislature after absenting himself from the relevant cabinet discussion (a long list of broad-ranging issues); he had to implement all cabinet decisions related to his portfolio areas, even if he had absented himself and dissented; and he could not threaten to resign in cabinet negotiations.

For Carnell, she was able to secure her position and add a more ideologically congruent voice to cabinet to balance the right wing, a tactic many have argued that UK Prime Minister David Cameron used in encouraging a coalition with the Liberal Democrats. Moore's health portfolio was also a more challenging portfolio for the government, and while Moore gained ministerial influence, he could also be blamed for failings. Moore emphasised that the success of the arrangement was highly dependent upon trust.

South Australian Labor Premier Mike Rann adopted a similar arrangement, but granted further dispensation to the non-government ministers. Under the agreements with the independent and National party ministers, they did not have to provide a list of issues that they could disagree with, however broad-ranging, and instead were effectively given *carte blanche*. They were also offered a ministerial position in a future Labor government if they served in line with the agreement.

The Western Australian Nationals copied these arrangements in entering a 'partnership', rather than a coalition, with a minority Liberal government in 2008. Notably, the Liberals had already secured the support of two independents without the need for formal agreements, and one entered the cabinet under traditional conditions. She was subsequently demoted, but did not bring down the government. While cabinet solidarity was varied in these arrangements, cabinet secrecy was still expected.

The 'Greens' first entered a parliamentary accord with Labor in Tasmania in 1989 while still known as the Green Independents. It was the first such written agreement focusing on parliamentary and accountability reforms, increased consultation and resources for non-government members, but also included many policy commitments. It broke down in acrimonious circumstances and, with Labor reluctant to govern with Green support after the 1996 election, the Liberals governed without a majority or an agreement with the Greens. The major parties again refused to cooperate with the Greens during the 2010 state election, and after they won the same number of seats, Labor premier David Bartlett advised the governor to commission a minority Liberal government as they won the most votes. Governor Peter Underwood released a statement, and under the sub-heading 'Irrelevant matters' stated that:

> In view of certain public statements made by some candidates in the lead up to the election I express my view that the commissioning of a person to form a government is entirely the Governor's prerogative and it is not within the gift of any political leader to hand over, or cede to another political leader the right to form a government, whatever the result of the election. For the same reason it is also appropriate to express my view that the total number of votes received by the elected members of a political party is constitutionally irrelevant to the issue of who should be commissioned to form a government.

Eventually, Bartlett continued as premier after inviting Greens into the cabinet. Like the Australian Capital Territory (ACT) arrangement, the Green ministers were required to provide a comprehensive list of matters of conscience where they would likely disagree, but were able to add to the list at a later date. There was also provision for 'matters of significant concern', which was open like the provisions in the South Australian and Western Australian arrangements, except it was framed in terms of party policy and acknowledged that Greens ministers were subject to their own internal party dynamics. The key difference from earlier arrangements was that resignation was acknowledged as an option, with the expectation that the Greens would if they could not abide by the other traditions of cabinet. While popularly described as a coalition, the other three Greens were not part of the government and could take a different position to their colleagues in cabinet. The Greens were eventually expelled from the cabinet prior to the 2014 election.

The Greens charted a similar path in the ACT. They had previously supported minority governments in the investiture votes, without entering formal agreements. After winning a record number of seats in 2008, they entered a parliamentary agreement to support a minority Labor government in exchange for parliamentary reform and one of the most extensive policy programmes contained in an Australian agreement. This was despite the Liberal leader offering cabinet positions. After the 2012 ACT election, despite losing three of their four seats, the Greens sole member entered cabinet and was explicitly subject to cabinet confidentiality but not solidarity on matters of serious concern. However, most of the agreement was, focused on specific policy commitments.

New Zealand has similarly experienced incremental changes in multi-party governance arrangements, beginning with traditional coalition and loosening in recent times. The first 'loosened' arrangement occurred after the 1999 election, with the coalition agreement between Labour and Alliance affirming the convention of collective cabinet responsibility.[2] However, in one of the longest parts of the agreement, exception was made for 'party distinction':

> Where either party leader considers that a distinctive policy matter raises an issue of importance to the party's political identity, the leader will raise

[2] Coalition agreement between the Labour and Alliance parties, 6 December 1999.

> this with the Coalition management committee, which will resolve an appropriate course of action, including possibly identifying the matter as one of 'party distinction'. In this event, there may be public differentiation between the parties in speech and vote which will not be regarded as being in breach of the convention. Such issues are expected to be infrequent and the parties recognise that dealing with them openly and responsibly is critical to the credibility of the Coalition. Differentiation on such issues will not detract from the overall acceptance that the two parties are taking joint responsibility for the actions of the Government.

Boston and Bullock (2010) contend that the previous coalition's tight discipline proved to be flawed due to inflexibility and inability of the minor party to differentiate itself, which led to this 'agree to disagree' provision. However the Alliance still struggled to maintain their identity and eventually split, with its leader forming the Progressives and again entering a coalition with Labour after the 2002 election. By this stage the Cabinet Manual had been updated to reflect changing governance arrangements, and thus a shorter provision on 'maintaining identity' was inserted into the coalition agreement:

> The coalition partners will work in good faith to further the objectives of government, while accepting the need for distinctive party political identities within government, especially in relation to the smaller party being able to maintain a separate but responsible identity. Agree to disagree provisions will apply where necessary and in such circumstances the Progressive Coalition will be free to express alternative views publicly and in Parliament.[3]

Labour and the Progressives then negotiated a confidence and supply agreement with United First, while Labour reached a 'cooperation' agreement with the Greens, in exchange for limited policy commitments. Both agreements bound United First and the Greens to publicly support the process and outcome of their own policy initiatives. After the 2005 election these agreements went further, and in doing so established a distinctive 'New Zealand model'. There were two elements: acceptance of ministers outside of cabinet being free from collective responsibility except for matters within their portfolio areas, and the establishment of a new class of 'minister', known as government spokesperson.

[3] Coalition Agreement between the Labour and Progressive Coalition Parties in Parliament, 8 August 2002.

The leaders of the United Future and New Zealand First parties became ministers outside of cabinet and were 'bound by Cabinet Manual provisions in respect of any areas within the[ir] portfolio responsibility' and required to 'fully represent the government's position'.[4] The 'cooperation agreement' with the Greens identified three levels of issues, with level one fully involving the Green Party spokesperson in the detailed development and implementation of policy proposals, thus becoming government spokespeople.[5]

The National Opposition Leader Don Brash was predictably critical in describing the arrangements as 'concerning from a constitutional point of view' (cited in Boston and Bullock 2010: 359). The party's position changed, however, by the time they won government at the following election, after the new approach proved to be practical and politically feasible, in addition to widespread acceptance from constitutional authorities and the media (Boston and Bullock 2010). The government was also creative in its management of potential areas of disagreement, carefully allocating the ministries and even removing contentious portfolios, while also narrowly interpreting what constituted a portfolio area (Boston and Bullock 2010). Significantly, Boston and Bullock identify the development of new 'informal rules' that facilitated the new arrangements, that arguably could be considered new 'conventions': firstly dissent within the executive would be limited to matters of party distinction, rather than ministers being able to take independent individual positions; secondly, the aim was always consensus with dissent accommodated only as a last resort; and thirdly, any criticism of government policy would be relatively muted compared to the opposition. As previously mentioned, when National won the 2008 election they opted for these arrangements with three parties, rather than just a traditional coalition with ACT. National even pioneered a new arrangement by negotiating a 'memorandum of understanding' with the seemingly ideologically incongruent Greens.

Stable yet adaptable conventions

The general trends in each of these two countries provide an interesting contrast. In Australia the trend had been for minor parties and

[4] Labour Confidence and Supply Agreement with United Future, 17 October 2005; Labour Confidence and Supply Agreement with New Zealand First, 17 October 2005.

[5] Labour-led Government Co-operation Agreement with the Green Party, 17 October 2005.

independents to incrementally gain more and more influence before finally gaining cabinet positions and then securing more and more opt-outs from collective responsibility. In New Zealand the starting point was full, traditional coalition with tightly prescribed agreement that has gradually loosened to protect cabinet's collective responsibility while accommodating or co-opting minor parties. Yet at the core, New Zealand has preserved traditional understandings of collective responsibility, while pioneering other innovative executive arrangements under cabinet; in Australia collective responsibility has been more compromised.

The United Kingdom has maintained the more traditional approach to collective cabinet responsibility. The formal agreement between the coalition parties stated that 'There is no constitutional difference between a Coalition Government and a single party Government, but working practices need to adapt to reflect the fact that the UK has not had a Coalition in modern times'. The deputy prime minister (the leader of the Liberal Democrats) had almost equal oversight as the prime minister. Each government department contained ministers from both parties to ensure that neither had complete control. The coalition agreement contained a comprehensive policy programme, noting likely and allowable disagreement on higher education funding and nuclear power plant construction. In this way, the coalition preserves the doctrine of collective responsibility by specifying minimal exemptions (Paun 2011: 451). The Cabinet Manual reflected this by noting the collective decisions of cabinet can be 'explicitly set aside'.[6] In the preface, Cabinet Secretary Sir Gus O'Donnell observed that:

> The content of the Cabinet Manual is not static, and the passage of new legislation, the evolution of conventions or changes to the internal procedures of government will mean that the practices and processes it describes will evolve over time. If the Cabinet Manual is to continue to play a useful role as a guide to the operations and procedures of government, it will need to be updated periodically to reflect such developments.

The conventions of executive government have evolved as the influence of third parties, minor parties and independents has grown.

The Westminster parliamentary system of an executive drawn from and accountable to the legislature remains stable, and the first minister

[6] Section 4.2 of the Cabinet Manual: A guide to laws, conventions and rules on the operation of government, 1st edition, October 2011.

and control of the treasury remains within one of the two major parties. Concessions have been made to the challenging actors, acknowledging the democratic and popular will of the people, but real power has remained within two parties in each of the four countries, while the challenger's influence has often been fleeting (see Brenton 2013). This has not stopped new challengers, nor necessarily arrested the longer-term decline in the major parties' share of the vote: the minor changes to conventions have provided a safety-valve ensuring their fundamental stability.

References

Boston, Jonathan 2001. 'Forming a Government', in R. Miller (ed.), *New Zealand Government and Politics*. Auckland: Oxford University Press.

Boston, Jonathan 2007. 'An Unusual Government: Coalition Politics and Inter-party Arrangements Following the 2005 General Election', in S. Levine and N. S. Roberts (eds.), *The Baubles of Office: The New Zealand General Election of 2005*. Wellington: Victoria University Press.

Boston, Jonathan 2011. 'Government formation in New Zealand under MMP: Theory and practice', *Political Science* 63 (1): 79–105.

Boston, Jonathan and Bullock, David 2010. 'Multi-party governance: Managing the unity-distinctiveness dilemma in executive coalitions', *Party Politics* 18 (3): 349–68.

Brenton, Scott 2013. 'Policy traps for third parties in two-party systems: The Australian case', *Commonwealth & Comparative Politics* 51 (3): 283–305.

British Broadcasting Corporation 2010. *UK Election Results through Time*. London: British Broadcasting Corporation, http://news.bbc.co.uk/2/hi/uk_news/politics/election_2010/.

Commonwealth of Australia Department of Parliamentary Services 2011. *43rd Parliament. Parliamentary Handbook of the Commonwealth of Australia 2011*. Canberra: Parliamentary Library, Department of Parliamentary Services.

Costar, Brian 2011. 'Australia's curious coalition', *Political Science* 63 (1): 29–44.

Curtin, Jennifer and Miller, Raymond 2011. 'Negotiating coalitions: Comparative perspective'. *Political Science* 63 (1): 3–9.

Lijphart, Arend 1999. *Patterns of Democracy: Government Forms and Performance in Thirty-Six Countries*. New Haven and London: Yale University Press.

Lijphart, Arend 2012. *Patterns of Democracy: Government Forms and Performance in Thirty-Six Countries*. New Haven and London: Yale University Press.

Parliament of Canada 2014. *Parliament File*. Ottawa: Library of Parliament (Bibliothèque du Parlement), www.parl.gc.ca/parlinfo/Lists/Parliament.aspx.

Paun, Akash 2011. 'After the age of majority? Multi-party governance and the Westminster model', *Commonwealth & Comparative Politics* 49 (4): 440–56.

Paun, Akash and Hazell, Robert 2010. 'Hung parliaments and the challenges for Westminster and Whitehall: How to make minority and multiparty governance work', *Political Quarterly* 8 (2): 213–22.

Strøm, Kaare, Budge, Ian and Laver, Michael J. 1994. 'Constraints on cabinet formation in parliamentary democracies', *American Journal of Political Science* 38 (2): 303–35.

7

Parliament

J. R. NETHERCOTE

This chapter examines constitutional and other conventions in the workings of parliaments, most notably the parliament at Westminster and the major institutions which trace their origins and character from it – the Canadian Parliament at Ottawa, the New Zealand Parliament at Wellington and the Australian Parliament, first at Melbourne and, since 1927, at Canberra, for sixty-one years in the provisional Parliament House and, since 1988, in the New and Permanent Parliament House.

The general approach is as follows: conventions figure prominently in explaining the workings of a parliament, but they are only one form of signpost affecting conduct and procedure. They are not necessarily in written form, and it is unusual for them to be formally adopted. There is much variation over time and from parliament to parliament. It is a reminder of the Anglican view of the traditions of the church as contained in Article 33 of the Articles of Religion: 'It is not necessary that Traditions and Ceremonies be in all places one, and utterly like; for at all times they have been divers, and may be changed according to the diversities of countries, times, and men's manners, so that nothing be ordained against God's Word.'

Conventions so described are more explicitly in evidence at Westminster than elsewhere. They attract greater interest from lawyers and academics than from parliamentarians and the clerks of houses of parliament. Neither the concept itself nor the conventions themselves are easily defined either as to formulation or to application. Their utility is, thus, often variable, uncertain and potentially obscure. Because of their elusive and possibly indefinite character, their utility may well be strengthened if they are viewed not so much as rules or obligatory precepts or maxims, but are seen instead as precedents, in particular circumstances guiding rather than prescribing conduct and behaviour.

The chapter concludes with a survey of the more prominent of what are viewed as conventions in Westminster parliaments, or function with the same effect.

The business of all institutions, especially those of ancient origin, indirectly as well as directly, is conducted according to a maze of rules, practices, customs, traditions, procedures, protocols, guidelines (guidances), courtesies and what Sidney Low called 'tacit understandings' (adding that 'the understandings are not always understood') (Loughlin 2013: 1). In relation to parliament, this feature is well-captured in the title of Erskine May's classic treatise: *A Practical Treatise on the Law, Privileges, Proceedings and Usage of Parliament* (Jack 2011).

A useful exposition of this aspect of the workings of a parliament has been provided by Reid and Forrest with regard to the conduct of debate. They wrote:

> Every deliberative assembly needs rules of debate. In some cases they are written and are public property; in some cases they are less formal and their declaration or interpretation is left to the will of the meeting or to a person nominated or elected to preside; in other cases their interpretation is seen to be something supernatural, under the influence of a hidden hand, or a matter of Divine guidance. But in all deliberative assemblies there is deference to perceived rules, and to their authorised interpretation. (1989: 132)

It is usually relatively easy to find the essential rules according to which a parliamentary institution works. Most (perhaps all) houses of parliament have published rules in the form of standing orders or a comparable document; such rules usually have the force of law. In the case of the Australian Parliament, the standing orders of both the Senate and the House of Representatives are made under the authority of the Constitution (s. 50) and cover the 'mode in which its powers, privileges, and immunities may be exercised and upheld', and the 'order and conduct of its business and proceedings either separately or jointly with the other House'. Standing orders may be supplemented by other orders which apply for a specified period of time.

Such orders rarely cover all eventualities, but they often contain guidance as to how a legislature should proceed if a matter not provided for arises. In the Canadian House of Commons, the occupant of the chair is directed to make decisions based 'on the usages, forms, customs and precedents of the House of Commons of Canada and on parliamentary tradition in Canada and other jurisdictions, so far as they may be applicable to the House' (SO 1). Comparable counsel was provided to the Australian Senate in *Australian Senate Practice*: 'It is a very sound Senate practice that, where there may be doubt with respect to the interpretation of a rule or order, the Chair leans towards a ruling which preserves or strengthens the powers of the Senate rather than towards a view which may weaken or lessen the Senate's powers' (Odgers 1991: 117).

Standing orders ought not be seen as a strait-jacket. A frequent device in many Houses is a resolution providing that such standing orders as would prevent achievement of a specified goal (for example, expeditious handling of a particular item of business) be suspended.

There are major treatises on the practice and procedure of all the major Westminster houses of parliament. These provide much valuable information about 'usages, forms, customs and precedents.' The most famous such treatise is now known as *Erskine May*. It dates from 1844 and is now in its twenty-fourth edition (Jack 2011). It mainly deals with the House of Commons at Westminster, whose Clerk is formally the editor, but includes extensive coverage of the House of Lords.

Among the houses of parliament which have successfully emulated the Westminster Parliament in producing a treatise on procedure and practice are the House of Commons in Ottawa (Marleau and Montpetit 2000); both the Senate (Evans and Laing 2012) and the House of Representatives (Wright 2012) in Canberra; the House of Representatives in Wellington (McGee 2005); and, at state level in Australia, the two chambers of the New South Wales Parliament (not an institution noted for the manifestation of parliamentary values).

These works, invariably written by clerks of the respective Houses, combine invaluable documentary information with much expository analysis. They are the most instructive of all the bridges between the formal (constitutional) framework, standing and other orders, and the manner in which the Houses of parliament actually work, including perceived conventions.

Beyond the formal rules and the treatises are various texts, of varying authority, by journalists and academics *Griffith and Ryle* (Blackburn et al., 2003).

Seventeen years after the first edition of *Erskine May*, in 1861, J. S. Mill wrote in *Considerations on Representative Government* that the 'conduct of the different political authorities is in fact regulated' by the 'legal provisions of the British Constitution, together with the unwritten maxims of the British Constitution' (229). Mill, an accomplished administrator and later a member of the House of Commons, knew well the nature, and the mystery, of 'unwritten maxims':

> Every branch of [government] is a skilled business, which has its own peculiar principles and traditional rules, many of them not even known,

> in any effectual way, except to those who have at some time had a hand in carrying on the business, and none of them likely to be duly appreciated by persons not practically acquainted with the department.

He wryly added:

> I do not mean that the transaction of public business has esoteric mysteries, only to be understood by the initiated. Its principles are all intelligible to any person of good sense, who has in his mind a true picture of the circumstances and conditions to be dealt with: but to have this he must know those circumstances and conditions; and the knowledge does not come by intuition. (231)

It may be seen from the foregoing that, in the intervening century and a half, there has been a good deal of codification, informal as well as formal. While there may still be maxims to guide procedure and practice, few of them are now still unwritten. But Mill's injunction about observing or applying a convention or like maxim necessitates having a 'true picture of the circumstances and conditions to be dealt with' retains its force.

Gaining such a 'true picture' is not easy. David Butler's observations of four decades ago about the deficiencies of research on Australian government not only still have much force in Canberra, not least where conventions are involved, but might well have been written about other major parliamentary jurisdictions. He wrote, with reference to the parliament, that:

> Nothing substantial seems to have been published on question time ... There is oddly little too, on the process of legislation ... There is the wider question of parliamentary procedure and its reform ... The role of the Speaker offers another worthwhile theme ... There is also the more political side of parliament. How do the Whips operate? ... What are the conventions that cover the relations between the leader of the House and the deputy leader of the opposition [who at that time was responsible for opposition interests in the conduct of business in the House]? (Butler 1973: 9)

In all the gaps to which Butler pointed, and many others he did not mention, what is at issue is not mainly the formal situation, but questions about the actual workings and conduct of parliament; there is not infrequently a substantial difference between the two. Butler himself explained: 'Politics and administration are messy businesses. Reality cannot be described in terms of formal blueprints' (1973: 8).

Conventions are often seen, not really convincingly, as the means of progressing beyond such formal blueprints. Sir Ivor Jennings contended that conventions 'provide the flesh which clothes the dry bones of the law; they make the legal constitution work; they keep it in touch with the growth of ideas' (1943: 80–1; cited Hughes 1980: 41). Another similarly eminent author wrote that they are 'rules of political conduct or binding usages', a definition almost immediately rendered otiose by the remainder of the sentence which states that they are 'capable of being varied or simply disappearing as political conditions and ideas change' (de Smith 1971: 37; cited Hughes 1980: 41).

The idea of 'conventions' is of academic provenance and is especially associated with A. V. Dicey. Dicey contended that conventions of the constitution are 'supported and enforced by something beyond or in addition to the public approval. What then is this "something"? My answer is, that it is nothing else than the force of law' (1948: 445–6; cited Hughes 1980: 43).

Conventions do not, however, figure so prominently in the professional material about either parliaments or the conduct of government. The main exception to that proposition in the past four decades has been the extraordinary endeavour by administrators in Canberra, possibly encouraged by Sir Paul Hasluck (1979: 17–18), to characterise what are basically rules and guidelines applicable between a dissolution of the House of Representatives and the commissioning of a new government after general elections as 'conventions'. Although very much the means by which administrators strive to regulate (restrain) the behaviour of incumbent ministers in an election period, inasmuch as they have ministerial authorisation, it is as self-denying ordinances. In their infancy they were described more accurately by the Royal Commission on Australian Government Administration as 'practices' (1976: 5.2.12, 121). While they have effect, they are only enforceable with the authority of the prime minister. The penalties for a breach are neither constitutional nor legal but political, electoral and reputational; in Dicey's approach, public disapproval. Neither the United Kingdom nor Canada has found it necessary to construct any comparable volume of rules and directions (notwithstanding occasional claims to the contrary). In these jurisdictions the term *caretaker conventions* is largely unknown, but some of the practices involved are extant (see Menzies and Tiernan in this collection).

House of Representatives Practice frankly faces the fuzziness surrounding the concept of constitutional conventions (Wright 2012: 48–9):

> The existence of a wide range of conventions of the Constitution plays a fundamental part in Parliament/Executive Government relations. These conventions are numerous, and in some cases there is no universal

> agreement that they exist. Conventions are based on established precedent and practice and in many respects have their foundation in British law and practice established before 1901. They are subject to change by way of (political) interpretation or (political) circumstances and may in some instances be broken.

The book wisely refrains from seeking 'to identify and separately examine in depth the full range and meaning of all of them, as they [are subject] to continuing political questioning which has left the status of many so-called conventions in doubt' (Wright 2012: 49). This perspective was shared, more than three decades ago, by two lawyers in a paper which sought to identify 'conventions associated with the Commonwealth Constitution'; in preparing the paper they were 'not concerned to draw fine distinctions between conventions and customary practices which may in time achieve the status of conventions' (Saunders and Smith 1980: 1).

Robert Hazell's chapter explains how, in British practice, those in authority such as ministers and possibly senior officials periodically declare conventions. In Westminster and Whitehall there is normally a high level of observance of any such declared convention.

In the newer nations of the Westminster world, the idea of conventions is less entrenched; and there are fewer statements of policy or practice formally described as conventions. If Australian government is taken as an example, there are, under the auspices of the Department of the Prime Minister and Cabinet, something of a library of booklets containing what is referred to as 'advice to other Australian Government agencies on many aspects of public administration'. These are various handbooks (*Cabinet Handbook, Federal Executive Council Handbook* and the *Legislation Handbook*), Guidelines (for post-election consultations with Independent Members; for Official Witnesses before Parliamentary Committees and Related Matters) and, best of all, *Guidance on Caretaker Conventions*. Though not law in a formal sense, these promulgations are authoritative and, if necessary, can be enforced by the prime minister.

Not everyone accepts the idea of conventions. This became very apparent in Australia in the wake of the controversies of October and November 1975 surrounding dismissal of the Whitlam Government. At that time much was made both of the existence and force of constitutional conventions especially regarding the powers of the Senate. G. S. Reid, a former Sergeant-at-Arms in the House of Representatives, concluded, however, that they were 'a chimera (a creation of the imagination, or a foolish fancy)'. He contended that, as foundations for argument, they were bound to lead to 'trouble in understanding the affairs of real government,' and considered this had been demonstrated in arguments about the fate of the Whitlam Government (1977: 243).

Describing use of the term as 'little more than an article of political rhetoric', he was especially critical of 'people who go beyond mere description and ascribe some prescriptive (or normative) quality to the practices of the past as obligatory rules for the future'. He pointedly challenged the view of several professors of law that: 'The unwritten rule in question ... is the convention that control of the supply of money to the Government ... should rest with the Lower House ... where Governments are made' (244).

His argument was that 'Every alleged convention in Australian government (that is, every established practice or method) is explicable in terms other than convention; that is, if we take the trouble to reason "why" ... The notion "convention of the Constitution" forecloses reasoning and bedevils our understanding of the processes of democratic government' (245).

This approach is consistent with the wisdom of *House of Representatives Practice* when it observes that 'Parliamentary convention may be considered to be synonymous with parliamentary practice which is, as the term implies, of very broad scope' (49). Convention in this sense is much less entrenched or binding and more capable of adaptation according to circumstances. A preferable term might be that used by Sir William Anson: 'custom'. Definitions of 'custom', however, frequently suggest a practice having the force of law.

Apart from what Canadians describe as the 'confidence convention', a good many claimed conventions in the workings of a parliament are, in fact, about inter-house relationships and, in particular, limiting or containing the role and rights of second chambers; in Australia, especially, claimed conventions often have the purpose of circumscribing the role of the Senate. The function of a convention in this situation is to place a restraint upon an express legal, even constitutional, power (in contrast to asserting a power or authority to do something not specifically provided for by law).

It is, accordingly, not surprising that *Australian Senate Practice* (since 1993, *Odgers' Australian Senate Practice*) has little to offer on the question of conventions. The 1976 (5th) edition, indeed, was clear in denying a number of claimed conventions which had currency in the controversies of the two previous years. Reflecting on those events, this edition declared that 'The power of the Senate to reject or defer any proposed law, including a money bill, was affirmed'. Again, 'the double dissolutions of 1974 and 1975 demonstrated that a Government which has been denied Supply by the Parliament cannot govern and should advise a general election or resign' (Odgers 1976: xix).

Contesting what many (including professors of law) regarded as entrenched conventions did not prevent the author from asserting a few of his own. One aim in 1976 was to argue that 'the Senate is as much a checks and balances House for the nation as it is a States' rights House' (xix).

This survey of the meaning and force of constitutional convention provides a necessary background to consider what are thought of as conventions even if not explicitly so in all cases. Consideration will be given to the formation of ministries (governments); the role of second chambers in the making of legislation; location of the prime minister in the lower house; the second chamber as a parliamentary base of ministers; governments and the confidence of the house; individual ministerial responsibility; parliamentary design; parliamentary colours; the Opposition; question time; and the Speakership.

First and foremost is the simple doctrine that ministries are formed in the lower house, the Houses of Commons in Westminster and Ottawa, the Houses of Representatives in Wellington and Canberra. The lower house is colloquially known as the 'people's house' on the basis that it is elected by the people (as is, on a State basis, the Australian Senate). Historically, in Britain, such a claim was made well before there was a democratic franchise. In the contest for power, the ambitions of the Commons prevailed partly because of its democratic (elective) character, but also because the second chamber, the House of Lords, was, in its composition, largely a hereditary/appointed chamber. The second chamber in Canada is appointed, as was that in New Zealand until its abolition in 1950 (Jackson 1972).

Ministries (governments), whether single-party, multi-party or coalition, will usually have a majority in the lower house though this is not essential in a formal sense. What is essential, at the very least, is sufficient support to introduce and secure passage of legislation appropriating funds, as the Constitution of Australia expresses it, for 'the ordinary annual services of the Government'.

This idea developed at Westminster in the late eighteenth century and has been adopted by most legislatures claiming a Westminster pedigree. In Australia's national parliament it is founded in the financial initiative embodied in the Constitution (s. 53). Such legislation must constitutionally commence in the House of Representatives; a similar requirement is to be found in the British North America Act and its successor (s. 53). A corollary of this feature is similar – namely the capacity to initiate revenue-raising legislation to fund public expenditure. That also has to commence in the lower house.

The role of the second chamber in the handling of such legislation varies. At Westminster, since the Parliament Act 1911, such legislation automatically becomes law one month after leaving the Commons. Prior to the 'Peers versus the People' battles of 1909–11, it was widely held that, in basic financial matters, the House of Commons was pre-eminent; one means of making the claim was by resolution of the Commons (Hanham 1969: 193, citing a resolution of 26 June 1907). The claim of the Commons was much contested and neither history nor precedent provided a conclusive guide, notwithstanding that as early as 1860, even before the second Reform Act, Walter Bagehot felt able to state that 'on great political questions [the House of Lords] have not the substantial power of beginning a bill. They are only a court of review' (Bagehot 1974 [1860]: 14).

The Canadian House of Commons likewise claims to be predominant in expenditure and tax legislation. The appointed Canadian Senate, however, has not always, historically, acquiesced in these claims. It 'has regularly asserted the right to amend money bills' (Marleau and Montpetit 2000: 712). It also initiates financial legislation, but 'such bills have been laid aside [in the House of Commons] on the grounds that they contravened the constitutional principles that financial bills originate in the Commons and are introduced at the initiative of the Crown' (Marleau and Montpetit 2000: 713).

An Australian ministry, to stay in office, needs to be able to secure passage of such legislation through the Senate as well. This is not a convention but a provision of the Constitution. Nevertheless, whatever the party numbers in the Senate, it has been usual for appropriation bills to pass on the voices. Oppositions have been very reluctant to use a majority in the Senate to challenge appropriation legislation; most such challenges come when the opposition lacks a majority, so the effect is essentially rhetorical. When the appropriation legislation was attacked in 1974 and 1975, the purpose was to bring on a general election (in both instances, a double dissolution ensued).

In retirement Sir Robert Menzies, prime minister 1939–41 and 1949–66, recalled that 'when Arthur Calwell was Leader of the Opposition, he would never tolerate the refusal of supply by the Senate; his view being, quite rightly, that the primary control of the finances was with the Lower House, and not with the Senate' (Henderson 2011: 262). This could be regarded as a convention of the self-denying type, and some have seen it as such; but it also represents prudence – oppositions too hungry for office do not readily win, and may quickly lose, the regard of voters.

Acknowledgement that the financial initiative rests in the lower house does not by any means eliminate scope for disputation. It usually takes two forms.

The first is argument about what qualifies for inclusion in legislation appropriating expenditure for the ordinary annual services of the government. In the Westminster Parliament, the certification of the Speaker settles the matter.

This has, by contrast, been a source of much friction between the House of Representatives and the Senate in Canberra. It was effectively settled by what became known as the Compact of 1965 which now provides the framework for resolving disputes about the content of financial legislation which may, and may not, be amended by the Senate.

In Canberra, the business of requesting amendments is a second source of tension. Under the Constitution, the Senate may not amend a variety of finance legislation, but it 'may at any stage return [such legislation] to the House of Representatives . . . requesting, by message, the omission or amendment of any items or provisions therein. And the House of Representatives may, if it thinks fit, make any of such omissions or amendments, with or without modifications' (s. 53).

When the House does not agree, the Senate will frequently press its case. The right of the Senate to 'press' requests has long been contested. The House has developed a suite of responses to Senate requests for amendment, including pressed requests; in particular, especially when there is some urgency about the legislation, the House will accept the amendment but will resolve to refrain from the determination of its constitutional rights (Wright 2012: 451). This suite of responses, in a sense, serves something of the same function as a convention even if not always to the advantage of the ministry. It provides a cover for retreat with dignity.

The view that the prime minister will be the leader of the party or parties with a majority in the House derives from the political strength conferred by the financial initiative. At its heart, it is a product of parliamentary power which some (unnecessarily) like to cloak with the respectability of convention. But in the democratic age it would be very unusual for the head of government not to come from the elected house.

But where, as in Australia, the second chamber is also elected, there is nothing to prevent appointment of a senator who remains a senator as prime minister. But the necessity of being able, if necessary, to control financial legislation makes such a course unlikely. It is now very rare for a head of government in a parliamentary system not to be a member of what is known as the lower (or 'popular') house. (This is a contrast to the congressional form as practised in the United States where congressional figures who emerge as candidates for the presidency invariably come from the Senate.)

A particular reason for prime ministers sitting in the elective House is simply to be able to confront, directly and personally, the main challenger for the office, the leader of the opposition. This, indeed, was the rationale for commissioning Stanley Baldwin instead of Lord Curzon, when, in 1923, Andrew Bonar Law stood down without advising the King about a successor.

The elective character of the Australian Senate, combined with effectively co-equal powers in legislation, confers a significance not enjoyed by appointed upper houses. About one-third of the ministry in 2014 was drawn from the Senate – sixteen out of forty-two: five ministers in Cabinet; six in the outer ministry; and five parliamentary secretaries. At Whitehall, of more than twenty ministers at a meeting of the Cabinet, only two were from the House of Lords (parliamentary under-secretaries in the main constitute ministerial numbers in the Lords). In Ottawa, there is often only one minister in the Senate, and never more than three (Marleau and Montpetit 2000: 27).

This practice has broadly prevailed for half a century. It is sometimes noted by observers, most frequently in Canada, but it is never raised to the level of a convention though why not is a reasonable question.

Ministries remain in office as long as they retain the confidence of the lower house. Tight – very tight – party discipline has characterised the Australian House of Representatives for more than a century so the risk of a defeat on any question great or small has become extremely slight. In the past century, Australian ministries have been defeated in the House on three occasions (1929 and 1931, which were followed by general elections; and 1941, the last time there was a change of government without an election). Confusion followed collapse of the Hughes Labor Government in 1916, but that particular realignment of parliamentary forces was settled by formation of the Nationalist government early in 1917.

In earlier times, defeat in virtually any vote was enough to end a ministry; elections never followed. In 1904, the Watson government, the first national Labor government in the world, was defeated on a procedural vote which discomforted even conservative members of the House. Merely the threat of a hostile vote brought its successor, the Reid-McLean ministry, to an end.

The strength of the Australian need for a visible majority in the House was evident in the 2010–13 parliament when neither the Labor party nor the Coalition parties had a majority. The incumbent Labor Prime Minister, Julia Gillard, thought it important to have, in writing, assured commitments to the government from sufficient crossbenchers to ensure a majority for votes on major questions in the House. As the parliament progressed some of these alliances dissolved, but they had served the purpose of securing Labor's hold on office in the immediate aftermath of the general election. Thereafter, had the opposition wanted to remove the government, the onus was on it to take the initiative with a vote of no confidence and win the votes of cross-benchers.

Canada, which has a more varied history of parliaments in which none of the major parties has had a majority in the House of Commons, has eschewed this approach. Coalitions are unknown in Canadian government and formal parliamentary alliances guaranteeing majorities are rare. In such circumstances, since 1957, the party with a plurality has formed the government. Half the ministries since 1957 have been minority governments. Parliaments in which no-one has a majority are usually short-lived and fresh elections accordingly follow well before the scheduled expiry of the parliament.

Today, a government could only be defeated on a major question; such a case was the defeat of the Fadden coalition government in Australia in October 1941. In March 1979, the Callaghan Labour government in the United Kingdom was defeated in a straight vote that the House had no confidence in the government; in a minority situation notwithstanding a pact with the Liberals, it had previously weathered the loss of several votes in the House in the preceding three years without having to contemplate a dissolution.

The Clark Conservative government in Canada was defeated in a vote on the budget at the end of 1979. The House of Commons was dissolved and an election called for the following February which brought the Liberal party back to office.

If a ministry were inadvertently defeated on a vote, the question would be recommitted or otherwise defused. Such a case occurred in the Canadian House of Commons in 1968 when, after defeat of a tax bill on the third reading, the House passed a motion stating that it did 'not regard' the vote on the tax bill 'as a vote of no-confidence in the Government' (Marleau and Montpetit 2000: 45).

Historically, ministries without majority support in the Australian House of Representatives were, when defeated, often succeeded by another ministry lacking a formal majority. This occurred when dissolutions were routinely refused, as they usually were other than at the end of a parliament. It is more likely nowadays that a dissolution would be granted except, possibly, in the highly unusual circumstances at the start of a new parliament when an incumbent ministry has decided to await a vote in parliament before resigning (a practice which once prevailed in the United Kingdom until the mid-nineteenth century when it was abandoned at Disraeli's instance). The view is now that the removal of governments is the business of the people rather than parliaments (St John-Stevas 1982: 18).

The confidence requirement comes very close to being what might be called a pure convention; that is, it is nowhere expressed in law or formally but, if successfully activated, has instant effect, usually bringing on a dissolution. A change of ministry remains a possibility, as Peter Russell's chapter in this volume shows.

It would also be possible, even if highly unlikely, for a ministry falling foul of a confidence vote to hang on, at least for a time. If it were able to withstand a very hostile press and public opinion in these circumstances, eventually the Dicey approach would kick in. The defeated ministry would later if not sooner have to face parliament, under the rules requiring annual sittings, and it would eventually have to seek appropriations to carry on the government.

Responsibility of individual ministers to the House is generally fairly straightforward. They answer questions relating to their portfolios put them in the House and in committee. They likewise oversee passage of legislation within their portfolio. But it is what happens when something goes wrong that is of greatest interest. The usual formula is that a minister losing the confidence of the House resigns.

It is a long time since there has been an express vote against a minister in her/his ministerial capacity in any house of parliament; government majorities and party discipline see to that. Sometimes the matter does not even come before the House unless a former minister who has resigned decides to make a statement. It is all settled by the prime minister outside parliament.

On other occasions the opposition will put no-confidence motions to the House. One or even two or three motions can be resisted;

this occurred shortly after the Howard government took office in 1996 when the Minister for Foreign Affairs was subject of much opposition criticism over some foreign aid matters. But, in other circumstances, a succession of such motions, though invariably defeated, can lead to a resignation. The political price of retaining a minister becomes too great for the government. (It is what the former Prime Minister of Australia, John Howard, has referred to as 'an important principle of the Westminster system: a minister should resign or stand aside when his or her continued membership of the cabinet is damaging the government' (Howard 2010: 216)). An example of a resignation of this sort is that of Ros Kelly in Australia in 1993 in what was referred to as the sports rorts (whiteboard) affair. Similar occurrences can be found in Westminster, Ottawa and Wellington.

In Australia, ministers in the Senate are also liable to censure in the House of Representatives and sometimes may face attack in both Houses. An important instance of such two-pronged assault was the events leading to Senator Graham Richardson's resignation from the Keating government in 1992.

In the realisation of traditional ministerial responsibility, the House of Representatives especially and the parliament generally is, contrary to the usual exposition, as much the forum as the instrument of execution. A besieged minister, to survive, must weather the storm in the House, and do so fairly quickly.

Governments have never acknowledged that ministers in the Senate are beholden to that chamber. In 1973, the Senate passed a resolution of no confidence in the Attorney-General in the Whitlam government, Senator Lionel Murphy. In response, the Prime Minister, Gough Whitlam, quickly marshalled his forces in the House to declare confidence in Murphy and, in doing so, to claim the supremacy of the House in such matters. The record shows that Senate ministers under sustained fire in the Senate may win the immediate contests, but they rarely survive for long.

It is a curiosity that in the analysis of conventions, kindred practices such as the physical context are rarely addressed. In 1943, Winston Churchill provided a powerful reminder of the importance of the physical scene to parliamentary and political practice: 'We shape our chambers and our chambers shape us'. However much the physical layouts of chambers differ from the shape and configuration of the House of Commons, they all resemble Westminster in one key feature: the ministry (government) faces off against the opposition.

In a physical sense, this is the feature which distinguishes Westminster parliamentary design from the semi-circular Greek style found in Continental assemblies, and also the Congress, where the division between the contestants for power is marked by the aisle rather than the table (physically if not rhetorically). Westminster parliaments are considered to be among the most adversarial of all representative assemblies, and these physical characteristics of the chamber, which represent a form of convention, would certainly not have the effect of ameliorating the vigour of the contest.

The signature colour of all such chambers is green. Again there can be variations. In the provisional Parliament House at Canberra, where the House met from 1927 until 1988, it was a deep green. The muted shades of green in the chamber in the New and Permanent Parliament House, to which the Parliament moved in 1988, were chosen as representing the tones of native eucalypts (Wright 2012: 107). (A suggestive speculation is to imagine the behavioural dynamics of a Westminster chamber in which members were seated alphabetically, or in order of election, instead of according to whether they support or oppose the ministry.)

The colour of the chamber sheds an instructive light on the character of parliamentary tradition. *House of Representatives Practice* states that, while the 'derivation of the traditional use of green is uncertain', green appears to have been the colour of the House of Commons since the thirteenth century (Wright 2012: 107).

As a matter of interest, and an example of the different explanations which may emerge in dealing with traditions of parliamentary institutions, *House of Commons Procedure and Practice* (Canada) states that the 'association of the colour green with the Commons is not so easily determined. The colour green has been linked to the Commons' meeting places at least since 1663 (date of the first authoritative written reference to green in the House of Commons) Marleau and Montpetit 2000: 232 (f/n 27).

That green should be the colour of the House is not stipulated anywhere in an authoritative way, and it was almost certainly never formally adopted; it would seem to have established itself by effluxion of time. Yet were a House to wish to change to another colour, perhaps to signal some decisive change in the nature of the House or the parliamentary regime, it is probable that some procedure would need to be followed, including but beyond a simple vote, before doing so.

The physical configuration of the lower house chamber, whether rectangular or horse-shoe, accords well with the familiar government-opposition dichotomy of Westminster politics. The opposition is the characteristic institutional artefact of a Westminster parliament which distinguishes it from both continental and congressional modes of political contest.

The whole opposition arrangement fits into the concept of convention although is only occasionally so recognised. Entrenched in a recognised role without roots in any constitution, it only gradually secured acknowledgement in standing orders and statute.

Opposition in a formal sense had its origins in the eighteenth century: Charles James Fox, Pitt the Younger's great adversary, is widely seen as the first leader of the opposition. But, at Westminster, it was not until the early twentieth century that the person leading the opposition in the House of Commons was perceived as the alternative prime minister. Although being so viewed, and enjoying a number of prerogatives in House proceedings, as late as 1937 it was still possible for the holder of the office, Labour leader C. R. Attlee, to state in the Commons that the 'Leader of the Opposition is a private Member... He is responsible only to his constituents and to the Members from whom he derives his position'. Attlee interestingly added: 'He is, I think, under a special obligation to defend the rights and privileges of private Members, particularly the right of every Member to express his opinion freely on all matters of public policy' (1937).

With the passage of time, the office took shape, moving from the realm of convention to the rule-book. With recognition (usually in standing orders) of a certain precedence in House proceedings came additional accommodation, staff and eventually a salary (which even in 1970 cut out when the House was dissolved, underlining the parliamentary nature of the office). In all jurisdictions it was usually by way of salary recognition that the office found its way into the statute books. In the United Kingdom, the leader of the opposition is sworn of the Privy Council if not already a member. As such, certain confidential matters can be shared.

The leader of the opposition in the Canadian House of Commons, like the Westminster counterpart, has roots in the practice of the House and was the first to be paid a special salary; the legislation dates from 1910, and the explanation given by Prime Minister Sir Wilfred Laurier gives the post an unmistakable constitutional cast. Today, the occupant receives the salary and allowances of a member of Cabinet; has an official residence in Ottawa (Stornoway); and becomes a member of the Privy Council of Canada.

The leader of the opposition in the Australian House of Representatives has been well-recognised in statute and standing orders for more than half a century. It was in 1912 that the Hansard reporters decided upon upper case to designate the office; and eight years later a special salary was appropriated in view of the additional work falling to the office-holder. Governmental practice makes provision for opposition leaders to be briefed on important matters, but they do not become members of the equivalent of the Privy Council, the Federal Executive Council. Nor does the leader of the opposition in Canberra have an official residence. The office is similarly structured in Wellington.

Question Time is widely seen as the most public part of the day in most parliaments. It is certainly the time when most members attend. Again, methods of handling questions, with notice and without, is a dynamic illustration of the workings of convention, especially in the extent to which practice conspicuously precedes formulation of rules. In this instance more than most others, it is tempting to write that such rules as evolve, whether located in standing orders or in the treatises on practice, seem to be far more honour'd in the breach than 'th'observance'.

In the Australian Parliament, provision was first made only for Questions on Notice. But as *House of Representatives Practice* records:

> in practice questions without notice were answered from the outset. During the first sitting days of the first Parliament the Speaker made the following statement in reply to a query from the Leader of the Opposition as to whether a practice of asking questions without notice should be created:
>
> There is no direct provision in our standing orders for the asking of questions without notice, but, as there is no prohibition of the practice, if a question is asked without notice and the Minister to whom it is addressed chooses to answer it, I do not think that I should object.

The practice of members asking questions without notice developed in a rather ad hoc manner. It was not until 1950 that the standing orders specifically permitted questions without notice or included them in the order of business, despite their long de facto status (Wright, 2012).

In Canberra, questions from the opposition have been increasingly asked by members of the front bench. Supplementaries are rare.

By contrast, in Ottawa, while the opposition party leadership may lead off, private members of the opposition still have a reasonable opportunity to put questions. Whereas in Canberra, the question is normally answered by the minister to whom it is addressed, this is not necessarily so in Ottawa; questions there are taken to be addressed to the ministry as a whole. Both in Ottawa and Wellington, supplementaries are conspicuously part of question time.

A curiosity about the evolution of Question Time in the derivative parliaments is that while they each developed what might be called a deregulated approach where all ministers were expected to be in attendance, from the very early years of the twentieth century the House of Commons was establishing a highly regulated approach to oral questions (or, more accurately, oral answers) in which ministers were rostered over a two–three-week period to take questions. At a later stage, Prime Minister's Question Time was introduced, initially twice a week for twenty minutes. Tony Blair changed this to once a week for half an hour.

A further prominent case where practice, convention and ideals interact with much variety is in the office of Speaker. At Westminster, the Speaker is seen as an impartial office, and the incumbent is expected to withdraw not only from party activity but also from much of the daily life of the House. Generally, the occupant contests his seat simply as Mr or Madam Speaker and other parties refrain from entering the contest. A Speaker if returned usually continues in office and most serve for two or three terms, often taking a seat in the House of Lords upon retirement.

At the other end of the spectrum, the Speaker of the House of Representatives in Canberra remains an active member, not least of the party. After elections, even if the incumbent Speaker has been returned, there will be a contest for the Speakership; and if there has been a change of government, a new Speaker will generally be elected from the ranks of the new party in government. When the House is finely divided, the government may seek to strengthen its position by looking to an opposition member to take the chair. This was attempted with only slight success by the Gillard government in the 2010–13 Parliament, when a former member of the Liberal Party (Peter Slipper) became Speaker for a time. Back in 1961, when the Menzies coalition government survived with a majority of one in the House, the then leader of the opposition, Arthur Calwell, stated that had he been successful in forming a ministry, he would have sought to persuade the incumbent Speaker, John McLeay, who had been in the chair since 1956, to remain, but it is not likely that he would have been successful.

One of the long-standing traditions of the Speakership is that a successful candidate for the office takes the chair with reluctance. This practice stems from much earlier times when the Speaker, as spokesman for the House to the monarch, encountered a measure of danger in carrying out such responsibility. In the New Zealand House of Representatives members now nominate themselves for election. As a consequence, since 1996, 'this pretence of a "reluctant" Speaker has been largely abandoned' (McGee 2005: 138).

Any systematic consideration of conventions in a parliamentary context underlines their elusive and generally indeterminate character. It certainly confirms Mill's counsel that they must be interpreted with a full regard for 'circumstances and conditions'. It may also be preferable to approach them not so much as rules or even as maxims, whether written or unwritten, but as precedents.

Loughlin has usefully observed that the 'British constitution is, at heart, an assemblage of customary practices, with the "rules" often amounting to no more than cribs distilled from such practices' (2013: 21).

Seeing conventions as precedents would allow a better match between prior experience and the application of any conclusion about their meaning to new circumstances and conditions. Conventions and like concepts (traditions, practices, customs, usages) would thus become guides – indeed, significant guides – to addressing new situations rather than dogmatic stipulations which, in a crisis, will not be accepted as binding.

References

Attlee, C. R. 1937. Cited in Le May, G. H. 1955. *British Government 1914–1963: Select Documents*. London: Methuen, 188–9.

Bagehot, Walter 1974 [1860]. 'The Financial Position of the House of Lords', in Norman St John-Stevas (ed.), *The Collected Works of Walter Bagehot*, vol 6. London: The Economist, 13–17.

Blackburn, R. and A. Kennon with Sir Michael Wheeler-Booth (eds.) 2003. *Griffith and Ryle on Parliament – Functions, Practice and Procedures*, 2nd edn. London: Sweet & Maxwell.

Butler, David 1973. *The Canberra Model*. Melbourne: Cheshire.

Coombs, H. C. 1976. *Report: Royal Commission on Australian Government Administration*. Canberra: Australian Government Publishing Service.

Evans, Harry and Rosemary Laing (eds.) 2012. *Odgers' Australian Senate Practice*, 13th edn. Canberra: Department of the Senate.

Franks, C. E. S. 1987. *The Parliament of Canada*. University of Toronto Press.

Hanham, H. J. (ed.) 1969. *The Nineteenth Century Constitution 1815-1914: Documents and Commentary*. London: Cambridge University Press.

Hasluck, Paul 1979. *The Office of Governor-General*. Melbourne University Press.

Henderson, Heather (ed.) 2011. *Letters to My Daughter: Robert Menzies, Letters, 1955-1975*. Sydney: Pier 9.

Howard, John 2010. *Lazarus Rising*. Sydney: HarperCollins.

Hughes, Colin A. 1980. 'Conventions: Dicey Revisited', in Patrick Weller and Dean Jaensch (eds.), *Responsible Government in Australia*. Richmond: Drummond, 41–9.

Jack, Sir Malcolm (ed.) 2011. *Erskine May's Treatise on the Law, Privileges, Proceedings and Usage of Parliament*, 24th edn. London: LexisNexis.

Jackson, W. K. 1972. *The New Zealand Legislative Council; a Study of the Establishment, Failure and Abolition of an Upper House*. Dunedin: University of Otago Press.

Loughlin, Martin 2013. *The British Constitution*. Oxford University Press.

Marleau, Robert and Camille Montpetit 2000. *House of Commons Procedure and Practice*. Ottawa: House of Commons.

McGee, David 2005. *Parliamentary Practice in New Zealand*, 3rd edn. Wellington: Dunmore Publishing.

Mill, J. S. [1861] 1910. *Considerations on Representative Government. Utilitarianism, Liberty & Representative Government*. London: Everyman's Library.

Odgers, J. R. 1976. *Australian Senate Practice*, 5th edn. Canberra: RAIPA (ACT Division).

Odgers, J. R. 1991. *Australian Senate Practice*, 6th edn. Canberra: RAIPA (ACT Division).

Reid, G. S. 1977. 'Commentary', in Gareth Evans (ed.), *Labor and the Constitution 1972–1975*. Melbourne: Heinemann, 240–6.

Reid, G. S. and Martyn Forrest 1989. *Australia's Commonwealth Parliament 1901–1988: Ten Perspectives*. Melbourne University Press.

Rogers, Robert and Rhodri Havard Walters 2006. *How Parliament Works*, 6th edn. London: Pearson/Longman.

Royal Commission on Australian Government Administration (Chair H.C. Coombs) 1976. *Report*. Canberra: Australian Government Printing Service.

Saunders, Cheryl and E. Smith 1980. *Paper Prepared for Standing Committee D of the Australian Constitutional Convention Identifying the Conventions Associated with the Commonwealth Constitution*. Melbourne: Victorian Government Printer.

St John-Stevas, Norman 1982. 'Government by discussion', in J. R. Nethercote, (ed.), *Parliament and Bureaucracy*. Sydney: Hale & Iremonger, 14–25.

Wright, B. C. 2012. *House of Representatives Practice*, 6th edn. Canberra: Department of the House of Representatives.

8

Upper houses

CAMPBELL SHARMAN

There is a clear inconsistency between a majoritarian tradition in parliamentary democracies and the existence of upper houses as autonomous actors in the legislative process. If an upper house is not controlled by the governing party, there is the potential for disruption of the government's legislative program and a break in the line of electoral accountability through the lower house. This can be seen as an unwarranted constraint on popular democracy, the likely view of a parliamentary executive faced with upper house opposition. Yet it can be argued that an upper house not under the control of the government provides the only avenue for effective parliamentary scrutiny of the executive in an age of disciplined political parties (Aroney, Prasser and Nethercote 2008). This clash of views can be characterised as part of a broader debate over the nature of limited government and the competing claims of majoritarian and consensus democracy (Lijphart 1999).

In British-derived parliamentary systems, upper houses have long been the subject of such disagreements. Given the propensity of parliamentary executives to cleave to a majoritarian model, it is no surprise that governments have worked consistently to limit the powers of upper houses, where constitutional constraints or political resistance have prevented outright abolition. Yet some upper houses have persisted and a number have been able to enhance their role and significance.

Where bicameralism continues, how is the cohabitation between the houses managed? For the reasons stated, the relationship is inherently unstable because there is a strong drive on the part of a government based on a lower house majority to dominate the parliamentary process. The success of an upper house is measured by the extent to which it can maintain some autonomy in the face of government pressure to conform to executive preferences. This measure of independent action is dependent on the ability of an upper house to work with the parliamentary executive to develop conventions, in the sense of rules of prudence, which manage conflict and set the limits to confrontations between the two houses. Where these rules fail or are absent, confrontation with a government majority in the lower house may prompt constitutional change to reduce the power of the second chamber, sometimes foreshadowing its abolition.

The range and nature of this accommodation has varied widely between institutions. Australia and Canada, with their national and subnational parliaments, provide a set of fourteen bicameral and formerly bicameral legislatures, seven of whose upper houses have survived.[1] Over the course of their existence, variations between the conventions of accommodation in upper houses have been shaped not only by their institutional design but also by the subtle influence of attitudes towards the role of government and the behaviour of previous regimes. In this respect, history is important. Differences in upper house traditions between Australia and Canada are the result, in large measure, of differences in the context of the grant of colonial self-government. Before looking in greater detail at current bicameral parliaments, these differences in historical context need to be explored; they have set the range of bicameral accommodations available in each system, and raise perennial questions about the operation of upper houses.

Upper houses designed as institutions for limiting popular government are quintessentially nineteenth-century institutions, created as a conservative response to the spread of representative democracy and the extension of the franchise. This period is sandwiched between an earlier one in which second chambers reflected theories of mixed government (note Fukuda 1997), and the current one in which constitution makers in parliamentary systems have favoured unicameral legislatures. In the British case, the House of Lords in the 1800s had evolved from a premodern version of parliamentary government but remained steeped in the idiosyncrasies of British history and social structure.

Pressure for a measure of effective popular self-government for British colonies in Australasia and Canada after 1800 presented unfamiliar problems of parliamentary design for both the colonists and the imperial government (Ward 1976). There was dispute over the way in which the practice of 'responsible government' could be implemented for the colonies and the constraints on popular majorities that might be

[1] Newfoundland is excluded from the Canadian count; although it had an upper house from 1854 until 1934 when parliamentary self-government was suspended, Newfoundland had a long history as an independent British colony and dominion, and joined the Canadian federation as a unicameral province in 1949.

required. But, by mid-century, the goal of the new system was clear; the operation of executive government would be dependent on ministers who, collectively, could secure majority support from a popularly elected assembly.

Such a system left open the question of a changed role for existing legislative councils. These bodies had begun as small committees of officials, supplemented by local notables, to advise the colonial governor on his executive and legislative functions. Over time, the importance of legislative councils grew, some acquiring an elective component. If responsible government implied a dominant role for the new assemblies in the process of parliamentary government, what was to become of the legislative councils? Should they be retained as a check on potentially radical measures proposed by assemblies or abolished as redundant and undesirable limits on popular government?

The Canadian model and its consequences

In the Canadian colonies, the fate of legislative councils was complicated by wide variations in the patterns of settlement and institutional traditions of the colonies, and in the role that legislative councils had played in some colonial governments. Fears of radical action by popularly elected assemblies had prompted the governors and legislative councils of Upper and Lower Canada to undermine the measure of representative self-government granted in 1791 (note Garon 1970) by circumventing the financial accountability of government to the elected assemblies (Ajzenstat 2007, 113–23). Popular agitation and a change of administration in Britain finally resulted in responsible government being implemented in Canadian colonies by 1850 (Dawson 1970: 5–19).

By the time of debates on Canadian confederation in 1865, there was a range of views on upper houses (Ajzenstat et al. 2003: 77–102; Moore 1998: 104–13). For some, the experience of legislative councils in undermining popular government had left a strong commitment to unicameral parliaments. Any upper house was seen as an unwarranted limitation on responsible government. Others thought that some form of upper house might be an appropriate component of a parliament as a limitation on hasty legislation. But few supported an elected house, most relying on executive appointment as the most suitable selection procedure to preserve the primacy of an elected lower chamber. At the time of confederation, however, the issue of some form of regional representation in the national parliament of a federated Canada overrode objections to bicameralism and persuaded almost all participants that an upper house of some kind was necessary.

A number of factors played an important role in the final choice for the design of the Canadian Senate. The first was the ability to look at the experience of existing upper houses operating in self-governing British colonies. The Province of Canada – the union of Upper and Lower Canada – had moved from an appointed to an elected Legislative Council in 1859. Nova Scotia, New Brunswick, Newfoundland and New Zealand had appointed upper houses with life membership as did two of Australia's five self-governing colonies, Queensland and New South Wales. The other Australian colonies had legislative councils elected on a restricted property franchise as did Prince Edward Island. The choice made for the Canadian Senate was an appointed house with life membership but with two modifications. The first was a regional basis for appointment; the second was a limitation on the size of the Senate; these conditions, together with constitutional entrenchment, were to play a critical role in the history of the Senate and its relationship with the executive.

The second factor was the role of political parties in Canada. Earlier than in the Australian colonies, broad party groupings had formed in some Canadian parliaments. This meant that Canadian politicians were more aware of the possibilities of partisan clashes between upper and lower houses on matters of government policy. An elected upper house might exacerbate these conflicts and give unwelcome legitimacy to critics of the government. For these reasons alone, appointment by the executive was the preferred option, but it could also provide the possibility of appointing additional upper house members to swamp persistent opposition after the fashion of Queensland and New South Wales. This was not a characteristic of Canadian legislative councils after self-government, but there was a special provision for the governor-general to appoint a limited number of additional senators in case of a deadlock between the Canadian Senate and the House of Commons.[2]

The Canadian model of parliamentary government that emerged by the 1900s was one that was majoritarian in its strong aversion to formal limits on the executive control of parliament that an upper house might provide (Docherty 2008). Ontario (1867) and British Columbia (1871) became provinces with unicameral parliaments and, with the exception

[2] Constitution Act, 1867, s. 26; see Franks (2003: 161–3) for description of its use in 1990, the only time the section has been invoked.

of the short-lived Legislative Council of Manitoba (1871–6; see Grebstad 2014), no province created from newly settled territory sought a bicameral parliament. Of those provinces that had upper houses at confederation in 1867, those of New Brunswick (1892) and Prince Edward Island (1893)[3] were abolished by the turn of the century. The Legislative Council of Nova Scotia survived until 1928, with abolition forced on it as the result of a controversial decision by the Judicial Committee of the Privy Council (Beck 1957: 231–52) and that of Quebec, the last province to retain an upper house, was finally abolished in 1968 (Orban 1969). Only the Canadian Senate survives today.

With governments predisposed against legislative councils, upper house obstruction and provincial financial difficulties were the usual reasons given for the abolition of Canadian legislative councils. Abolition was usually accompanied by financial arrangements to induce a majority of councillors to abolish the upper house. In this respect, Quebec is a partial exception. The Legislative Council of Quebec had a structure that mirrored the Canadian Senate – a fixed number of members appointed for life but chosen from specified districts within Quebec. As Orban (1969) explains, the Council persisted as a result of partisan convenience, the accommodation of the economically influential Anglophone minority, and the interlocking interests of social and commercial elites. For most of its existence the Council was politically quiescent, saved from abolition by partisan self-interest and the difficulty of persuading thirteen of the twenty-four members to agree to disband the Council. In the end, a broadly based agreement that such an upper house was inconsistent with current views of democratic representation led to its abolition in 1968.

But the most important factor explaining the abolition of Canadian provincial upper houses, Prince Edward Island excepted, was the appointed nature of their membership which simultaneously denied any democratic legitimacy to the chambers and made them the object of patronage appointments. It is possible that a self-denying government might have aimed to create some partisan balance in the chamber, but the temptation to use a place in the legislative council to accommodate powerful political interests and to reward partisan benefactors proved hard to resist. In other words, successive governments had no interest in establishing conventions for appointments that maintained a partisan

[3] Prince Edward Island is a special case: in 1892, both the Assembly and the Legislative Council were abolished and a new Legislative Assembly was created, half elected on the previous Assembly franchise, half on the Council franchise (MacKinnon 1951: 210–15).

balance or that furthered the parliamentary function of the upper house; partisanship and patronage were the operating principles. This tradition has been continued in the Canadian Senate. As a consequence, the conventions that have developed in the Canadian Senate are not ones that have been designed to enhance the parliamentary process but to further the primacy of the House of Commons and the executive's dominance of the Senate.

Before analysing how this tradition has played out in the current relationship between the executive and the Canadian Senate, an alternative model of parliamentary bicameralism needs to be examined.

The Australian model; strong parliamentary bicameralism

The British settlement of Australasia took place in the first half of the nineteenth century, a much shorter time span than in Canada. While there were some differences in the pattern of settlement and the social structure of the colonies, the linguistic and sectarian divisions and the institutional variations that coloured colonial politics in Canada were largely absent from Australia and New Zealand. There was a strong similarity in both the timing and the demands for self-government in the Australasian colonies, the five Australian colonies[4] and New Zealand, all gaining responsible government between 1854 and 1857. They also had the advantage of being able to benefit from the experience of the Canadian colonies in framing their requests for a system of responsible government. Even so, there were significant differences between the design of colonial parliamentary institutions, the most important one being the selection of members for their upper houses.

There had not been the aversion to bicameralism in Australia and New Zealand that had coloured the debate in Canada. While legislative councils were often seen as dominated by a conservative economic and social elite, the stress was on the creation of a popularly elected assembly rather than the abolition of legislative councils. The problem facing both the colonists and the Colonial Office was how to reframe legislative councils as upper houses in a bicameral parliament.

[4] New South Wales, South Australia, Tasmania and Victoria; Queensland separated from New South Wales in 1860, but its residents had enjoyed responsible government since 1856 as part of New South Wales. Western Australia did not gain self-government until 1890.

One solution was to follow the Canadian model and appoint members for life to the upper house. This practice was followed by New Zealand in 1854, New South Wales in 1856 and Queensland when it separated from New South Wales in 1860. For the Australian colonies, and after much debate (Clune and Griffith 2006: 66–71), a minimum number of councillors was specified but no maximum, a feature adopted by New Zealand after 1862 (Jackson 1972). This opportunity to swamp an Opposition majority in the legislative council by appointing additional members, while it required the consent of the governor which was not always forthcoming,[5] eventually led to the demise of these legislative councils or, in the case of New South Wales, to its transformation.

The problems of patronage, partisanship and frequent parliamentary stagnation that characterised appointed houses in Canada were present in the Australasian chambers, with a corresponding lack of incentive for the executive to develop conventions for partisan balance in appointing councillors. A fiercely partisan campaign to abolish the Queensland Legislative Council eventually succeeded in 1922 despite strong controversy (Carney 2008: 262–7; Harding 2000). A less controversial abolition occurred in 1950 in New Zealand (Jackson 1972). After avoiding several abolition attempts, the New South Wales Legislative Council was transformed into an indirectly elected house in 1934 (Turner 1969) and finally into a directly elected house in 1976 (Clune and Griffith 2006: 494–515). As such, New South Wales joined South Australia, Tasmania, Victoria and Western Australia, which had all been designed at their founding to have parliaments with elected upper houses.

Strong, elective parliamentary bicameralism has become the hallmark of the Australian parliamentary tradition. Before federation in 1901, powerful upper houses elected on a restricted franchise operated as a conservative brake on colonial governments, often amending or blocking legislation, sometimes leading to major political controversies, and occasionally to constitutional crises.[6] Pressures for abolition were thwarted by the legislative councils themselves but, as the franchise for upper houses was widened and organised party groupings

5 Such decisions often involved the governor in political controversy, especially so when the governments of Queensland and New South Wales moved to abolish the upper house.

6 One of the most serious of these occurred under the premiership of James McCulloch from 1863 to 1868 (see Wright 1992: 77–80).

emerged, conflict between the chambers began to acquire an overtly partisan flavour. When conservative parties were in government, legislative councils became quiescent, only to spring into action if a Labor government was elected.

Notwithstanding the checkered history of elective bicameralism in the Australian colonies before 1900, the model of strong elective bicameralism that characterised the majority of Australia's colonial parliaments was adopted for the Australian Senate in 1901, but with universal franchise and the states as electoral districts with equal representation. As with Canada, this was the result of both the demands for territorial representation in the national parliament, particularly from the smaller states, as well as support from those who wanted limits on the legislative power of the lower house. The subsequent trajectory for elected upper houses in Australia since 1901 has been well described by Stone (2002). In spite of a steady move to universal franchise for state upper houses, both state and federal upper chambers were seen, until the 1960s, as either redundant when they shared a partisan majority with the governing party, or highly partisan when they were controlled by the opposition party.

This began to change after proportional representation was adopted for Australian Senate elections from 1949 and accelerated as state upper houses adopted similar institutional changes in the decades following 1970. The fact that minor parties and independents began to hold the balance of power in upper houses, with no governing party likely to have a partisan majority in the chamber, had the effect of transforming the legislative role of upper houses and greatly enhancing the accountability of the executive to parliament (Mulgan 1996; Sharman 1999). This process has been uneven, but the expectation is now that upper houses are an important part of parliamentary democracy in Australia. Executive government must, more often than not, have to deal with a powerful legislative chamber over which it has no partisan control. Moreover, with proportional representation, upper houses often have a stronger claim to more accurate partisan representation than governments based on lower house majorities.

Conventions for accommodating conflict: elected upper houses

All Australian upper houses have extensive constitutional powers, now reinforced by the political legitimacy of direct election and fair representation.[7] All can seriously embarrass a government by amending its legislative programme and inquiring into government activities which the executive would prefer unexamined, and some can force a government to the polls by denying the executive the authority to spend money. This creates the potential for serious political clashes between a government with a partisan majority in the lower house and an upper house controlled by opposition parties. Disciplined political parties can be seen as the drivers for such disagreements, but parties also have worked out conventions in the sense of accommodations to avoid or constrain conflict.

Even before proportional representation and the rise of smaller parties holding the balance of power in upper houses, the two largest party groupings had to tread carefully in partisan clashes between chambers. Given that the same political parties fielded candidates at both upper and lower houses during elections, a party contesting a lower house election would not wish to be too closely linked to upper house obstruction to popular measures. There could also be intra-party resistance to the upper house being used to further the goals of a lower house opposition. Some upper houses have their own party caucuses which resent being dictated to by their lower house colleagues, especially when it is upper house members who would be the target of political criticism. And at joint house caucus meetings, upper house members can be more anxious to arrive at a compromise with the government, pointing out political costs that may be less obvious to lower house members. Strong and persistent disagreement between the chambers is something that both major parties view, whatever the short-term partisan gains, as having the potential for serious political costs; constraining the level of conflict is important to both major parties.

This has been reinforced by the disruptive effects of those few occasions when partisan hostility has led to serious governmental crises. The refusal of the Australian Senate to pass a supply bill in 1975 was a precursor for the dismissal of the Whitlam Labor government and a subsequent level of partisan bitterness that all parties regarded as dysfunctional. This traumatic event demonstrated that, when the practice of partisan accommodation fails, constitutional change may be an option in some cases but not in others. In filling casual vacancies for the Australian

[7] The Tasmanian Legislative Council is the only Australia upper house not elected by proportional representation but, with the removal of malapportionment, its idiosyncratic structure produces highly representative results (Sharman 2013).

Senate, state governments had accepted a practice of appointing senators of the same partisan colour. When this practice was ignored after 1973, setting up the preconditions for the blocking of supply bills in the Senate, both major parties agreed to a constitutional amendment in 1977 requiring the maintenance of the partisan balance in the chamber. On the larger question of reducing the Senate's powers, no agreement on constitutional change could be reached, and other attempts after 1975 to reduce the influence of the Senate have failed to gain popular support. Nonetheless, the costs of reckless partisan hostility have been learnt, both by the parties and by the wider public.

But the biggest changes to the operation of the Senate have followed the representation of minor party and independent members in the chamber. These members see legislative politics and not the capture of government as their major concern. With the collusion of senators from the lower house opposition party, the Senate has progressively negotiated with a reluctant executive since the late 1960s to achieve fundamental changes to the role of the Senate in the legislative process and to the Senate's committee system.[8] This is not something any executive government would choose, but it has greatly enhanced the quality of parliamentary democracy in Australia and, as Stone (2008) has shown, provided a model that state upper houses have begun to emulate.

Accommodation between the chambers is not easy to maintain, and there is always a flurry of controversy when a change of government – or a newly elected upper house – has to learn that success will usually follow negotiation rather than confrontation. Even though there is a lack of detailed research on the way disagreements between the chambers play out,[9] the pattern of partisan accommodation is now established with a wealth of agreed procedures, both formal and informal, to keep inter-house conflict within bounds. Both the executive and the upper house can live within the partisan conventions they have established.

Conventions for accommodating conflict: an appointed upper house

The UK House of Lords looks as though it is a model of how an appointed upper house can be reformed by a combination of structural

[8] For reviews of the operation of the Australian Senate and its committee system, see Bach (2003), Odgers (1976) and Reid and Forrest (1989).

[9] An exception is the study by Young (1999) of the negotiations over the passage of the 1993 Budget.

change and the development of conventions to deal with inter-house conflict in a bicameral parliamentary system. It is true that the current House of Lords makes a constructive contribution to legislation and the parliamentary process in general, and that this situation is largely dependent on the agreement of recent governments that there should be some partisan balance in the composition of the Lords (Russell 2010). This has been achieved by supplementing government appointees with members chosen by an independent commission. But however distinguished the nature of its membership and the moral authority of its arguments, the House of Lords is a weak upper chamber both in its constitutional inability to enforce its opposition to the House of Commons, and in its lack of direct electoral representation to provide political legitimacy. The way in which conflict between the houses in the UK Parliament has been managed has been to reduce the power of the upper house by constitutional change, a process that is continuing as successive UK governments grapple with the design of an upper house that has democratic legitimacy without being too strong a rival to the House of Commons or an impediment to executive control of the parliamentary process (note Russell 2012).

By contrast, the Canadian Senate's extensive powers over legislation and the parliamentary process are undiminished since 1867, and its mode of appointment unchanged except for the requirement that senators must retire at the age of seventy-five years. The many attempts at reform of the Senate have foundered on its constitutional entrenchment; the procedure requires a degree of regional unanimity and common purpose among the provinces and both houses of the Canadian Parliament that have always been elusive.[10] This has left the Senate as an appointed chamber with wide powers but little political legitimacy. As with the history of previous appointed houses in British-derived parliamentary systems, patronage and partisanship have dominated to the detriment of the role of the chamber and its public image.

This is not to deny that the Senate has performed some useful functions (see generally Joyal (2003)), particularly in its committee reports and in its treatment of some legislation that has generated wide public interest (note Smith 2003: 131–45). But its performance has been fitful at best (Franks 2003; Heard 2014: 141–53), asserting its ability to embarrass

[10] The entrenchment of any change to the structure and composition of the Senate has recently been confirmed by the Supreme Court of Canada; see *Reference re Senate Reform* (2014 SCC 32).

the government only when emboldened by an opposition majority for its stance on an issue that its partisan masters in the lower house consider popular. But making an accurate assessment of the role of the Canadian Senate and its relations with the Canadian House of Commons has been hampered by a lack of research on the activities of the Senate and the nature of its interactions with the lower house and the executive.

The deadening hand of patronage has limited the Senate's ability to act independently in the parliamentary process since its inception. Recommendations for appointment to the Senate by the governor-general are the personal prerogative of the prime minister; no reference to any other body is required. The choice of speaker of the Senate is made by the prime minister, as is the leader of the governing party in the Senate, and there appears to be little willingness on the part of the great majority of senators – in spite of the absence of any need to be re-elected – to take control of their own chamber. Indeed, Senate party discipline under the direction of the leader of the lower house[11] is a further indication of the absence of any convention of independence. Party provides the conventions for the relationship between the executive and the Canadian Senate, but it is the prime minister's party and the party leadership in the prime minister's office who make the rules.

The Harper Conservative government came to power in 2006 with a strong commitment to Senate reform. Harper's base in Alberta had had a commitment to Senate reform since the 1980s, the goal then being to legitimise the Senate through some electoral process, and to reduce the heavy over-representation of the Eastern provinces. Unwilling to engage in formal constitutional amendment, and facing a hostile Liberal majority in the Senate from 2006 to 2010, Harper proposed a series of changes, the key element of which was a change in the convention governing the process of appointment. The proposal was that Harper, as prime minister, would agree to appoint as senators those who had been elected by special elections held in those provinces that agreed to hold such elections.[12]

[11] In January 2014, Justin Trudeau, the leader of the Liberal party in the Canadian House of Commons, decided that Liberal senators should no longer be members of the Liberal party caucus, and should be regarded as Independents, although it was unclear whether they remained members of the Liberal party. Some Liberal senators promptly formed their own Senate Liberal caucus, but there is little indication of the extent to which they will ignore direction from the Liberals in the lower house. If Justin Trudeau becomes prime minister, it will be interesting to see whom he appoints.

[12] For analysis of this and related proposals made by Prime Minister Harper, see Sharman (2008).

He left vacancies in the Senate unfilled while this proposal was debated – and ultimately rejected – by the Liberal-dominated Senate. It is unclear whether the prime purpose of this original proposal was to achieve some change to the composition of the Senate or to embarrass the Liberal opposition in the lower house whose senators held a majority in the Senate. Once the Conservatives had majority support in the House of Commons and retirements had thinned the ranks of Liberal senators, Harper filled all the Senate vacancies, gaining control of the Senate. Senate reform then lost much of its urgency.

The interest of this episode is that it presented, however briefly, the prospect of changing the role of the Senate by changing the conventions surrounding appointment rather than through constitutional change. Unfortunately, there was no suggestion that Harper was interested in a bipartisan Senate, and no attempt was made to persuade other parties that some move in this direction was desirable. There is considerable irony in the fact that the issue of Senate reform returned in 2013 as a consequence of investigations into political scandals involving misuse of Senate allowances and possible criminal behaviour on the part of a Conservative senator in his dealings with the prime minister's chief of staff. Other than tighter administrative regulation of Senate expenditure, it is unclear what plans any party now has for the role of the Senate in the parliamentary process.

Conventions and upper houses

Bicameralism was a feature of the constitutional settlement of both the Australian and Canadian federations but, as with many aspects of British-derived parliamentary government, its precise role was not formally specified. This silence resulted from an awareness of the range of opinions about the place of upper houses in parliament, and the belief that any attempt to be more specific would make clear the anomalous aspects of the institutions that had been created. As Foley has argued in his brilliant essay (Foley 1989), at the base of constitutionalism is a willingness to defer or obscure consideration of deeply controversial issues and to avoid attempts at resolving constitutional ambiguities likely to generate severe conflict.

It is argued here that bicameralism has been just such an issue in the government of British colonies in Australia and Canada since the coming of self-government after 1840. The stress on the history of responsible government in this chapter has been used to show the origins of the anomalous role of upper houses, and how each system has responded to the potential conflict between parliamentary executives and powerful upper houses. For some, their political and governmental traditions have resulted in the absence of upper houses or their abolition. Others, as the result of constitutional entrenchment or public resistance, have been faced with bicameral systems that have required the cohabitation between governments based on lower house majorities and powerful upper houses with the constitutional potential to use the parliamentary process to embarrass the executive and block its legislative program.

The way in which bicameral systems have coped with this problem reflects the differing constitutional traditions in Australia and Canada (note Sharman 1990), but in both federations, the role of political parties has been critical. In Canada, the belief in the primacy of lower house majorities and the unwillingness to grant legitimacy to upper house opposition beyond minor amendment and delay (Smith 2003) has led to the Senate, as the sole surviving Canadian upper house, being dominated by the partisan preferences of the governing party. By comparison Australia, whose politics superficially appear more majoritarian, now views bicameralism as an important component of parliamentary government. The partisan battle continues, but the public acceptance of parliamentary bicameralism is secure.

For Australia, coping with bicameralism has generated a settled repertoire of rules and conventions that permit some parliamentary autonomy for upper houses within a system that is otherwise dominated by powerful executives, both state and federal. For Canada, partisanship and patronage have almost completely undermined the legitimacy of the Senate and made it a perennial issue for reform. Only a change in the conventions of partisanship has any prospect of giving the Canadian Senate the public acceptance that its constitutional entrenchment implies.

References

Ajzenstat, Janet 2007. *The Canadian Founding: John Locke and Parliament*. Montreal: McGill Queen's University Press.

Ajzenstat, Janet, Romney, Paul, Gentles, Ian and Gairdner, William D. (eds.) 2003. *Canada's Founding Debates*. University of Toronto Press.

Aroney, Nicholas, Prasser, Scott and Nethercote, J. R. (eds.) 2008. *Restraining Elective Dictatorship: The Upper House Solution?* Perth: University of Western Australia Press.

Bach, Stanley 2003. *Platypus and Parliament: The Australian Senate in Theory and Practice*. Canberra: Department of the Senate.

Beck, J. Murray 1957. *The Government of Nova Scotia*. University of Toronto Press.

Carney, Gerard 2008. 'Abolition and Restoration of a Legislative Council: Queensland and Other States', in Aroney, Nicholas, Prasser, Scott and Nethercote, J. R. (eds.), *Restraining Elective Dictatorship: The Upper House Solution?* Perth: University of Western Australia Press.

Clune, David and Griffith, Gareth 2006. *Decision and Deliberation: The Parliament of New South Wales 1856–2006*. Sydney: Federation Press.

Dawson, R. MacGregor 1970. *The Government of Canada*, 5th edn., revised by Norman Ward. University of Toronto Press.

Docherty, David C. 2008. 'Upper Houses in the Canadian Provinces', in Aroney, Nicholas, Prasser, Scott and Nethercote, J. R. (eds.), *Restraining Elective Dictatorship: The Upper House Solution?* Perth: University of Western Australia Press.

Foley, Michael 1989. *The Silence of Constitutions: Gaps, 'Abeyances' and Political Temperament in the Maintenance of Government*. London: Routledge.

Franks, C. E. S. 2003. 'The Canadian Senate in Modern Times', in Joyal, Serge (ed.), *Protecting Canadian Democracy: The Senate You Never Knew*. Montreal: McGill-Queen's University Press.

Fukuda, Arihiro 1997. *Sovereignty and the Sword: Harrington, Hobbes and Mixed Government in the English Civil Wars*. Oxford University Press.

Garon, André 1970. 'La fonction politique et sociale des chambres haute canadiennes, 1791–1841', *Histoire Sociale (Social History)*, 5 (April): 66–87.

Grebstad, David 2014. 'A Tale of Two Houses: The Rise and Demise of the Legislative Council of Manitoba, 1871–1876', *Manitoba History*, 75: 2–12.

Harding, Justin 2000. 'Ideology or Expediency? The Abolition of the Queensland Legislative Council 1915–22', *Labor History*, 79: 162–78.

Heard, Andrew 2014. *Canadian Constitutional Conventions: The Marriage of Law and Politics*. Ontario: Oxford University Press.

Jackson, W. K. 1972. *The New Zealand Legislative Council: A Study of the Establishment, Failure and Abolition of an Upper House*. University of Toronto Press.

Joyal, Serge (ed.) 2003. *Protecting Canadian Democracy: The Senate You Never Knew*. Montreal: McGill-Queen's University Press.

Lijphart, Arend 1999. *Patterns of Democracy: Government Forms and Performance in Thirty-Six Countries*. New Haven: Yale University Press.

MacKinnon, Frank 1951. *The Government of Prince Edward Island*. University of Toronto Press.

Moore, Christopher 1998. *1867 How the Fathers Made a Deal*. McClelland & Stewart.

Mulgan, Richard 1996. 'The Australian Senate as a "House of Review"', *Australian Journal of Political Science*, 31 (2): 191–204.

Odgers, J. R. 1976. *Australian Senate Practice*, 5th edn. Canberra: Australian Government Printer.

Orban, Edmund 1969. 'La fin du bicaméralisme au Québec', *Canadian Journal of Political Science*, 2 (3): 312–26.

Reid, G.S. and Forrest, Martyn 1989. *Australia's Commonwealth Parliament 1901–1988: Ten Perspectives*. Melbourne University Press.

Russell, Meg 2010. 'A Stronger Second Chamber? Assessing the Impact of House of Lords Reform in 1999 and the Lessons for Bicameralism', *Political Studies*, 58 (5): 866–85.

Russell, Meg 2012. 'Elected Second Chambers and Their Powers: An International Survey', *Political Quarterly*, 83 (1): 117–29.

Sharman, Campbell 1990. 'Parliamentary Federations and Limited Government: Constitutional Design and Redesign in Australia and Canada', *Journal of Theoretical Politics*, 2 (2): 205–30.

Sharman, Campbell 1999. 'The Representation of Small Parties and Independents in the Senate', *Australian Journal of Political Science*, 34 (3): 353–61.

Sharman, Campbell 2008. 'Political Legitimacy for an Appointed Senate', *Choices*, 14 (11): 1–27 (Montreal: Institute for Research on Public Policy). Available at: www.irpp.org/assets/research/strengthening-canadian-democracy/political-legitimacy-for-an-appointed-senate/vol14no11.pdf.

Sharman, Campbell 2013. 'Limiting Party Representation: Evidence from a Small Parliamentary Chamber', *Legislative Studies Quarterly*, 38 (3): 327–48.

Smith, David E. 2003. *The Canadian Senate in Bicameral Perspective*. University of Toronto Press.

Stone, Bruce 2002. 'Bicameralism and Democracy: The Transformation of Australian State Upper Houses', *Australian Journal of Political Science*, 37 (2): 267–81.

Stone, Bruce 2008. 'State Legislative Councils – Designing for Accountability', in Aroney, Nicholas, Prasser, Scott and Nethercote, J. R. (eds.), *Restraining Elective Dictatorship: The Upper House Solution?* Perth: University of Western Australia Press.

Turner, Ken 1969. *House of Review? The New South Wales Legislative Council, 1934–68*. Sydney University Press.

Ward, John Manning 1976. *Colonial Self-Government: The British Experience 1759–1856*. University of Toronto Press.

Wright, Raymond 1992. *A People's Counsel: A History of the Parliament of Victoria, 1856–1990*. Melbourne: Oxford University Press.

Young, Liz 1999. 'Minor Parties and the Legislative Process in the Australian Senate: A Study of the 1993 Budget', *Australian Journal of Political Science*, 34 (1): 7–27.

9

The United Kingdom

ROBERT HAZELL

Britain's twenty-year constitutional revolution

Other chapters in this book record the common principles underlying the Westminster system of government, and the conventions which other countries have inherited or adapted from Westminster since the nineteenth century. This chapter has no such grand historical sweep, but focuses just on the last twenty years. Since the advent of the first Blair government in 1997 the United Kingdom has gone through an unprecedented period of constitutional change, which has seen the creation of important new conventions; modification of old conventions; codification of many conventions; and the demise of conventions rendered obsolete. So the United Kingdom's recent history is a test bed for the birth, death, evolution and codification of constitutional conventions. There have been so many changes to our conventions that coverage of each must necessarily be brief.

The constitutional reforms can be divided into four successive waves, linked to the different prime ministers in charge. Blair's first government (1997–2001) introduced the first big tidal wave of reforms, with the creation in 1998 of devolved governments and legislatures in Scotland, Wales and Northern Ireland; a directly enforceable bill of rights in the Human Rights Act 1998; and removal of the hereditary peers in 1999, leaving the House of Lords an almost entirely appointed House. His second government (2001–2005) introduced a second wave of judicial reforms in the Constitutional Reform Act 2005, with the Lord Chief Justice replacing the Lord Chancellor as head of the judiciary, introduction of a Judicial Appointments Commission, and creation of the new Supreme Court, separate from the House of Lords. Then under Gordon Brown (2007–2010) a third wave focused mainly on codifying the prerogative powers, but with only modest results in the Constitutional Reform and Governance Act 2010. It was not until the fourth wave under David Cameron (2010) that the most important prerogative powers (appointing and dismissing a prime minister, summoning and dissolving parliament) were codified in the new Cabinet Manual; dissolution of parliament was brought under statutory regulation by the Fixed Term Parliaments Act 2011; and old conventions were tested in the new context of coalition government.

These big constitutional reforms have led to changes in the main conventions governing the Monarch, executive, legislature and judiciary. The sweep of this chapter is deliberately wide, to remind readers that conventions operate in all branches of government. In all cases conventions are a code of self-restraint: about not exercising powers to the full, not abusing power and respecting the constitutional role and functions of the other branches of government. So to take just four examples covered in this chapter, there are conventions limiting the Monarch's choice of prime minister, conventions restraining the prime minister's power to make war, conventions constraining the Westminster parliament's exercise of its legislative power, and conventions regulating the conduct of the judiciary. In most cases conventions have been developed as a self-denying ordinance by one branch of government to restrain its own behaviour but occasionally in consultation with, or at the instigation of, others. At the end of the chapter we consider who the guardians of each different convention are. Conventions may not be legally enforceable, but that does not mean they do not have enforcers.

New conventions resulting from United Kingdom's constitutional reform programme

These big constitutional changes have given rise to some important new conventions to guide the behaviour of government and parliament in the new reformed world. The first two conventions discussed below arise from new processes required by devolution; the third from managing the composition of the new House of Lords; and the fourth from the operation of the Human Rights Act. They illustrate how conventions are created, some instantly but others more gradually. They also illustrate the fluidity of conventions; not everyone would agree that the second, third or fourth items yet count as conventions.

Devolution conventions: the Sewel convention

This convention was created instantly, on the floor of the House of Lords, during the passage of the Scotland Act 1998. Unlike in federal systems, the UK Parliament may still legislate on matters which are within the competence of the Scottish Parliament: Section 28(7) of the Scotland Act makes that clear. However, during the passage of the Scotland Act, Lord Sewel (a government minister) announced that the UK government 'would expect a convention to be established that Westminster would not normally legislate with regard to devolved matters in Scotland without the consent of the Scottish Parliament.' This became known as the Sewel Convention, and was subsequently given more formal expression in the Memorandum of Understanding (MoU) between the UK government and Scottish government, first issued in 2001 (UK Government 2013: para 14). Under the convention, legislative consent motions are tabled before the Scottish Parliament for any UK legislation that trespasses on devolved matters, and it has become a convenient device for Westminster to legislate for Scotland, saving the Scottish Parliament the time and trouble of doing so.

Devolution conventions: the need for referendums

The requirement for referendums is less clear cut, and a convention which has grown more by usage than by declaration. Referendums were held in Scotland, Wales and Northern Ireland in 1997 and 1998 before legislating to establish the devolved institutions, and in 1998 before the creation of the Greater London Authority with a directly elected mayor (the first in the United Kingdom). A referendum was also held (and defeated) on the proposal for an elected Regional Assembly in the north-east of England in 2004. Have these precedents created a convention that devolution will not be introduced into any part of the United Kingdom without a referendum? And if established by referendum, is there an implied convention that devolved institutions will not be abolished or significantly altered without a further referendum? A referendum was subsequently held in Wales in 2011 before the Welsh Assembly was given primary legislative powers, but there was no referendum before the fiscal powers of the Scottish Parliament were extended in the Scotland Act 2012. (But, under the Sewel convention, the Scottish Parliament had given its consent to Westminster legislating to amend its powers).

In 2010 the House of Lords Constitution Committee held an inquiry into the use of referendums in the United Kingdom. Their report opened with a list of all the referendums held so far, and asked to what extent these created precedents for the future. In evidence, Professor

Bogdanor suggested that 'conventions have grown up', that a referendum is required before any 'significant devolution of powers away from Westminster', or 'when a wholly novel constitutional arrangement is proposed'. But although eight out of the nine referendums held in the United Kingdom since 1973 had related to devolution, the committee did not include devolution in its list of 'fundamental constitutional issues' which would require a referendum (2010 HL 99: Box 1, paras 89, 94).

Proportionality convention for appointments to the House of Lords

With the departure of almost all the hereditary peers in 1999, the House of Lords has become an all-appointed chamber, save for the ninety-two remaining hereditary peers and the twenty-six bishops. Appointments to the Lords are made on the advice of the prime minister. There is no limit to the size of the House, so it is open to the prime minister to pack the Lords with as many of his own party supporters as he likes. Aware of this danger, the Labour party declared in its 1997 election manifesto that 'No one political party should seek a majority in the House of Lords... Our objective will be to ensure that over time party appointees as life peers more accurately reflect the proportion of votes cast at the previous general election' (Labour Party Manifesto 1997). In office Blair remained true to this principle, and despite accusations of the appointment of Tony's cronies, it was not until 2006 that the Labour group for the first time outnumbered the Conservative group in the Lords. Brown was similarly restrained, and under his premiership the net increase in the Labour group was five members (Hazell 2010: ch 4.4 and fig 4.1; Russell 2011). The coalition government in 2010 repeated the proportionality principle that 'Lords appointments will be made with the objective of creating a second chamber reflective of the share of the vote secured by the political parties in the last general election' (Conservative/Liberal Democrat Coalition Agreement, 2010).

This is another example of a convention emerging through usage and the declaration of a principle which is then followed in practice. It has been followed by three prime ministers. So long as the House of Lords remains (almost) all appointed, it is hard to see any future prime minister departing from the proportionality principle. How many more instances do we need before it is considered to be a convention? (For a contrary view, see Russell 2011: 10–11).

Human Rights Act convention: responding to declarations of incompatibility by the courts

Under s. 4 of the Human Rights Act 1998, courts may make a declaration of incompatibility, which is a finding that a law does not comply with the European Convention on Human Rights (ECHR). This ruling does not invalidate the law, but constitutes formal notification to government and parliament that the law is incompatible with the Convention rights. It is an invitation to the political branches of government to legislate to remedy the breach. There is no legal obligation on them to do so, but a convention has developed that government and parliament will respond to declarations of incompatibility. Compliance is monitored by the parliamentary Joint Committee on Human Rights, to which the government submits an annual report. The 2013 annual report records that of twenty-eight declarations of incompatibility made by the courts since 2000, nineteen had become final, that is had not been overturned on appeal or subject to appeal. Of those nineteen final declarations of incompatibility, eighteen had been remedied by primary or secondary legislation, with just one outstanding (Ministry of Justice 2013).

Again, this is an example of a convention developing through emerging practice. The one exception is an important one, on prisoner voting rights, where the government has been very slow to respond to a series of judgements by the European Court of Human Rights and the UK Supreme Court that the blanket ban on prisoner voting is incompatible with the ECHR. The eventual outcome of that issue is still unknown. Amongst academic commentators, Jeff King believes that there is a convention of compliance with declarations of incompatibility (King 2015); Francesca Klug is not so sure (Klug 2015).

Convention requiring parliamentary vote before going to war

One other new convention deserves mention, which does not originate from recent constitutional reform, but from changes in parliamentary practice. Following the parliamentary debate and substantive motion approving the invasion of Iraq in 2003, the bombing of Libya in 2011, and the disapproval by the House of Commons of the government's proposed bombing of Syria in 2013, it has been argued that there is now a convention requiring prior parliamentary approval before military action overseas, save in cases of urgent necessity (Phillipson 2013).

Old conventions that have been modified

As other chapters have said, conventions are flexible and may need to be modified to adapt to changed circumstances. The United Kingdom provides two recent examples of changing conventions under the coalition government of 2010–15. The first is the relaxation of collective responsibility under the coalition. The coalition's procedural agreement provided that 'The principle of collective responsibility, save where it is explicitly set aside, continues to apply to all Government Ministers' (Prime Minister's Office et al. 2010). The coalition's programme for government mentioned five issues on which the coalition partners and their ministers would be able to vote on opposite sides: the referendum to change the voting system for the House of Commons to Alternative Vote (AV), raising student tuition fees, introducing a married couple's tax allowance, renewing civil nuclear power and replacement of Trident nuclear missiles. There have also been two occasions when the coalition parties have formally voted on opposite sides. The first was in 2013, when Liberal Democrats voted to delay the boundary review reducing the House of Commons from 650 to 600 members of parliament (a Conservative policy) after Liberal Democrat proposals for an elected House of Lords had to be withdrawn following a rebellion by Conservative backbenchers. The second was in 2014, when the Liberal Democrats voted with Labour to support modification of the 'bedroom tax'.

A second convention which has been modified to reflect changed circumstances is the Salisbury convention. This is a self-denying ordinance of the House of Lords that the Lords will not block or wreck a bill in the governing party's manifesto. It originates from 1945, when the Labour government had just 15 Labour peers facing hundreds of Conservative peers, and the opposition leader in the Lords, Lord Salisbury, gave an assurance that the Conservatives would not wreck the Labour government's post-war legislative programme. But with the removal of the hereditary peers in 1999 the Lords no longer has a built-in Conservative majority. This has led the Liberal Democrats to suggest that the convention no longer applies, and the Lords could be more assertive. But when the convention was reviewed by a joint parliamentary committee (see below), the opposite occurred: the committee restated the convention, with modifications, and added that in recent years the practice had emerged that the House of Lords would usually give a second reading to any government bill, whether or not it was in the governing party's manifesto (Joint Parliamentary Committee on Conventions 2006: paras 98, 102).

Codification of conventions

Recent years have seen the codification of many conventions, in different ways. This has not always been in the form of executive guidance, or 'soft law'. Conventions in the United Kingdom have been codified in statute; in intergovernmental agreements; in the reports of parliamentary committees; and in guidance issued by other branches of government, such as the judiciary. Examples of each are given below.

Codification in statute

After an initial fanfare (Ministry of Justice 2007) and comprehensive review of the prerogative powers (Ministry of Justice 2009) the Brown government's ambitious plans for constitutional reform ended with a whimper in the Constitutional Reform and Governance Act 2010. But the Act codified two of the prerogative powers, and thereby codified two conventions: on the neutrality of the civil service, and the 'Ponsonby rule' on the ratification of international treaties. Part 1 of the Act put management of the civil service on a statutory footing, and enshrined in statute the civil service values of integrity and honesty, objectivity and impartiality. Part 2 codified the Ponsonby rule (first stated by Arthur Ponsonby MP, Under Secretary for Foreign Affairs in 1924) that treaties should not be ratified by the government unless they have first been laid before parliament, and twenty-one sitting days have been allowed for either House to object.

Two broader conventions have been codified in statute, about upholding the rule of law and the independence of the judiciary. Section 3 of the Constitutional Reform Act 2005 requires that 'The Lord Chancellor, [and] other Ministers of the Crown ... must uphold the continued independence of the judiciary'. It goes on to specify that 'The Lord Chancellor and other Ministers of the Crown must not seek to influence particular judicial decisions through any special access to the judiciary' (s. 3(5)), and lays on the Lord Chancellor a particular duty to defend judicial independence (s. 3(6)).

Codification in intergovernmental agreements

We have already noted how the Sewel convention, now known as the Legislative Consent convention, has been codified in the MoU between the UK and the Scottish governments. The MoU provides that 'The UK

Parliament retains authority to legislate on any issue, whether devolved or not. . . However, the UK government will proceed in accordance with the convention that the UK Parliament would not normally legislate with regard to devolved matters except with the consent of the devolved legislature' (Cm 7864 2013: para 14). The MoU is supported by Concordats and other procedural agreements to underpin the devolution settlement. Recognising that these procedural agreements are like conventions, the MoU explains that it is not intended that the agreements should be legally binding.

Codification by parliamentary committees

The most notable example of codification by a parliamentary committee is the Joint Committee on Conventions in 2006. The committee was expressly established 'to consider the practicality of codifying the key conventions on the relationship between the two Houses of Parliament which affect the consideration of legislation'. It was asked to look in particular at the Salisbury convention, conventions on secondary legislation, the convention that the Lords dispatch government business in reasonable time and conventions on the exchange of amendments between the Houses. While emphasising throughout that conventions are flexible and unenforceable, the committee did clarify and sharpen three of the conventions under examination. They offered a definition of the Salisbury convention, and suggested that it be renamed the Government Bill convention, to reflect their view that it had been extended to all government bills, not just manifesto bills. They also suggested six exceptional circumstances in which the Lords might be justified in defeating secondary legislation; and while protesting that it was impossible to define 'reasonable time', they suggested that 80 sitting days might be long enough for government bills to spend in the Lords (2006 HL 265; HC 212: paras 97–115, paras 229 and 283, paras 153–7).

The Lords Constitution Committee's inquiry into referendums in the United Kingdom was less successful in trying to identify the circumstances in which a referendum might be required. They concluded that referendums should be required for 'fundamental constitutional issues', and as examples listed proposals to abolish the Monarchy, leave the European Union, for any of the nations of the United Kingdom to secede from the Union, to abolish either House of Parliament, change the electoral system for the House of Commons, adopt a written constitution or change the United Kingdom's currency (2010 HL 99: para 94).

Codification by executive guidance

This is the most common way in which conventions are codified, in codes of conduct or other forms of 'soft law'. Such codes are not just issued by the executive. The judiciary have produced codes to regulate judges' behaviour, and these codes incorporate conventions. The Guide to Judicial Conduct, first issued in 2004 and revised in 2013, contains a detailed codification of all the conventions, great and small, which help to ensure the integrity and impartiality of the judiciary. The 2012 Guidance to Judges on Appearances before Select Committees sets out the 'long-standing constitutional conventions' which prevent judges from commenting on individual cases, the merits of other judges or politicians, the meaning of provisions in bills or pending legislation, or the merits of government policy (Judicial Executive Board 2012: 2, para 3). The counterpart convention, that ministers do not criticise individual judges for their decisions, is harder to find in any executive guidance.

The most frequent form of codification of conventions is in guidance issued by the executive. The more important codes include the Ministerial Code of Conduct, the Civil Service Code of Conduct and most recently the Cabinet Manual. There is not enough space to discuss the conventions codified in the Ministerial and Civil Service Codes. Because of the interest generated in other countries (see, for example, Peter Russell's Chapter 13), discussion here focuses on the Cabinet Manual.

The Cabinet Manual

The Cabinet Manual owes its origin to widespread fears before the United Kingdom's 2010 election about the uncertainty that might follow a 'hung parliament' in which no party commanded an overall majority. The process of appointing a new prime minister seemed shrouded in mystery, leading to speculation that an uncertain result would lead to political and economic chaos, or that the Queen herself might be forced to choose. In December 2009 the Constitution Unit published a report explaining the conventions about the appointment of a new prime minister, and urged the government to publish clear guidance about the process to be followed in a hung parliament, pointing to the New Zealand *Cabinet Manual* as an excellent model (Hazell et al. 2009). In February 2010 the Cabinet Secretary Sir Gus O'Donnell, with the consent of Prime Minister Gordon Brown, published *Elections and Government Formation* as an advance chapter of a new cabinet manual, just in time for the election. The guidance proved invaluable when there was a hung parliament two months later, leading to negotiations between the three main political parties over five days before the new government was formed. The beneficiary of those negotiations, the new Prime Minister David Cameron, endorsed the cabinet manual project. A consultation draft was issued in late 2010, which was scrutinised by three parliamentary committees, and the first edition of the *Cabinet Manual* was published in October 2011 (Cabinet Office 2010, 2011).

Many of the chapters in the Cabinet Manual contain relatively little that is new. The chapters on the executive and ministers, cabinet decision making, parliament, the law, the civil service, relations with the devolved administrations and the EU, government finance and official information draw heavily upon guidance already published elsewhere; what is valuable is drawing all the guidance together in one place. The new material is to be found in Chapter 1 on the Sovereign and Chapter 2 on elections and government formation. For our purposes, Chapter 2 is the most important, because it codifies for the first time the key conventions about the formation, resignation and dismissal of governments, and the summoning and dissolution of parliaments.

Parliamentary scrutiny of the Cabinet Manual focused mainly on Chapter 2. Three committees conducted separate inquiries, but came to similar conclusions (2011 HL 107; 2011 HC 734; 2011 HC 900). They were concerned that the Cabinet Manual should record rules and precedents, but not itself be the source of any rule: it should be descriptive, not prescriptive. Where there was uncertainty about a convention, the manual should be open about the areas of doubt or disagreement. As one example of that, the committees focused on the question of whether, in the event of a hung parliament, there was a duty on the incumbent prime minister to remain in office until it was clear who could command confidence in the new parliament. In response, the government softened the drafting so that it now reads:

> It remains a matter for the Prime Minister, as the Sovereign's principal adviser, to judge the appropriate time at which to resign ... Recent examples suggest that previous Prime Ministers have not offered their resignations until there was a situation in which clear advice could be given to the Sovereign on who should be asked to form a government. It remains to be seen whether or not these examples will be regarded in future as having established a constitutional convention.
>
> (*Cabinet Manual* 2011: para 2.10)

The Political and Constitutional Reform Committee criticised the government for omitting any mention of the new convention that there should be a parliamentary debate before going to war. In response the government inserted a new section recording previous precedents, and concluding:

> In 2011, the Government acknowledged that a convention had developed in Parliament that before troops were committed the House of Commons should have an opportunity to debate the matter and said that it proposed to observe that convention except when there was an emergency and such action would not be appropriate.
>
> (Cabinet Office 2011: para 5.38)

The two Commons committees disagreed about the constitutional status of the Cabinet Manual. The Political and Constitutional Reform Committee toyed with the notion that the manual should be subject to parliamentary approval, or at least regular parliamentary debate, but the Public Administration Committee was clear that it was not appropriate for parliament to endorse the Cabinet Manual. The government agreed, and in its response to all three committees stated firmly:

- The Cabinet Manual is a document written by the Executive, for the Executive. It represents the Executive's best understanding of the laws, conventions and rules which govern the conduct of the Executive's business.
- The Cabinet Manual is primarily for Ministers and the Civil Servants that advise them. However, publishing the document will help aid good government and increase transparency.
- Cabinet should own and endorse the text. It would not be appropriate for the Civil Service to own the Cabinet Manual . . .
- Parliament should not endorse the Cabinet Manual.

Although the government accepted that the Cabinet Manual should be purely descriptive, and not break any new ground, Chapter 2 did sneak in three innovations. The first was an extension of the caretaker convention, so that it applies in three circumstances: once an election has been called; after an election, until it is clear who can command confidence in the new parliament; and following a mid-term loss of confidence (Cabinet Office 2011: paras 2.27–2.31). Second was enforcement of the caretaker convention by the permanent secretary as accounting officer requesting a formal direction for any ministerial instruction deemed improper, with immediate publication of the direction, and notification to the auditor general and both houses of parliament (paras 2.32–2.33). The third innovation was to mention the role of the civil service in supporting negotiations between the parties as part of the process of government formation (paras 2.13–2.14).

Coalition government and its effect on conventions

The coalition government of 2010–15 has had surprisingly little effect on constitutional conventions in the United Kingdom. It is a majority government, with a comfortable majority of seventy-six seats in the House of Commons, and it has governed in a majoritarian way. There have been plenty of rebellions by both Conservative and Liberal Democrat backbenchers, in both houses, but the conventions of Westminster parliamentary government have been maintained. When the House of Lords Constitution Committee conducted an inquiry in 2014 into the constitutional implications of coalition government, they found relatively little to say. They rejected calls for an investiture vote to decide who could command confidence in a hung parliament, or for the opening debate on the Queen's Speech to become a debate on the coalition agreement when a coalition government had been formed (2014 HL 130: paras 52 and 60). They reserved their main strictures for the coalition's departures from collective responsibility, and suggested that the cabinet as a whole should agree on any future departures (paras 77–9); but that was already provided for in the coalition government's procedural agreement (Prime Minister's Office et al. 2010: para 5.1). That procedural agreement remains a good starting point for any future coalitions: it covers all the main points, and has a clear exposition of the need for collective cabinet responsibility and party discipline (paras 2.1 and 5.1–5.5).

The one big change to conventions under the coalition was the introduction of fixed-term parliaments in the Fixed Term Parliaments Act 2011. This Act removes the power of the prime minister to call an early election and transfers the power to dissolve parliament from the prime minister to the House of Commons. In future, parliament can be dissolved for early elections in only one of two circumstances: following a successful no-confidence motion, if no alternative administration is formed within fourteen days; or if the House of Commons votes by a two-thirds majority for its own dissolution. The prerogative power of dissolution is abolished: not expressly, but by implication in s. 3(2), which provides that 'Parliament cannot otherwise be dissolved'. So long as the Fixed Term Parliaments Act remains part of the United Kingdom's constitutional arrangements, all the academic writing about the circumstances in which the Monarch might properly accept or reject a request for dissolution is now obsolete.

Conclusions

This chapter has given an overview of the many changes to constitutional conventions in the United Kingdom in the last twenty years, which have happened as a result of the major constitutional reforms under the Blair, Brown and Cameron governments. This has led to the creation of important new conventions; modification of old conventions; the codification of many conventions; and the demise of conventions rendered obsolete.

The most important development has been the codification of conventions. This has been undertaken by all three branches of government: the executive, parliament and the judiciary. It is helpful if conventions can be codified, in terms of public understanding, transparency and accountability. The strongest example of that was the codification in the Cabinet Manual of the conventions governing the appointment of the prime minister, which proved of real value when the 2010 election resulted in a hung parliament with no clear winner. Conventions which had been shrouded in mystery, understood only by a few constitutional experts, became public property when put into the public domain in the Cabinet Manual. The work of codification also generated political and public debate about the scope and meaning of the conventions. The Cabinet Manual was scrutinised and commented on by three parliamentary committees. Amongst the judges, the Guide to Judicial Conduct was the product of a working group which consulted with all levels of the judiciary, leading to lively professional debate about the conventions which underpin judicial independence (Judges' Council 2013: 3–5).

One argument against codification is that conventions become set in stone, and lose their flexibility. The British experience shows that fear to be groundless. Codified conventions do not become set in stone, as can be demonstrated by the two examples given above. The Judges' Council set up a standing committee of nine judges to keep the Guide to Judicial Conduct under review, and in 2013 they produced a revised and updated version of the Guide, first published in 2004. It is the same with the Cabinet Manual, which was revised following comments on the consultation draft, and will periodically be revised in future.

The New Zealand *Cabinet Manual* is now in its fifth edition, with significant changes made with each version.

Another criticism levelled at the Cabinet Manual was that it was wrong for the executive unilaterally to determine the scope and meaning of conventions governing executive behaviour (Blick 2014). Constitutional conventions, it is said, are indeterminate and difficult to codify, and shaped by the wider political environment: they cannot be monopolised by the executive. This kind of argument often comes from constitutional lawyers, who have a particular suspicion of the executive. They would not criticise the judiciary for producing the Guide to Judicial Conduct; nor would they criticise parliament for trying to codify the Salisbury convention which governs the relationship between the two houses. But each branch of government must take responsibility for its own behaviour, and for explaining the conventions which it will observe as restraints on that behaviour. The government was right to say, in response to suggestions that parliament should share ownership of the Cabinet Manual, that the Manual is a document written by the executive, for the executive. It represents the executive's best understanding of the laws, conventions and rules which govern the conduct of the executive's business.

This is not to say that other branches of government do not have an interest in the drafting and codifying of conventions, and in their observance. This is the final point to be made in these conclusions: that conventions have multiple guardians. We have seen examples of that throughout the chapter. Some conventions have very specific guardians: the main guardians of the caretaker convention in the United Kingdom are permanent secretaries blowing the whistle as accounting officers (and exemplifying the argument made in Chapter 6 that public officials have become the interpreters and enforcers of the caretaker convention). But most conventions have multiple guardians, in other branches of government, amongst other political actors (such as opposition parties), the media and the wider public. There is no shortage of critical commentators to cry foul when conventions are flouted. The fact that conventions are not legally enforceable does not mean that they lack enforcers. Prominent amongst the guardians of conventions in the United Kingdom are now a series of specialist parliamentary committees, in particular the Lords Constitution Committee, the Joint Committee on Human Rights, the Commons Public Accounts Committee and the Commons Political and Constitutional Reform Committee. It is no coincidence that their reports are also prominent in the References which follow.

References

Blick, Andrew 2014. 'The Cabinet Manual and the Codification of Conventions', *Parliamentary Affairs* 67: 1.

Cabinet Office 2010. *Draft Cabinet Manual*, December 2010.

Cabinet Office 2011. *Cabinet Manual*, 1st edition, October 2011.

Hazell, Robert et al. 2009. *Making Minority Government Work: Hung Parliaments and the Challenges for Westminster and Whitehall*. London: The Constitution Unit and Institute for Government.

Hazell, Robert 2010. *The Conservative - Liberal Democrat Agenda for Constitutional and Political Reform*. London: The Constitution Unit.

House of Commons Political and Constitutional Reform Committee 2011. *Constitutional Implications of the Cabinet Manual: Sixth Report of Session 2010–11*. London: House of Commons. HC 734.

House of Commons Public Administration Committee 2011. *The Cabinet Manual*. HC 900.

House of Lords Constitution Committee 2010. *Referendums in the UK*. HL 99.

House of Lords Constitution Committee 2011. *The Cabinet Manual*. HL107.

House of Lords Constitution Committee 2014. *The Constitutional Implications of Coalition Government*. HL 130.

Joint Parliamentary Committee on Conventions 2006. *Conventions of the UK Parliament*. HL 265; HC 212.

Judges' Council 2013. *Guide to Judicial Conduct*, 2nd edition. Judiciary of England and Wales.

Judicial Executive Board 2012. *Guidance to Judges on Appearances before Select Committees*.

King, Jeff 2015. 'Parliament's Role Following Declarations of Incompatibility under the Human Rights Act', in Hunt, M., Hooper, H. and Yowell, P. (eds.), *Parliaments and Human Rights: Redressing the Democratic Deficit*. Oxford: Hart Publishing.

Klug, Francesca 2015. *A Magna Carta for Humanity, Homing in on Human Rights*. London: Routledge.

Labour Party Manifesto 1997. *New Labour because Britain Deserves Better*.

Ministry of Justice 2007. *The Governance of Britain*. Cm 7170.

Ministry of Justice 2009. *Review of Executive Royal Prerogative Powers*.

Ministry of Justice 2013. *Report to the Joint Committee on Human Rights on the Government's Response to Human Rights Judgements 2012–13*.

Phillipson, Gavin 2013. '"Historic" Commons' Syria vote: the constitutional significance (Part I)' 'Part II: the Way Forward', UK Const. L. Blog (19 September 2013; 29 November 2013).

Prime Minister's Office, Deputy Prime Minister's Office, Cabinet Office 2010. *Coalition Agreement for Stability and Reform*. London: Cabinet Office.

Russell, Meg 2011. *House Full: Time to Get a Grip on Lords Appointments.* London: The Constitution Unit.

UK Government 2013. *Memorandum of Understanding and Supplementary Agreements between the UK Government, Scottish Ministers, Welsh Ministers and Northern Ireland Executive.* Cm 7864.

10

Canada

ANDREW C. BANFIELD

Canada is a Westminster-derived parliamentary democracy with a constitutional monarchy. At its founding in 1867, three British colonies were united: the Province of Canada, New Brunswick and Nova Scotia (Ajzenstat et al. 1999). Canada's constitutional structure is a combination of British and American elements. Like the United States, for example, Canada is a federation. Over time, Canada's political ties to Westminster have diminished, despite having the preamble of the British North America Act saying Canada has a 'Constitution similar in Principle to that of the United Kingdom'.

Canada and the United Kingdom share a head of state, the British monarch, who is represented by the governor-general, and at the provincial level by lieutenant governors. Canada's bicameral legislative structure is overtly British: the lower house, the House of Commons, contains 338 seats, filled by members of parliament (MPs) who are elected by a single-member plurality electoral system. The upper house, the Senate, contains 105 appointed members who represent the four original regions of Canada: Ontario, Quebec, the maritime provinces and the western provinces. Six additional seats were granted to Newfoundland and Labrador in 1949 when they joined confederation and one seat each for the three territories: Yukon, North West Territories and Nunavut. The governor-general, on the advice and consent of the prime minister, appoints senators, who may serve until the age of seventy-five.

This chapter unfolds in two parts. First, I outline some of the constitutional conventions that operate in Canada with regard to formation of parliament and executive function, and I examine the role that the Supreme Court of Canada has played in codifying and/or clarifying these conventions. In the second part, I examine the role of constitutional conventions during a minority parliament, paying special attention to the prorogation crisis of 2008. I then draw some broad conclusions about constitutional conventions in Canada.

Convention versus custom

Like other Westminster-derived systems, constitutional conventions play a critical role in the day-to-day operation of the Canadian constitution. Conventions are distinguishable in Canada from other codified sets of rules, like common law, as they are enforceable neither by the courts nor by the speaker of the House of Commons. If there is a conflict between a formal rule and a convention, both the speaker and courts will tend to enforce the formal rule over the convention. Thus conventions exist, change and are modified by political actors. For our purposes, an easy way to distinguish between a convention and a formal rule is that formal rules are enforced by the officers of parliament and the courts, whereas conventions are accepted and enforced by the political actors in the system.

Importantly, conventions are seen as both 'morally and politically binding' (Wheare 1964: 122). One cannot understand the form and function of the Canadian political system without understanding the roles that constitutional conventions play. Sir Ivor Jennings (1959: 81) once observed that conventions 'provide the flesh which clothes the dry bones of the law [keeping] it in touch with the growth of ideas'. Put another way, constitutional conventions make the 'formal rules' of the *Constitution Act, 1867*[1] 'tolerable' (Heard 2005: 19).

Before outlining the various conventions that operate in various ways in Canada, it is worth drawing a distinction between custom and convention. There is a common misconception that all customs are conventions. While it is true that conventions can morph into customs, the converse is not always the case. Take, for example, the custom of the speaker being dragged to the chair at the start of a parliamentary session. This is a custom, rather than a convention. The key difference is the hurdle outlined by Wheare (1964: 122): conventions are 'meant to be a binding rule, a rule of behavior accepted as obligatory by those concerned in the working of the constitution'. Customs are only symbolic or 'pleasing rituals whose observation or abeyance has no substantial impact on the operation of constitutional rules and principals' (Heard 2005: 20). Therefore, if the speaker willingly walked to the chair – as in some subnational legislatures – no one

[1] The original name of the Canadian Constitution was the *British North America Act*. It was renamed *Constitution Act, 1867*, in 1982 as part of the 'patriation' of the constitution.

would argue that a convention has changed. They may lament the demise of a longstanding ritual, but no one would claim that the machinery of the constitution had changed.

An important aspect of conventions is the way they operate in relation to constitutional law. While in some cases conventions provide the framework to understand the law (the principle of responsible government, for example), in other instances conventions can make a functioning part of the constitution inoperable. According to Wheare, a 'convention paralyses the arm of the law: does not amend or abolish the law' or, put another way, 'it does not amputate the limb; it merely makes its use impossible' (Wheare 1964: 123). An example from the *Constitution Act, 1867* makes this point well.

Sections fifty-five, fifty-six and fifty-seven of the *Constitution Act, 1867* provide mechanisms by which the governor-general may override or refuse assent to bills passed in the provinces. Section ninety extends these powers to the lieutenant governor and the federal government. Reservation is the process whereby the governor-general, rather than refusing to give assent, can refer the matter to the imperial government (that is, Westminster) for a final decision. Disallowance, by contrast, is the practice in which a passed law can be declared null and void by the imperial government, even if the governor-general has given assent.

At the time of confederation, the inclusion of these sections seemed uncontroversial. Indeed, giving the powers of reservation and disallowance to the federal government was seen as a natural extension of the existing arrangements in the Dominion of Canada. However, it was clear that their inclusion violated the federal principle. The Macdonald (1867–73 and 1878–91), Mackenzie (1873–8) and Laurier (1896–1911) governments extensively used reservation and disallowance, especially against the western provinces. Over time, however, invoking these constitutional powers was seen as increasingly illegitimate, to the point where a convention of non-use developed. Indeed, the last uses of reservation and disallowance were in 1961 and 1943, respectively. Simply put, no prime minister who wishes to be re-elected would consider using the powers of disallowance in the modern age (for a detailed discussion, see Vipond 1991).

Yet Sections fifty-five, fifty-six and fifty-seven and ninety remain a part of the Constitution Act, 1867. During the constitutional negotiations of the 1970s and 1980s it was proposed to eliminate them (Russell 1993: 89). Given the length of time since they had last been used, this was an easy proposal for the federal government to make, but the provincial premiers wisely declined to have them removed, as a constitutional convention of non-use had been well established.

Executive conventions

If you were to read the *Constitution Act, 1867*, you would be right to conclude that the governor-general holds a great deal, indeed perhaps all, of power over the daily functioning of the Canadian polity. Take, for example, the formation of government. The text of the constitution says that the governor-general invites the government to form. The conventions that underpin the Canadian constitution help clarify how that text operates. In this case, convention says that the party which has secured the most seats in the previous election is invited to form government.

Like other Westminster-derived systems – Australia, for example – the Canadian constitution makes little mention of the cabinet and ministry. The appointments, dismissals and overall function of the cabinet are left to constitutional convention. As Matheson (1976: 1) observes, 'there is no law or document that specifically defines the cabinet or its responsibilities'. Indeed, composition, size and portfolio allocation are entirely left to the prime minister, whose own constitutional basis is nearly non-existent (Kerby 2014: 265). There are no formal rules dictating which specific ministers need to be drawn from either the House or the Senate. However, the convention is that ministers without a seat in either chamber will seek to secure one. Moreover, the number of unelected ministers should be kept relatively low.

The form and function of executive government in Canada are governed by the conventions of collective and individual ministerial responsibility. These conventions originated in the United Kingdom, and were formally transplanted to Canada in 1867. A loss of confidence in the House of Commons usually results in dissolution of the House and a subsequent general election. In only one instance (1873) has the governor-general asked the second-largest party to form government (Kerby 2014: 265).

A related example occurred in 1926 and has come to be known as the 'King-Byng Affair'. After the October 1925 election, the incumbent Liberal party, led by William Lyon Mackenzie King, was returned with only 101 seats and second place status. The Conservative party, led by Arthur Meighen, secured the most seats at 116. Backed with the support of the Progressives (28 seats), the Liberal party held onto power until

June 1926 when they were defeated on a censure motion. Before the vote took place, however, King asked Governor-General Lord Julian Byng of Vimy to dissolve parliament and call a new election, which Lord Byng denied. It was unheard of to request dissolution while a motion of censure was under debate. When the censure vote passed, resulting in a vote of no confidence, Byng asked the Conservative opposition to form government. The Conservative party held onto power through four censure votes but eventually fell on a fifth. Meighen then asked the governor-general for a dissolution and an election which was granted. The King-Byng affair eventually came to an end when King a majority election in September 1926. Since 1926, no governor-general has publically refused the advice of a sitting prime minister (for a full discussion see Russell 2008, especially chapter 3).

During elections and after

Chapter 6 by Menzies and Tiernan fully outlined comparative Westminster-derived caretaker conventions; the Canadian experience is entirely consistent with their account, but a reminder is in order. During the election campaign or the 'caretaker period', it is expected that the governing party (which remains the governing party during the writ period) will not undertake any major spending projects. This is because once parliament has been dissolved, the ministers are no longer accountable to parliament; it would be unfair if the governing party were defeated, having saddled the incoming government with large financial burdens not present before the writ was passed. Indeed, it would be reasonable for the governor-general to decline or defer the action (appointments, for example) until after the election (see also t'Hart and Uhr 2011).

Constitutional conventions, inherited from Westminster, determine events in the aftermath of an election. Contrary to widely held opinion, the voters of Canada do not elect the government. They elect their local member, who is almost always a member of a political party. Once the outcome of the election is known, the constitutional convention is that the governor-general extends a formal invitation to the leader of the political party that is best able to secure the confidence of the House of Commons. This typically means the party that has secured the largest number of seats. In Canada single-party majorities are the norm, but in those instances where a single party has not secured a majority of the seats in the House of Commons, the party with the most seats is invited to form government either as a minority or as a coalition. As I shall discuss below, this convention may lead to difficult situations in the early days of a government.

There is nothing in the Canadian constitution that says a defeated prime minister *has* to resign in the aftermath of an election. Yet, in the aftermath of the 1993 election, no one seriously suggested that the prime minister, Kim Campbell, should remain in power after her party was reduced to a mere two seats. Indeed, as Heard (2005: 20) notes, '[h]ad she done so, the Governor General would have been justified in firing her and appointing Jean Chrétien as Prime Minister'. Nevertheless, according to constitutional convention, the incumbent prime minister has the right to remain in office and face parliament if there is a belief that he or she can secure a confidence vote (Heard 2005: 21).

Responsible government

The principle of responsible government is upheld by the government's need to retain the confidence of the members of the House of Commons. In Canada, this is manifested in a number of ways: the Crown will only act on advice from the ministry; ministers of the Crown answer questions on the floor of the House of Commons (Question Period); if the ministry is defeated on a confidence measure, it must resign, resulting in an election or a new ministry trying to secure the confidence of the House.

Ministerial responsibility

The guiding principles that inform executive function in Canada are the twin conventions of individual and collective ministerial responsibility, which originated in Britain and were transplanted to Canada in 1867 (for further discussion, see Kerby 2014). In the simplest form, the convention of individual ministerial responsibility holds that ministers must answer questions in the House of Commons on issues for which their department is responsible. In Canada this happens during Question Period. Ministers are fully responsible for wrongful actions which occur in their department: they must correct the wrong or resign over the consequences. Moreover, ministers are held accountable for personal errors, which may include anything from private indiscretions which are said to interfere with the minister's public credibility to political misjudgements where ministers act in their public capacity without the backing of their department (Heard 1991). The modern incarnation of individual ministerial responsibility is less strict. MPs still rise to ask questions of ministers regarding their administrative responsibilities, but there is reasonable debate about whether ministers are politically responsible for *everything* that happens in their departments (Kerby 2014: 267).

Most Canadian scholars agree that ministers are not politically responsible for everything that happens in their departments. Kenneth Kernaghan (1980: 130), for example, argues that ministerial responsibility does not extend to departmental underlings: 'in practice, ministers do not resign or atone for either serious mismanagement by their officials or personal administrative mistakes'. Yet individual ministerial responsibility still exists in the liable sense, especially when ministers have done something wrong personally rather than administratively. Heard (1991: 55) suggests that 'personal wrongdoing' which 'demonstrates the basic unfitness of an individual to be entrusted with the management of the affairs of the state' is still a reason for a minister to resign. Often, however, this is due to political pressure from the party rather than a sense of moral rightness.

Related to the notion of individual ministerial responsibility is collective ministerial responsibility, which dictates that a minister must resign following public clashes with cabinet colleagues over policy. Marshall and Moodie (1971: 71, quoted in Kerby 2014: 268) observe of the UK practice:

> collective responsibility provides a definition of what a government is in our system: The substance of the Government's collective responsibility could be defined as its duty to submit its policy before the House of Commons and resign if defeated on an issue of confidence.

The most obvious aspect of collective cabinet solidarity is the 'all for one and one for all' presentation in public. Ministers do not dispute collective decisions outside the cabinet chamber. Moreover, all ministers must vote in favour of governmental policies. As Heard (1991: 62) writes:

> If a government is held collectively responsible to the legislature, one cannot have individual ministers saying: 'Well, don't condemn me along with the rest of the Cabinet, because I disagree with that decision, and argued all along that another course of action should be followed.

Cabinet solidarity in Canada has produced a number of additional rules which have been elucidated by Forsey and Eglinton (1985, quoted in Kerby 2014: 269). Among them are the following:

- Government advice to the Crown must be unanimous, even if arrived at after the consideration of strongly held but opposing views.

- A minister must loyally support and defend any cabinet decision and not quaver by suggesting he was compromised or reluctantly persuaded.
- A minister must not only refrain from publicly criticising other ministers but also defend them publicly.
- A minister must not express private views on government policies.

In the Canadian case, violations of collective ministerial responsibility are rare. This is due largely to the strong leadership of the prime minister and the single-plurality electoral system. Ambitious ministers know that their fortunes are tied to both their current party and the prime minister. Thus, if a minister cannot support the government in public, especially in the House of Commons, then he or she must resign the cabinet position. As Savoie (1999: 82) says, 'the prime minister appoints Cabinet ministers . . . [if they] disagree with government policy, he or she has two choices – keep quiet and bear it or resign'. Ultimately both individual and collective ministerial responsibility reflect the increasingly professional nature of politicians. Kerby (2014: 270–1) notes that Canada is more compliant with individual ministerial responsibility in cases of 'personal fault, or lapses in person or political morality' and that 'collective cabinet responsibility appears to be strong and readily enforced'.

Courts

Given that the political actors enforce constitutional conventions in a system, it seems odd that a discussion of the judiciary is needed. Such is the Canadian way. Unlike other Westminster-derived political systems, like Australia and New Zealand, there exists a blurred separation of powers doctrine in Canada. This is primarily seen through the use of advisory, or reference, opinions (Hausegger et al. 2009: 242–3).[2] In these cases, the Supreme Court of Canada, at the federal level, and the provincial courts of appeals at the provincial level, may be asked by their attorney generals to provide a non-binding legal opinion on the constitutionality of a potential bill. While technically non-binding, these opinions are frequently cited in subsequent case law and more often than not are followed to the letter by politicians when drafting the response to a bill. Indeed, the Supreme Court Act sets out in the widest possible terms what types of questions may be asked. The Court does, however, reserve the right to refuse a question, often on the basis of non-justicibility.

[2] The United States explicitly rejected this procedure under Article three of its Constitution.

Any discussion of Canadian constitutional conventions would be incomplete without a discussion of the Supreme Court's *Patriation Reference (1981 1 S.C.R. 753)* regarding the amendment to the Canadian Constitution. The lead-up to the *Patriation Reference* occurred during the 1970s and early 1980s when there was a push by the prime minister, Pierre Trudeau, to 'bring home' the Canadian constitution from Westminster (for a discussion of these events, see McWhinney 1982; Hogg 1983). A number of items were on the constitutional negotiating table, including an amending formula, fiscal equalisation and, of course, the *Charter of Rights and Freedoms*. A resolution was drafted and initiated through federal parliament, requesting that the Queen 'lay the *Constitution Act* before the United Kingdom Parliament' (Russell et al. 2008: 493).

The provinces immediately objected to this departure from the constitutional convention of provincial consent for amendments affecting provincial responsibilities. Indeed, only two provinces – Ontario and New Brunswick – supported the unilateral move by the federal government. But the prime minister claimed that the number of failures during the constitutional negotiations justified federal unilateralism and that the constitutional convention required the Westminster Parliament to 'automatically pass any amendment of the Canadian Constitution requested by the federal Parliament regardless of provincial objections' (Russell et al. 2008: 493).

Three provinces sought judicial opinion via a reference case to their respective courts of appeal on:

1. Whether the *Constitution Act, 1981* affects the federal provincial relationship or provincial powers;
2. Whether there is a convention requiring provincial consent for such an amendment;
3. Whether provincial consent for such an amendment was a 'constructional requirement'.

The provincial courts divided on the critical third question and both the federal government and the provincial governments appealed the decision to the Supreme Court of Canada.

On Monday 28 September 1981, the Supreme Court of Canada released its decision. On the first question, the justices agreed that the federal government's proposed amendments did potentially alter the federal–provincial relationship. On the second and third questions, however, a decidedly mixed result was delivered. On the second question, the Court (6–3) held that there was a constitutional convention that required 'a *substantial* degree of provincial consent' (emphasis added) for federal requests made to the United Kingdom. On the third question the justices held (7–2) that, although this convention was a 'constitutional requirement', observance of the convention was not 'legally required' (Russell et al. 2008: 495). As Peter Russell (1993: 119) has observed, the decision amounted to 'a legal green light but a political red light'.

The Court divided the ruling into constitutional law and constitutional conventions. It found that because constitutional conventions are part of the constitutional framework of Canada, 'they may be more important than some of the laws', and the failure of politicians to observe them is tantamount to constitutional violation. Thus the enforcement and remedies of breaching constitutional conventions are political, not legal. The Court was placed in a difficult situation when it was asked to rule on the legality of constitutional conventions, but circumvented a possible institutional crisis by 'giving half a loaf to each side'. Again, Peter Russell (1985: 164) sums it up best when he said 'the decision was bold statecraft, but poor jurisprudence'.

Conventions in minority government and the prorogation crisis

As outlined above, some of the most important constitutional conventions govern the days following an election and the beginning of a new parliamentary session: the governor-general's appointment of a new prime minister and the parliamentary votes on the Speech from the Throne and Address in Reply to the Speech from the Throne. Where a majority government is won, as is often the case in Canada, there is no question: either the incumbent prime minister continues or, in the case of defeat, the prime minister visits the governor-general and resigns the post. However, in a minority government situation, where there is doubt surrounding who may form government, the prevailing custom suggests that the leader of the party with the largest number of seats is called on to form government.

Andrew Heard (2005: 21) observes that this prevailing custom is incorrect, noting that 'it [is] irresponsible, even, for Prime Ministers to resign simply because they finished second in situations where they knew full well that a smaller party was prepared to support them'.

Thus, in the aftermath of the 2004 election, some have suggested that Paul Martin could have delivered a Throne Speech to see if he could win the confidence in the House (Heard 2005: 21). However, custom prevailed: he resigned that night and the governor-general called on Stephen Harper and the Conservatives to form government.

The Speech from the Throne lays out the broad agenda of what the government intends to do. The vote on the Address in Reply is the judgement of the House and whether it has confidence in the government's plans. If the opposition party successfully adds words to the Throne Speech, that constitutes a vote of no confidence and the government must resign. The process starts again, and the opposition parties 'has a go'.

The 2008 'constitutional crisis'

After the election of 2008, the Conservative government of Stephen Harper delivered an economic update. Embedded in it was an indication that the Conservatives would cut the public subsidy to political parties. After each election, the parties are awarded $1.75 per vote (adjusted for inflation), until the next election. The Conservatives, who are very effective at raising money from small donors and least reliant on the subsidy, decided that it should be scrapped as a cost-saving measure (Valpy 2009). This set the parliamentary 'crisis' in motion.

The opposition parties announced they would not support the economic update, and called for a confidence vote in the government. They further announced that they would introduce a no confidence motion at the first opportunity (the following Monday) during their next opposition day. The government, realising it was about to be defeated, delayed the vote on the economic update for a week. It also delayed an opposition day for one week. That week in November 2008 proved to be a watershed in Canadian parliamentary history. The governor-general cut short an official visit to Europe to come home, and for the first time in collective memory constitutional conventions, such as the governor-general's reserve powers, were brought into the spotlight (Valpy 2009).

The two centre-left parties, the Liberal Party of Canada and the New Democratic Party, signed an agreement to govern as a coalition for a period of two years (with Liberal leader Stéphane Dion as prime minister), supported on confidence measures by the separatist party Bloc Québecois (which was not part of the governing coalition). The prime minister announced that he would ask the governor-general to prorogue parliament a mere seven weeks after the Throne Speech. The opposition parties countered that they should be given a chance to see if they could command the confidence of the House of Commons (which they could). After a week of political posturing, Stephen Harper had a meeting with the governor-general; after two hours he emerged and announced that parliament was suspended until early 2009. What went on during those two hours no one but the governor-general and the prime minister knows. As in other Westminster nations, there is a convention of non-disclosure of the proceedings of such meetings (Valpy 2009).

The aftermath

The question remains as to whether the governor-general ruled correctly in favour of prorogation. There are two schools of thought: the first suggests that the governor-general had no choice but to grant prorogation to the prime minister. It was the latter's decision alone, barring something remarkable, such as a no confidence measure on the floor of the House. In the absence of an extraordinary event of this kind, the governor-general was bound by convention to follow the advice of her chief advisor (Franks 2009; Heard 2009).

The other school of thought suggests that the governor-general should have declined the request for prorogation and instead asked the prime minister to face the Commons and continue with the pending vote of no confidence. Given the agreement signed by the opposition parties, it would seem likely that the prime minister would have been defeated (Weinrib 2009).

Those who argue in favour of the second option may be missing a key point. If the governor-general had declined the request, the convention would have been for the prime minister and cabinet to resign *en masse*, because the governor-general indicated she no longer had confidence in her chief minister. She would have then been forced to call on the opposition parties to see if they could secure the confidence of the House of Commons. At best, Canada would have been governed by a coalition of parties for two years. At worst, parliament would have ground to a halt, in a way reminiscent of the King–Byng Affair in 1926.

It was clear that the Canadian public was dissatisfied with the idea that the opposition parties could have been handed the keys to the peaceable kingdom without an election in which the government was defeated. Moreover, we may further hypothesise that the prime minister would not have gone quietly into the night, and that the Queen may have been called on to dismiss the governor-general. This would have led to a *real* constitutional crisis that may have had lasting effects on Canada, like the 1975 constitutional crisis in Australia.

The fallout of the prorogation crisis was perhaps predictable. The Conservative party was painted as a villain, and the coalition partners were seen as unsuitable to lead. The holiday season distracted public attention; then, early in 2009, the largest economic crisis since the great depression hit and the prorogation crisis was forgotten. Indeed, the House was prorogued again during the 2010 Vancouver Winter Olympics (Mendes 2010). There were protests, but not on the scale of those of 2008. The question of prorogation was barely raised during the 2011 federal election. The one legacy of lasting significance is the call for constitutional conventions to be codified in a cabinet manual as outlined by Peter Russell in Chapter 13. The success of that endeavour remains to be seen.

Conclusions

This chapter began by highlighting the many constitutional conventions that influence the day-to-day operation of the Canadian regime. As is the case with other Westminster-derived constitutions, conventions in Canada have evolved as they are needed. With the expansion of the state, combined with the increasingly complex nature of governing, the constitutional conventions have facilitated the workings of the constitution, enabling it to remain vibrant.

This lesson was acute during the 2008 prorogation crisis in Canada. The wording of the *Constitution Act, 1867* would have been little or no help in this situation. Indeed, too often the constitution is silent. Yet, thanks to the conventions that inform political realities, Canada moved forward, no worse for wear. It is clear that constitutional conventions in Canada play a significant role in the day-to-day operation of the political machinery. It is equally clear that they are poorly understood, and often misinterpreted. Our knowledge of the past suggests we should expect nothing less of the Canadian polity.

References

Ajzenstat, Janet, Romney, Paul, Gentles, Ian and Gairdner, William D. 1999. *Canada's founding debates*. Toronto: Stoddart.

Franks, C. E. S. 2009. 'To prorogue or not to prorogue: did the Governor General make the right decision?', in P. H. Russell and Lorne Sossin (eds.), *Parliamentary democracy in crisis*. University of Toronto Press.

Hausegger, Lori, Hennigar, Matthew and Riddell, Troy 2009. *Canadian courts: law, politics, and process*. Oxford University Press.

Heard, Andrew 1991. *Canadian constitutional conventions: the marriage of law and politics*. Toronto: Oxford University Press.

Heard, Andrew 2005. 'Constitutional conventions and parliament', *Canadian Parliamentary Review* 28: 19–22.

Heard, Andrew 2009. 'The Governor General's suspension of parliament: duty done or perilous precedent?', in P. H. Russell and Lorne Sossin (eds.), *Parliamentary democracy in crisis*. University of Toronto Press.

Hogg, Peter H. 1983. 'Patriation of the Canadian constitution', *Queen's Law Journal* 8: 123.

Jennings, Ivor 1959. *The law and the constitution*. University of London Press.

Kerby, Matthew 2014. 'Canada', in Keith Dowding and Patrick Dumont (eds.), *The selection of ministers around the world*. London and New York: Routledge.

Kernaghan, Kenneth 1980. 'Power, parliament and public servants in Canada: ministerial responsibility reexamined', in H. D. Clarke, C. Campbell, F. Q. Quo and A. Goddard (eds.), *Parliament, policy and representation*. Toronto: Methuen.

Marshall, Geoffrey and Moodie, G. C. 1971. *Some problems of the constitution*, 5th edn. London: Hutchinson University Library.

Matheson, William A. 1976. *The prime minister and the cabinet*. Toronto: Methuen.

McWhinney, Edward 1982. *Canada and the constitution, 1979–1982: patriation and the Charter of Rights*. University of Toronto Press.

Mendes, Errol P. 2010. 'Prorogation redux: Harper in contempt of parliament', *Toronto Star*. www.thestar.com/opinion/2010/01/05/prorogation_redux_harper_in_contempt_of_parliament.html.

Russell, Peter H. 1985. 'The Supreme Court and federal–provincial relations: the political use of legal resources', *Canadian Public Policy* 11(2): 161–70.

Russell, Peter H. 1993. *Constitutional odyssey: can Canadians become a sovereign people?*, 2nd edn. University of Toronto Press.

Russell, Peter H. 2008. *Two cheers for minority government: the evolution of Canadian parliamentary democracy*. Toronto: Emond Montgomery Publications.

Russell, Peter H., Knopff, Rainer, Bateman, Thomas M. J. and Hiebert, Janet (eds.) 2008. *The court and the constitution: leading cases*. Toronto: Edmond Montgomery Publications.

Savoie, Donald J. 1999. *Governing from the centre: the concentration of power in Canadian politics*. University of Toronto Press.

t'Hart, Paul and Uhr, John (eds.) 2011. *How power changes hands: transition and succession in government*. New York: Palgrave Macmillan.

Valpy, Michael 2009. 'The "crisis": a narrative', in P. H. Russell and Lorne Sossin (eds.), *Parliamentary democracy in crisis*. University of Toronto Press.
Vipond, Robert C. 1991. *Liberty and community: Canadian federalism and the failure of the constitution*. Buffalo: SUNY Press.
Weinrib, Lorraine E. 2009. 'Prime Minister Stephen Harper's "timeout": a constitutional revolution in the making?', in P. H. Russell and Lorne Sossin (eds.), *Parliamentary democracy in crisis*. University of Toronto Press.
Wheare, K. C. 1964. *Modern constitutions*. Oxford University Press.

11

Australia

NICHOLAS BARRY AND NARELLE MIRAGLIOTTA

One of the important features of Australia's constitutional arrangements is the extent to which it rests upon conventions in addition to a written constitution. This chapter considers the impact of conventions on the operation of Australia's constitutional system through revisiting what is arguably this country's most dramatic constitutional moment: the 1975 constitutional crisis. We suggest that this crisis underlined the three main fault-lines intrinsic to a mixed constitutional system[1]; first, the conflict between conventions and the written constitution; second, the tension between conventions with competing implications; and third, disagreements over how conventions should be invoked and applied in particular situations. However, we argue that, in polities with a strong commitment to constitutionalism, disputes over conventions are inevitable and do not weaken the integrity or legitimacy of the constitutional system.

This chapter is divided into three sections. Section one examines the characteristics of constitutional conventions and their relationship to other elements of the constitutional order in Australia. Section two uses the events of the 1975 constitutional crisis to illustrate the challenges that a mixed constitutional system can engender, especially when that system is reliant on conventions. Following on from this discussion, the third section considers what lasting impact the crisis had on the constitutional and political system.

Constitutional conventions in Australian practice

Constitutional conventions refer to a specific type of convention that is designed to regulate the discretionary power vested in offices or

[1] We concede that all constitutional systems contain a mix of written and unwritten elements; however, what is distinctive about Australia's constitutional arrangements is the extent to which central aspects of the system, including many of the central principles of responsible government, were purposely left unstated by those who drafted the constitution.

institutions listed in the constitution (Cooray 1979: 68–9). They furnish rules where the formal constitutional text is silent and fill natural gaps that may or may not have been deliberately intended by those who drafted the formal document (Jennings 1938: 80). In doing so they 'provide a means for harmonising relations where a purely legal solution of practical problems was impossible, would have impaired free development or would have failed to catch the spirit that gives life to institutions' (Jennings 1938: 20). They animate the austere sections of the formal constitution to produce a functional and flexible constitutional system of government.

However, the centrality of constitutional conventions to the performance of the constitutional system does not insulate them from the usual challenges that confront other types of informal rules or ordinary conventions (Wheare 1951). Conventions are the product of explicitly 'political influences and considerations' (Quick and Garran 1901: 60), and their interpretation is contestable because, much like any convention, the 'test' used to establish them is 'less systematic and less determinate' than in the case of formal legal rules (Sampford 1987: 377; see also Heard 1989 for a treatment of the difficulties of identifying the source of conventions). Even if there is little doubt as to the existence of a convention, 'many of its applications to particular factual situations may be open to argument' (Marshall 1985: 34).

It is also generally accepted that constitutional conventions are not legally binding (Forsey 1984: 12; but see Maley 1985 and Heard 1989). The non-justiciable quality of conventions renders their observance dependent on the continuing cooperation and perceptions of self-interest of those who command them (Marshall 1984: 4). As a result, the interpretation of constitutional conventions are subject to prevailing situational and contextual forces and at the mercy of the preferences of the dominant political actors.

Constitutional conventions must also be understood and interpreted alongside other legal frameworks, including the written constitution and statute law. In Australia, tensions can arise between constitutional conventions and the formal constitution because conventions can transform the literal everyday meaning of the written text. In certain circumstances, conventions also conflict directly with statute law.[2] Resolving such conflicts is often difficult. While constitutional conventions are not

[2] See Sirota (2011: 35–6) for a dissenting view on this subject.

justiciable they do possess moral and political authority and a degree of binding force, particularly when they are well established and widely accepted (Dicey 1897; Killey 2009: 20). As a consequence, those pressing the primacy of conventional rules over the written constitution laws can reasonably defend the former on constitutional, moral and political grounds.

Moreover, no constitutional convention operates in isolation from other governmental conventions. There are many constitutional conventions that exist to regulate the discretionary power of those institutions and agents named in the written constitution. These constitutional conventions function alongside an assortment of governmental conventions that relate to the workings of government and apply to critical matters such as the position of the prime minister in cabinet and the functioning of the cabinet system. As Cooray argues, while most governmental conventions address fairly routine matters of government, the non-observance of some can have serious implications for the stability of the constitutional system (Cooray 1979: 73–4).

In systems that rely heavily on conventions, it is likely that the meaning and interpretation of one convention will conflict with the meaning and interpretation of one or more other conventions. It may prove even more difficult to reconcile these competing conventions than it is to reconcile conflicts between conventions and the written constitution. Although some conventions are regarded as more established, more accepted and more fundamental, there is no official hierarchy of conventions (see, for example, Heard's (1989) efforts to develop a taxonomy of conventions). Moreover, the Australian High Court's decision to block consideration of advisory opinions on these and other such constitutional matters removes the prospect of political actors having recourse to authoritative legal guidance to resolve disagreements over conventions (Sampford and Wood 1987: 231).

The importance of constitutional conventions to the operation of government and the constitution means that the derogation of conventional rules can significantly unsettle the constitutional status quo. When this occurs, the sense of crisis is amplified because in the absence of an authoritative third-party adjudicator, the solutions brokered are expressly political in character. This in turn can invoke a particularly heightened feeling of injustice among the vanquished about the outcome that may linger for much longer than when the matter is resolved by the Courts.

The next section of this chapter demonstrates these challenges in practice through an examination of the 1975 constitutional crisis.

Challenges in practice: the 1975 constitutional crisis

While the singular is often used as a scholarly shorthand, the 1975 constitutional crisis describes what was in fact a series of four interlocking crises. These crises culminated in the dismissal of the Whitlam Labor government by the governor-general in 1975. The genealogy of the crisis has been outlined in other chapters in this volume and described in forensic detail in the scholarly literature (Archer and Maddox 1976; Sawer 1977; Kelly 1995), but particular aspects are highlighted below that underpin the following analysis of constitutional conventions in Australia.

The first hint of crisis emerged in May 1974 when the opposition, led by Liberal party leader William 'Bill' Sneddon, threatened to use its dominant position in the Senate to block passage of supply. This prompted the Whitlam Labor government to seek and to receive permission from the governor-general, John Kerr, to hold a double dissolution election. Yet the elections did little to improve Whitlam's position. While the government support in the House of Representatives meant it retained office, the Senate remained dominated by the major opposition grouping of the Liberal and National Country party coalition.

In the intervening months, deepening economic problems, coupled with a number of scandals involving government ministers, strengthened the opposition's commitment to using this strategy to bring down the Whitlam government. Against this backdrop of confrontation and division, the second crisis occurred in February and September of 1975 when the New South Wales and Queensland state parliaments selected non-Labor replacements to fill vacancies occasioned by the departure of Labor senators. This had the effect of delivering a clear majority to the opposition in the Senate. The third crisis was sparked in October when the opposition voted to defer supply in the Senate. The opposition agreed to support the budget if the government agreed to a House of Representatives election in the first half of 1975, even though the government's term was not due to expire until May 1977. The Whitlam Government refused to accede to this ultimatum and the opposition refused to commit to the passage of supply.

The final act in the affair occurred on 11 November when the governor-general acting with the advice of Chief Justice dismissed Whitlam. The governor-general appointed the newly installed Liberal opposition leader, Malcolm Fraser, as caretaker prime minister on condition that he obtain supply and then advise a double dissolution election. In a public statement announcing his decision, the governor-general said:

> The only solution consistent with the Constitution and with my oath of office and my responsibilities, authority and duty as Governor-General is to terminate the commission of the Prime Minister Mr Whitlam and to arrange a caretaker government able to secure supply and willing to let the issue go to the people. (Kerr 1975)

The election was held on 13 December 1975, and resulted in a landslide victory for the Liberal coalition with the National Country party. However, the partisan rancour generated by the crisis endured, as did the debate it prompted over the adequacy of Australia's constitutional arrangements. In large part, this was because the crisis illustrated the challenges that arise in a system that draws heavily on constitutional conventions in order to function.

First, the crisis illustrated how difficult it can be to invoke conventions. This is particularly evident from the controversy surrounding the replacement of Senate casual vacancies. Although s. 15 of the Constitution gives state parliaments the power to fill casual vacancies that arise in the Senate, since 1951 the convention was that state parliaments would appoint a replacement from the same party as the senator being replaced (Rydon 1976). However, when the New South Wales government appointed independent Cleaver Bunton to replace outgoing Labor Senator Lionel Murphy in 1975, it claimed this was justified because Murphy's departure was contrived (he had been appointed to the High Court), and that the convention only applied when the casual vacancy was involuntary (Winterton 2003: 234–5). Seven months later, when the Queensland parliament appointed Whitlam adversary and ex-Labor member Albert Field to fill the casual vacancy that had arisen as a result of the death of Labor Senator Bert Milliner, the state government defended its decision because of the circumstances of the case. It rejected Labor's nominee, Mal Colston, claiming that he was of doubtful integrity, and Labor refused the premier's request to provide another nominee, instead putting Colston forward again. In both cases, the Whitlam government rejected the arguments of the states, claiming that the failure to replace Labor casual vacancies with Labor nominees represented clear breaches of the convention (Whitlam 1979: 37-40).

The disagreement among New South Wales, Queensland and the Whitlam government over the casual vacancies convention reflected, in part, the less systematic and less determinate character of conventions. It also reflected the relatively recent origins of the convention, which had only been in place since 1951, prompted in part by the adoption of proportional representation for Senate elections in 1949. This meant that the convention was less well established and that it had been tested in fewer situations, leaving greater room for disagreements over how it should be applied in particular cases.

Second, the 1975 crisis exemplified the challenges that can arise when constitutional conventions clash with the text of the written constitution. The Constitution confers on the governor-general an extensive array of formal powers, including the power to dissolve the House and call elections, but the long-standing convention is that the governor-general uses these powers on the advice of the prime minister, except in certain unusual circumstances when he/she can unilaterally decide to exercise his/her reserve powers, dismissing the prime minister and dissolving the House. In 1975, Prime Minister Whitlam argued that the convention was dominant, and that the governor-general could only act on his advice. This was one of the factors that led the prime minister to dismiss the possibility that the governor-general would invoke his formal constitutional power (Kelly 1995: 304). This illustrates the complications that can arise when there is tension between constitutional conventions and the written constitution and few precedents to provide guidance to the actors involved in the dispute.

Third, the constitutional crisis demonstrated the uncertainty created by conflict between different constitutional conventions. In 1975, the principle that the government must retain supply to remain in office clashed with the convention at the heart of responsible government – that the government requires the confidence of the lower house to remain in office. Disagreement arose when the Senate, not the House of Representatives, blocked supply, which meant that the upper house was able to force the government to an election. The tension between these two principles was also apparent on the afternoon of 11 November when the House of Representatives passed a no-confidence motion in the new caretaker, Prime Minister Fraser, who could secure supply but lacked the confidence of the House (Winterton 2003: 239–40). Adding to the confusion, some players in the 1975 crisis (most notably, Prime Minister Whitlam) argued that the Senate was breaking convention by blocking supply and that the principle of responsible government was preeminent, while others (including Governor-General John Kerr, opposition leader Fraser and High Court Chief Justice and former Coalition minister Sir Garfield Barwick) claimed that the Senate did have the power to block supply and that the federal government therefore, in a sense, needed to have the confidence of both houses of parliament (Winterton 2003: 237–8). When such long-standing conventions come into conflict, it is often unclear which should prevail.

Fourth, the constitutional crisis illustrated the challenges that the political nature of conventions can produce. As constitutional conventions are non-justiciable, the High Court cannot authoritatively resolve disagreements over how they should be understood and applied, and it often falls to politicians to resolve these disagreements. This means that pragmatic political considerations strongly shape how conventions are interpreted, and whether they are upheld. For example, in the 1975 crisis, it was in the Fraser opposition's interest to claim that the Senate had the right to block supply and that the government had an obligation to resign when this occurred, as it knew that the government was unpopular and likely to lose the election. Conversely, it was in the interest of the Whitlam government to claim that the Senate was breaking convention in blocking supply, and that the preeminent principle was that the government enjoy the confidence of the lower house. Similarly, it was in the interest of Coalition state governments – strongly opposed to the Whitlam Labor government's centralist tendencies – to claim that the manufactured nature of the casual vacancy invalidated the conventions surrounding partisan composition, while the Whitlam government clearly had a motivation to criticise the appointment of non-Labor senators to fill the casual vacancies. In these cases, both contenders defended their positions citing convention in order to further their own interests.

The legacy of the crisis

The constitutional crisis exemplified the complexities and ambiguities that can surface in a system that is dependent on constitutional conventions. In light of these challenges, some scholars (including Peter Russell in Chapter 13) have argued for codification of key constitutional conventions in order to avoid future constitutional crises (for Australian examples see Sawer 1983 and Ward 2000; also note Sharman 1998). In this section, we consider the impact of the 1975 crisis on the constitutional system and whether the Australian reliance on conventions poses a challenge to the coherence, stability and legitimacy of the constitutional system.

One of the core functions of a constitution is to outline clearly how a system of government should function. As Waldron puts it, the aim is 'to redress that sense of the mercurial character of politics. The idea is that certain aspects of the political process should be made stable and put somewhat beyond the challenge of ordinary politics, precisely so there can be a known and predictable framework for substantial political debate' (Waldron 1990: 80). However, as the discussion in the previous section established, the reliance on conventions can lead to uncertainty over key elements of the political system. There can be ambiguity about how conventions will be interpreted and operationalised, how they relate to the written constitution, how they relate to each other and whether they will be followed when they clash with political self-interest. In the 1975 crisis, this led to disagreement over how Senate casual vacancies should be filled, whether the Senate could block supply, whether a government that enjoyed the confidence of the House should call an election if it were unable to secure supply, and whether the governor-general should dismiss the government and force an election in such a situation. This uncertainty seems inconsistent with the idea of a stable and predictable framework for government, so, to that extent, the heavy reliance on conventions could be argued to undermine one of the main purposes of a constitution.

The 1975 crisis also showed that conventions can both ignite and inflame a constitutional crisis. Some of the problems in 1975 arose because key actors operated from very particular but also very different understandings of the relationship between different elements of the system, or because they misjudged how other actors would behave. For example, Prime Minister Whitlam believed that the governor-general could only act on the advice of the prime minister, and this was one of the factors which led him to dismiss the possibility that he would be removed from office by the governor-general. Kelly suggests that 'Whitlam made little or no effort to persuade Kerr to accept the Prime Minister's view of the crisis, namely that it was a threat to responsible government which Whitlam felt an obligation to defend. Instead Whitlam delivered public and private homilies that Kerr could only act on the advice of his ministers' (Kelly 1995: 304). Another key factor was the governor-general's failure to warn Prime Minister Whitlam in advance that he would be dismissed if he were unable to secure supply. This also reflected the ambiguity surrounding the relationship between the governor-general and the prime minister, with the governor-general claiming that he could not have warned the prime minister because Whitlam would have dismissed the governor-general instead (Kerr 1978; Kelly 1995: 300–1; Winterton 2003: 247–8). In this way, the lack of clarity in aspects of the relationship between the prime minister and the governor-general led to strategic miscalculations by the key actors involved, which ultimately inflamed and deepened the crisis.

The constitutional crisis also raised doubts over the extent to which constitutional conventions can effectively restrain power. Without judicial review, there is no body to directly sanction actors who depart from long-standing conventions. This problem is evidenced by the Fraser opposition's decision to block supply in 1975 as part of a deliberate tactic to bring down the Whitlam government. This strategy had been discussed by the opposition as early as 1973, and it was also used prior to the 1974 double dissolution (Winterton 2003: 232). In this case, those within the Fraser opposition clearly believed that it was in their political interest to block supply to bring down the government, forcing an election which they were likely to win. Even if there had been widespread agreement that this was a breach of convention, conventions are non-justiciable and the Constitution gives the Senate this power, so there is no legal sanction that could have been used against the Fraser opposition, or that could be used against any future opposition who wished to engage in similar actions. Similarly, although many experts (e.g. Winterton 2003: 234-5) regarded the actions of the New South Wales and Queensland parliaments as a breach of convention, there was no sanction that could be used against them. In addition, although there continues to be controversy over the governor-general's decision to dismiss Prime Minister Whitlam, the dominant view is that the governor-general acted prematurely in dismissing the prime minister but not unconstitutionally (see Kelly 1995: 290–306 and Winterton 2003: 243–8; but cf. Smith 2013 for a dissenting view). Once again, the ambiguity surrounding the use of the reserve powers and the fact that conventions are non-justiciable meant that the governor-general's actions did not face legal censure.

However, it is important not to exaggerate the lasting impact of the 1975 crisis on the stability of the constitutional system. Although the dismissal generated outrage, ended Whitlam's prime ministership, and on many accounts hampered Fraser's effectiveness as prime minister, ultimately, the governmental and constitutional system was not irreparably damaged. An election was held, a new government was elected and Governor-General Kerr remained in his position until he resigned in 1977. Subsequent governors-general also placed great importance in rebuilding faith in the office of governor-general, and key figures within Labor embarked on a period of reflection that, on some accounts, helped set them up for the electoral success they enjoyed during the Hawke-Keating years (Kelly 1995: 309–12; Winterton 2003: 250–1). This exemplifies the virtue and the resilience of constitutional conventions, and the importance of having a strong culture of constitutionalism.

Constitutional crises are not phenomena that occur only in those systems that depend on conventions. What matters is whether constitutional disagreements can be resolved peacefully and democratically without causing fundamental, long-term damage to the system.

It is even possible that the Australian constitutional system is more stable now than it was in 1975 because although another constitutional crisis is a technical possibility (Winterton 2003: 251–2), there has been no genuine risk of the Senate blocking supply or of the government being dismissed by the governor-general in the four decades since Prime Minister Whitlam's dismissal. In fact, the experience of the 1975 crisis might actually have reduced the likelihood of a similar crisis occurring because it helped to resolve some dimensions of the Australian constitutional system that were previously untested. It starkly illustrated that the Senate does have the power to block supply and that the governor-general does have the power to dismiss the prime minister. It is hard to imagine any future prime minister sharing Whitlam's apparent sense of assurance that the governor-general would not act in this way. Successive generations of politicians appear to have learned the lessons of the crisis and have modified their behaviour and their expectations accordingly. Thus, in a sense, developments since 1975 illustrate the advantages of having the flexibility associated with a system that is based heavily on constitutional conventions. But perhaps more importantly, the crisis served to finally expose the latent tensions bubbling within the sub-structure of the Australian Constitution, while helping to resolve those unsettled points of issue that exist within the written text (Foley 1989: 9–10).

Conclusion

The constitutional crisis was in every respect the perfect storm. The events that transpired in the final three months that led to the Government's dismissal in 1975 very clearly underlined the challenges facing a constitutional system that relies heavily on constitutional conventions. While the integrity of the constitutional system remained intact, the crisis did leave a lasting imprint. Aspects of the relationship between conventions and law that had long been acknowledged by lawmakers and constitutional scholars as problematic were clarified. At a minimum, the crisis made very plain that interventions in the constitutional rules carry penalties for all concerned, even for those who ostensibly emerge triumphant.

To date, the only constitutional amendment that occurred as a result of the 1975 crisis was the amendment codifying the convention surrounding the replacement of Senate casual vacancies. The issue was discussed at the October 1976 Constitutional Convention, held in Hobart, and the Fraser government held a referendum on the amendment in 1977 (along with three other constitutional amendments which were considered simultaneously) (Williams and Hume 2010: 154). The *Constitution Amendment (Senate Casual Vacancies) Bill* passed through Parliament largely unopposed, and the proposal was passed at a referendum with a majority in all six states, and 73.3 per cent of the nation-wide vote. Even then, the subsequent entrenchment of the principle of filling vacancies from the same political party did not solve the problem of politicking in relation to the replacement of senators in every case. State parliaments adapted to the changed constitutional realities by failing to select replacements or delaying the appointment of new senators when it suited their political purposes to do so.

In the wake of 1975, there were also calls for other constitutional reforms. For example, the Labor party argued for constitutional reform to remove the Senate's power to block supply, to prevent a repeat of the 1975 crisis (Kelly 1995: 312; see also Sawer 1983: 100). This amendment has never been put to referendum, partly because Labor feared that it would not win sufficient support. Supporters of the Senate have also criticised this proposal on the grounds that it could be manipulated by governments. Labor no longer campaigns actively for this reform, although it does occasionally resurface (Australian Broadcasting Corporation 2003). The most controversial reform proposal was to codify the relationship between the governor-general and the prime minister, including the reserve powers which were exercised in 1975 (Sharman 1998; Ward 2000).

However, at the national level, there has been little sustained interest from politicians in codifying these conventions. Between 1973 and 1985 a series of constitutional conventions were held in order to build bipartisan support for constitutional reform, and eighteen constitutional conventions were eventually 'recognised and declared' in 1985. However, the most controversial proposals pertaining to the power of the governor-general over ministers failed. Moreover, there was no statement in support of incorporating these conventions into the formal constitution beyond a resolution that entrenchment 'might eventually' follow (Sampford and Wood 1987: 233–5).

Four main reasons explain this reluctance to entrench conventions. First, there are logistical and practical hurdles in formulating a form of words that adequately capture the full extent of the meaning of a convention, and difficulties enacting it through the constitutional amendment process required by s. 128. Second, and notwithstanding the events of 1975, there is a widely held view that constitutional conventions are only marginally more uncertain than the formal constitutional rules, and so instances of instability arising from their contestation are generally rare (Cooray 1979: 76–7). Third, there is little political will for entrenchment among lawmakers because it would mean having to surrender their interpretative discretion over such matters if conventions are entrenched.

The fourth reason, and possibly the most compelling of them all, is that entrenchment is not considered to be a morally desirable option by political elites. Successive generations of parliamentarians in Australia have shared a normative commitment to a constitutional order that rests on both written and unwritten pillars. Despite the shock of the 1975 constitutional crisis, this preference for a mixed constitutional system seems unlikely to change in the near future.

References

Archer, Jeffrey R. and Maddox, Graham 1976. 'The 1975 Constitutional Crisis in Australia'. *Journal of Commonwealth and Comparative Politics*, 14 (2): 141–57.

Australian Broadcasting Corporation 2003. 'PM Releases Senate Reform Proposals'. 8 October. www.abc.net.au/news/2003-10-08/pm-releases-senate-reform-proposals/1489962 (accessed 18 July 2014).

Cooray, Leonard J. M. 1979. *Conventions, the Australian Constitution and the Future*. Sydney: Legal books.

Dicey, Albert V. 1897. *Introduction to the Study of the Law of the Constitution*, 5th edition. London: Macmillan and Co.

Foley, Michael 1989. *The Silences of Constitutions: Gaps, 'Abeyances' and Political Temperament in the Maintenance of Government*. London: Routledge.

Forsey, Eugene A. 1984. 'Courts and the Conventions of the Constitution'. *University of New Brunswick Law Journal*, 33: 11–42.

Heard, Andrew D. 1989. 'Recognizing the Variety among Constitutional Conventions'. *Canadian Journal of Political Science*, 22 (1): 63–82.

Jennings, W. Ivor 1938. *The Law and the Constitution*. London University Press.

Kelly, Paul 1995. *November 1975: The Inside Story of Australia's Greatest Political Crisis*. Sydney: Allen and Unwin.

Kerr, John 1975. 'Statement by the Governor-General, 11 November 1975'. In H. Mayer and H. Nelson (eds.), *Australian Politics: A Fourth Reader*. Melbourne: Cheshire.

Kerr, John 1978. *Matters for Judgement*. Melbourne: Macmillan.

Killey, Ian 2009. *Constitutional Conventions in Australia: An Introduction to the Unwritten Rules of Australia's Constitutions*. North Melbourne: Australian Scholarly Publishing.

Maley, William 1985. 'Laws and Conventions Revisited'. *The Modern Law Review*, 48: 121–39.

Marshall, Geoffrey 1984. *Constitutional Conventions: The Rules and Forms of Political Accountability*. Oxford: Clarendon Press.

Marshall, Geoffrey 1985. 'What Are Constitutional Conventions?' *Parliamentary Affairs, 38* (1): 33–9.

Quick, John and Garran, Robert 1901. *The Annotated Constitution of the Australian Commonwealth*. Sydney: Legal Books.

Rydon, Joan 1976. 'Casual Vacancies in the Australian Senate'. *Politics*, 11 (2): 195–204.

Sampford, Charles 1987. 'Recognise and Declare: An Australian Experiment in Codifying Constitutional Conventions'. *Oxford Journal of Legal Studies*, 7 (3): 369–420.

Sampford, Charles and Wood, David 1987. 'Codification of Constitutional Conventions in Australia'. *Public Law*, 137: 231–44.

Sawer, Geoffrey 1977. *Federation under Strain, Australia 1972–1975*. Melbourne University Press.

Sawer, Geoffrey 1983. 'The Constitutional Crisis of Australian Federalism'. In Allan Patience and Jeffrey Scott (eds.), *Australian Federalism: Future Tense*. Melbourne: Oxford University Press.

Sharman, Campbell 1998. 'Over Powered and Under Legitimized: Redesigning the Australian Head of State'. In Andrew Murray (ed.), *Trusting the People: An Elected President for an Australian Republic*. Cottesloe: Optima Press.

Sirota, L. 2011. 'Towards a Jurisprudence of Constitutional Conventions'. *Oxford University Commonwealth Law Journal*, 11 (1): 29–51.

Smith, David 2013. 'Labor's Selective Constitutional Conventions'. *Quadrant*, 57 (5): 71–4.

Waldron, Jeremy 1990. *The Law*. London: Routledge.

Ward, Alan J. 2000. 'Trapped in a Constitution: The Australian Republic Debate'. *Australian Journal of Political Science*, 35 (1): 117–23.

Wheare, Kenneth C. 1951. *Modern Constitutions*. London: Oxford University Press.

Whitlam, E. Gough 1979. *The Truth of the Matter*. Ringwood: Penguin.

Williams, George and Hume, David 2010. *People Power: The History and Future of the Referendum in Australia*. Sydney: University of New South Wales Press.

Winterton, George 2003. '1975: The Dismissal of the Whitlam Government'. In Hoong Phun Lee and George Winterton (eds.), *Australia's Constitutional Landmarks*. Melbourne: Cambridge University Press.

12

New Zealand

GRANT DUNCAN

New Zealand lacks a supreme legal document called 'the Constitution of New Zealand' with a capital *C*. The 1840 Treaty of Waitangi permitted, but did not constitute, the Crown's government of the embryonic colony. The institution of responsible government was originally achieved by an Act of the UK Parliament, the Constitution of New Zealand Act 1852. In 1947 New Zealand ratified the Statute of Westminster 1931 and the UK Parliament granted to the New Zealand General Assembly full powers to amend the 1852 Constitution Act. The New Zealand Parliament then used those powers to abolish its own upper house in 1950, and it has remained unicameral ever since. More recently, the Constitution Act 1986 'revoked the continuing application of the 1852 Act but preserved intact Parliament's plenary powers of legislation' (Joseph 2007: 115). The Constitution Act 1986 and the New Zealand Bill of Rights Act 1990 are not entrenched, however.

Having experienced no historical moment of federation or revolution that called compellingly for a founding or framing document to entrench legitimate powers and rights, New Zealand has 'muddled through' without a written over-arching constitution and without resolving many underlying problems. Recent public deliberation about adopting a written constitution wound up inconclusively (Constitutional Advisory Panel 2013). Most of the significant features of New Zealand's constitutional conventions, institutions and norms can be found written in various places, however, including the Letters Patent that appoint the governor-general, key Acts of Parliament, the Standing Orders of Parliament and the Cabinet Manual. But, taken all together, they are a constitutional 'work in progress'.

New Zealand has, moreover, adopted features that diverge radically from its Westminster 'cousins'. Since 1867, a separate Maori electoral roll and Maori parliamentary seats, of which there are now seven, have existed. And a mixed-member proportional (MMP) electoral system based upon the German model has been in operation since 1996.

Another innovation, the Cabinet Manual, has evolved over time and now describes and clarifies constitutional conventions. But this Manual has been re-edited and updated by successive governments to accommodate political pressures.

Sir Geoffrey Palmer sums up New Zealand's Constitution as: 'a "political" constitution in the sense that political developments shape it and change it on a continuing basis and there are few fixed principles' (Palmer 2013: 337).

Few fixed principles mean it is adaptable. The politics of managing minority and coalition governments under MMP has led to important adaptations to the principle of cabinet collective responsibility and greater stress upon caretaker conventions. But MMP may also have increased the risk that the governor-general may one day exercise reserve powers if a minority government should fail a vote of no confidence in the House of Representatives or an election produce a stalemate. To negotiate such terrain, political actors are (or ought to be) guided by conventions; and in turn, conventions are shaped and reshaped by the exigencies of political events and accommodations. To understand the evolution and observance of constitutional conventions, one needs to understand the political history and context. Developments in this small but innovative jurisdiction illustrate how conventions and politics are interwoven. An understanding of one requires an understanding of the other.

This study of constitutional conventions in New Zealand investigates and places in their political context the following issues:

- Mid-term crises of government and the avoidance of recourse to reserve powers;
- The clarification of caretaker conventions;
- The status of the Cabinet Manual;
- Exceptions to cabinet collective responsibility arising from the politics of MMP.

Constitutional conventions evolve because they serve a purpose for the orderly conduct of government. While the courts may recognise conventions as relevant to their decision making, conventions themselves are not enforceable in the courts. They may evolve by practice and repeated usage; they may be created by precedent or by agreement (Joseph 2007). Conventions are thus customary and often unwritten. Their recognition as conventions depends upon their being perceived by the actors involved and by informed observers as positive obligations or correct ways to proceed, necessary for the orderly conduct of government. The latter quality helps to distinguish constitutional conventions from other nonetheless important rules (such as those about ministerial travel expenses) upon which the constitutional order does not really depend. The aim of the following is to illustrate how political events have necessitated close observance of and changes to constitutional conventions in New Zealand. The driving force for both continuity and change has ultimately been the political parties' fear of voters' displeasure at the ballot-box.

> The main restriction upon the power of government in New Zealand is the state of public opinion rather than the presence of formal constraints upon the powers of government. (Palmer 2013: 338)

This eminently political motive has nonetheless led to stable government under sometimes trying circumstances.

Mid-term crises

So far, reserve powers have not been used in New Zealand to intervene in a mid-term or post-electoral crisis. On two occasions (1912 and 1998), however, political discord led to mid-term change of government (or, in 1998, change in the composition of government) without resort to fresh elections. These illustrate how the political actors resolved matters among themselves, *without* the need for vice-regal intervention.

Following the cliff-hanger election of 1911, incumbent Premier Sir Joseph Ward sought to prorogue parliament for more than six months in order to delay facing a no-confidence vote. The governor-general, Lord Islington, however, 'protested at the constitutional impropriety of retaining office for so long in such circumstances' (Hamer 1988: 342). According to Lord Islington's own account, he told Ward that, while the governor-general's duty is to be guided by the advice of the Executive, this is always conditional upon the confidence of the House, a matter about which no one had any definitive knowledge at the time. Hence there was no option but to reassemble parliament at the earliest opportunity in order to 'clear up the doubt' (Lord Islington, quoted by Bassett 1982: 6). The new parliament was duly assembled. The incumbent minority Liberal government won the inevitable no confidence vote in February 1912, on the casting vote of the Speaker; but, after a change of leader and the defection of several supporters, it was defeated in a second vote in July that year (Hamer 1988). A mid-term change of government was then effected, and without recourse to reserve powers. While the governor-general had 'protested' at the initial advice of the incumbent prime minister to prorogue parliament, he had not had to override his advice and use discretion. Nonetheless the threat of reserve powers (to refuse prorogation) was implicit in the governor-general's account of the post-electoral situation.

The period from 1911 till 1935 saw a three-party system (Liberal, Reform and Labour). Single-party minority (often supported by Independent members) and coalition majority governments were common. The minority government formed in the hung parliament after the 1928 election was only the most remarkable example. There was one instance (1912) of a complete change of government mid-term; and there were three occasions (1915, 1919 and 1931) when the party composition of government changed, but without threat to the continuity of government (Church 2000). Throughout this, it was in the parliament itself that governments were 'revealed, patched together, or sacked as the case may be' (Bassett 1982: 65). Reserve powers were not called for. Between the sweeping Labour victory of 1935 and the advent of MMP in 1996, however, New Zealand's voters and politicians had become accustomed to knowing (normally on election night) who had 'won' – meaning, which leader of which political party (Labour or National) would form the next majority government. MMP brought back uncertainty, as proportionality is unlikely to give a single party a majority in the House. Hence the conventions of government-formation and the role of the governor-general came under the spotlight for the first time in more than a generation.

The lengthy negotiations following the 1996 election tested the patience of the public, and required a steady hand from the governor-general of the day, Sir Michael Hardie Boys. But an agreement was reached in time for the first sitting of the new parliament, which, under Section 19 of the Constitution Act 1986, 'shall meet not later than 6 weeks after the day fixed for the return of the writs'. This date acted as 'an informal deadline' for the coalition negotiations (Hardie Boys 1997). During this bedding-in phase of MMP, Sir Michael made a number of public statements that clarified conventions of government-formation and the respective roles of elected politicians and the governor-general. Essentially nothing had changed since the decades of three-party politics. As long as it remains unclear in which direction the support of the majority of the House lies, the incumbent government remains in office in a caretaker capacity, and the negotiations among political parties proceed until 'a coalition (or . . . a minority government with support) identifies itself and its leader' (Quentin-Baxter, quoted in Hardie Boys 1997: 15). The outcome should be – and, through the public statements of political leaders, be seen to be – the responsibility of the democratically elected representatives. Once it is clear who commands the confidence of the House, the governor-general can swear in the new ministry.

Following the first MMP election in 1996, the upshot was a formal coalition government (with shared seats in cabinet) led by Jim Bolger of the National Party, with Winston Peters, leader of the New Zealand First Party, as deputy prime minister. Politically, this particular coalition came as a surprise, given that Peters had made statements before the election suggesting that he would not negotiate with Bolger as incumbent prime minister, and was committed to removing the National Party from office. Nevertheless, the National–NZ First Coalition depended heavily upon the working relationship between Bolger and Peters. But the National caucus replaced Bolger as leader and prime minister with Jenny Shipley in November 1997 in an effort 'to distance itself from coalition with [NZ First]' (Boston, Church and Pearse 2004: 588). The coalition itself broke down in August 1998.

On 12 August 1998, a government supply bill was passed, and so the Shipley government did not expect to face another vote of confidence until the following February. Conflict within the coalition came to a head that same day over the proposed sale of a state-owned asset, however, and the NZ First members walked out of the cabinet meeting called to consider the matter. According to the coalition agreement, that departure should have ended the meeting due to loss of a quorum; but the prime minister continued with the meeting, relying upon the convention, as described in the Cabinet Manual, that a quorum requires half the full membership of cabinet plus one. The prime minister had sought advice from the cabinet secretary and the solicitor-general that the Cabinet Manual, which states constitutional convention, is not over-ridden by a coalition agreement, and that the meeting was quorate even after the departure of members of the coalition partner. But the prime minister was breaching the political agreement that had constituted the coalition, and thus precipitating the coalition's demise. Subsequently, on 14 August, the government concluded the controversial asset-sale, and Mr Peters was sacked from cabinet on the grounds that he had breached cabinet unanimity by publicly criticising government policy. The following week, seven of NZ First's sixteen members of parliament resigned from their party, formed a new party and pledged their support to the recomposed National-led minority government. What remained of the NZ First Party went into opposition.[1] Prime Minister Shipley could rely upon the ACT Party and two other MPs to support the government on confidence, but she initially resisted calls for a confidence vote. On 30 August the composition of the new ministry was announced, and sworn in the next day. On 8 September, Shipley moved a vote of confidence in 'the National-led minority Government', and that was passed (Stockley 1999; Boston, Church and Pearse 2004).

Taken all together, these events saw a change of prime minister followed by the recomposition of a majority National–NZ First coalition into a minority National-led government with support. This mid-term change was achieved by the political actors concerned, and the governor-general – who no doubt had been observing events and public statements closely – was only called upon to conduct the normal duty of swearing in ministers. The government was not seriously challenged on confidence. A confidence vote was needed, however, to erase any doubt that the new ministry enjoyed the support of the House and that the governor-general was not without responsible advisers.

These events show that MMP may have increased the risk that the governor-general may one day need to exercise reserve powers if, for instance, a minority government should fail a no-confidence vote (with no obvious alternative leader in sight) or an election produce a stalemate in the House of Representatives. But they also illustrate how New Zealand's politicians have managed to avoid that. Still, the full set of possible outcomes had yet to be explored in political practice. Thus far, for instance, no governor-general has refused a prime minister's advice to dissolve parliament. It is not unusual for prime ministers to call early elections, as New Zealand does not have fixed election dates. Governors-general have accepted prime ministers' advice to dissolve the parliament early provided the government still enjoys, for the time being, the confidence of the House. Naturally, though, prime ministers normally seek early elections for *political* reasons. And a prime minister could advise dissolution in order to avert a no-confidence motion that the government lacks the numbers to defeat, seeing it as electorally advantageous to campaign early without the embarrassment of losing the House's confidence. If, however, an alternative administration that could command the majority of the House appeared to be waiting in the wings, this

[1] NZ First's behaviour cost it dearly at the polls, sinking from 13.4 per cent of the party vote in 1996 to 4.3 per cent in 1999.

would place the governor-general in a very difficult position indeed. And the Cabinet Manual provides no description of convention for guidance under these particular circumstances. To refuse the prime minister's advice on dissolution would force his or her resignation and precipitate either the change of administration or, failing that, a fresh election. Either way, the governor-general could be accused of intervening in political matters. A safe alternative would be for the governor-general to *defer* the request for dissolution, and place the matter back before the House for the political parties to resolve (Joseph 1998). The desire to hold office and the fear of eventual sanction at the ballot-box would conspire to force those parties within reach of an agreement to conclude one.

It is also possible that a new parliament may assemble (according to the statutory deadline) before there is any signed agreement to form a government. In that case, the incumbent prime minister would present the governor-general with the Speech from the Throne that explains to the House the reasons for its being summoned. The House would then assemble for the Address in Reply debate. Most probably, a motion that the government does not have the confidence of the House would immediately follow. If the incumbent government were defeated, 'it would be expected that the Prime Minister would resign or advise the Governor-General to dissolve Parliament so that a new election could be held' (McGee 2005: 146). A resignation may allow for an alternative coalition that can command the confidence of the House to come forward. Or, if no such credible alternative has yet emerged, a fresh election may be needed. There is a political imperative hanging over the parties to resolve matters well before this stage, however. To be seen by the public to have prevented the formation of a stable government and/or to have forced the country to return so soon to the polls would be electorally damaging to any political party.

The conventions of democratic government and the desire of parties to be seen to be acting responsibly (even if only to avoid punishment at the next election) oblige the political actors to settle differences and reach an arrangement without undue delay. New Zealand's historical record shows that, even under three-party politics and proportional representation, workable governing arrangements can be found.

Caretaker conventions

Caretaker conventions were forged when former Prime Minister Robert Muldoon was defeated in the 1984 election. In the face of significant speculative outflows of capital, Muldoon disagreed with officials about the need to devalue the dollar.[2] He wanted to dissuade the incoming government from doing so too. According to his biographer, immediately after the defeat at the polls, Muldoon 'found it difficult to come to terms with the fact that the decision [about devaluation] was no longer his to make. . .' (Gustafson 2000: 389). Muldoon stated on television the day after the election that he would not devalue 'so long as I'm Minister of Finance' (quoted in Gustafson 2000: 392). In the tense two days following this, the governor-general, Sir David Beattie, was kept informed. The deputy prime minister, Jim McLay, met with Mr Muldoon to persuade him to accept the advice of officials and the wishes of the incoming government, and to devalue the currency. In doing so, he invoked the 'caretaker' principle, and thus:

> McLay creatively conjured up a new constitutional convention that had not existed in New Zealand before, but for which there was some overseas support, particularly in Australia. He simply announced it. (Palmer 2013: 340)

If this had failed, McLay had a 'plan B':

> I would advise the Governor General that Muldoon no longer had the confidence of Cabinet, that he should be dismissed, that I should be appointed as Prime Minister for the few remaining days of the National administration, and that we'd undertake no new policies and would implement any wishes of the incoming Government. (Quoted in Young 2012)

To have dismissed the incumbent prime minister on the advice of his deputy, the governor-general could have relied upon the fact that Mr Muldoon no longer enjoyed the confidence of either the House of Representatives or his own cabinet colleagues. The use of reserve powers was averted, however, when Muldoon reluctantly agreed to implement the instructions of the incoming government on the Tuesday after the election.

These events 'highlighted some serious weaknesses in the New Zealand arrangements for the handover of power after the defeat of a government in an election' (Palmer 2004: 208). In reaction to this and other constitutional chicanery by Muldoon, the fourth Labour government introduced and passed the Constitution Act 1986. This Act sets out the basic

[2] Exchange rates at that time were fixed.

institutions of parliamentary government. Section 6 codifies one of the key conventions of responsible government: 'A person may be appointed and may hold office as a member of the Executive Council or as a Minister of the Crown only if that person is a member of Parliament.' The Act does not 'codify' the caretaker convention, but s. 6 does allude to it by providing that a minister may remain in office for up to twenty-eight days after losing his or her seat in an election.

Subsequent events have refined the practice of caretaker government in New Zealand. Immediately after the 1993 election, the outcome was unclear, and it required the counting of special votes to ascertain (eleven days later) whether or not the incumbent National administration would continue to govern. While the results remained unclear, the incumbent prime minister and cabinet, in accordance with convention, adopted a caretaker role – even though the result eventually went in their favour and they retained office.

Given this experience, and in anticipation of the first election under proportional representation in 1996, a revision of the Cabinet Manual included a section on caretaker government (McGrath 1999). As it happened, following the 1996 election, New Zealand experienced its longest-ever period of caretaker government, due to protracted coalition negotiations lasting eight weeks (Hardie Boys 1997). Since then, after six more MMP elections, politicians and public servants have acquired considerable experience of governing and managing in transitional situations under the caretaker conventions while the outcomes of negotiations to form a government are finalised. And the Cabinet Manual now contains general advice for ministers and public servants, including a statement of the convention itself:

> During such periods, the incumbent government is still the lawful executive authority, with all the powers and responsibilities that go with executive office. However, governments in this situation have traditionally constrained their actions until the political situation is resolved, in accordance with what is known as the convention on caretaker government (Cabinet Office 2008: 77–8).

Political considerations, and the fact that decisions must be made in the light of evolving circumstances, make it impossible to generate a complete set of rules in advance, and the Cabinet Manual does not attempt to do that. The post-electoral requirement for conditional restraint is governed by convention, not law, and so the limits observed on particular decisions are ultimately political, to be answered for in the House or 'tried in the court of public opinion'.

The resolution of the 1984 crisis set a precedent. Subsequent post-electoral events have seen successful political navigation of sometimes lengthy periods of uncertainty about government formation. And general principles of caretaker government are now clarified in the Cabinet Manual, a document to which we turn next.

The Cabinet Manual

The Cabinet Manual is an authoritative, but not prescriptive, guide that provides clarity in moments of political flux as it sets out clear descriptions of the key constitutional conventions observed in New Zealand. It includes descriptions of and advice about reserve powers, government-formation, caretaker governments, relations between ministers and public servants, general ministerial conduct and more. It is readily available, and so it also provides clarity for the public. The Manual is commonly seen as an authoritative statement of the sources of New Zealand's constitution and the best practical guide to the conduct of executive government (Constitutional Arrangements Committee 2005; Palmer 2006b), but its constitutional status has attracted little academic inquiry (McLeay 1999). The development of a similar Manual in the United Kingdom, by contrast, led to parliamentary inquiries by both Houses (2011 HC 734; 2011 HL 107) and to wider debate and academic inquiry (Blick and Hennessy 2011; Blick 2014). Concerns were raised as to whether putting constitutional conventions into writing (even though this is well short of legal codification) would run the risk of consolidating biased interpretations of conventions, or possibly hindering their 'natural' evolution. Moreover, would such a Manual unduly hinder ministerial action?

The fact that the New Zealand Cabinet Manual is regularly updated and changed with the approval of the cabinet allows for pragmatic and prompt adaptation to changing circumstances or norms. The adaptations made around cabinet collective responsibility are the best example (described below). The Cabinet Manual is considered to be a 'descriptive' guide that follows, rather than leads, accepted practices, and not a prescriptive codification of conventions. It is described as 'not law' (Palmer 2006a: 3), and neither is its production required by law. It is not tabled in the House of Representatives. As it has served the purposes of governments of both the left and the right, its existence and contents have not become objects of political controversy. As described in its own preface, it is adopted by a new government at the first meeting of the cabinet. But because of that now routine adoption, I argue, New Zealand's Cabinet Manual has created at least one new constitutional convention: that, by convention, each new government moves, at the first meeting of its cabinet, to adopt the Cabinet Manual as its operating guidelines. This may seem at first a trivial, even tautological, assertion. But a failure or refusal to adopt the Manual could be due to incompetence or unintentional omission, or it could be deliberate. If the latter, it could mean that the prime minister prefers a new set of rules, or wishes to go back to the 'unwritten' practices of the past. In theory, the Cabinet Manual is only a description of constitutional conventions, and hence a failure or refusal by a new government to endorse it does not mean that conventions are nullified or changed in any way. As McLeay puts it, 'it is the conventions that help stamp authority on the *Manual*, rather than the other way around' (McLeay 1999: 15, original italics). But, if the Cabinet Manual were ignored or discarded as the government's official guidelines, there would be, at the very least, a period of uncertainty for the senior public service. One can only speculate about this, though, because no government so far has declined or failed to endorse the Manual. And the very fact that this has not happened suggests that not to do so is almost unthinkable due to the Manual's central role in government-formation and the functioning of the executive – and hence that the adoption of the Cabinet Manual has in itself achieved the status of a constitutional convention in New Zealand.

Moreover, due to the uncertainties created around government-formation by the advent of MMP, the Cabinet Manual has boldly included statements about reserve powers. It both describes reserve powers and interprets their scope: 'In only a very few cases may the Governor-General exercise a degree of personal discretion, under what are known as the "reserve powers". Even then, convention usually dictates what decision should be taken' (Cabinet Office 2008: 9).

Reserve powers are thus a rarely used vice-regal discretion, normally constrained by conventions. One of those conventions is that the governor-general 'avoids becoming involved in the party politics of government' (Cabinet Office 2008: 8). Another is that, in appointing the prime minister, the governor-general is required to 'act on the outcome of the electoral process and subsequent discussions between political parties [. . . and] the political process by which the individual who will lead the government as Prime Minister is identified' (Cabinet Office 2008: 17–18). While a prime minister-designate is not yet sworn in as a 'responsible adviser' to the governor-general, his or her appointment is in effect an exercise of reserve powers. But this is hedged in by constitutional convention, partly to ensure that political events do not compromise the governor-general's constitutional role.

Political uncertainty arising from MMP in New Zealand, and the lack of a written constitution to spell out matters such as the appointment of the prime minister, have led to clarifications in the Cabinet Manual. Even if governors-general are perfectly well versed in the conventions and do not need the Manual to guide them, the existence of these guidelines is nonetheless useful for clarity among political circles and in the media. As will be seen in the following section, moreover, the Manual has proven to be easily amended in response to the political pressures of managing coalition and minority governments, and this has facilitated adaptations of some key conventions as need has arisen.

Cabinet collective responsibility

The convention of cabinet unanimity is integral to responsible government. The governor-general in Council and the House of Representatives need to feel assured that policy statements made by a minister represent the position of the government. But this convention has been significantly modified in New Zealand to accommodate the political imperatives of multi-party governance arrangements brought about by MMP since 1996. The break-up of the National–New Zealand First Coalition in 1998 (related above) was partly fuelled by accusations of breaches of cabinet collective responsibility. Winston Peters, the leader of NZ First, had publicly expressed strong objections to the disputed asset-sale, and had even proposed voting for legislation that would overturn the government's decision to sell. This blatant breach of cabinet unanimity gave the prime minister cause to sack him (Stockley 1999).

The election of 1999 led to a change to a Labour–Alliance coalition government, led by Prime Minister Helen Clark, leader of the Labour Party, with deputy prime minister Jim Anderton, leader of the Alliance Party. The two leaders signed an admirably clear and brief coalition agreement that concentrated on inter-party processes rather than detailed policy commitments. The agreement affirmed that cabinet decisions would be made by consensus and that, subject to provisions within the agreement, cabinet collective responsibility would be observed. A key provision recognised that occasionally there would arise a policy issue that would trigger a political concern for 'party distinction'. The agreement then allowed for one party (in practice the smaller party, the Alliance) to express publicly a differing view, without this being regarded as a breach of collective responsibility. Such issues, as they arose, would need first to be put to the coalition management committee. Moreover, the two parties would still accept joint responsibility for actions taken as a government. And the Cabinet Manual was subsequently amended to reflect this new adaptation of the long-standing convention. The coalition crisis of 1998 had proven that the Manual, as a description of constitutional convention, took precedence over a political coalition agreement. Hence it was practical to amend the Manual to reflect this new approach to managing the political pressures that can arise within a coalition government.

The subsequent two elections (2002, 2005) led to the formation of Labour-led minority governments. These governments relied upon agreements with minor parties guaranteeing support on confidence and supply votes, rather than formal coalitions with shared seats in cabinet. Senior members of these minor supporting parties did, however, gain ministerial portfolios outside of cabinet. This led to a further variation in the convention of collective responsibility. In these cases, the ministers outside cabinet are bound by collective responsibility only in respect of matters within their portfolios, and of course on matters of confidence and supply. Unless there is a working agreement on a particular issue that requires the minor party's support, matters outside of those areas are open to disagreement and party-political differentiation (White 2005). These exemptions were first formalised in post-electoral political agreements and, in due course, appropriate amendments were made to the Cabinet Manual (Cabinet Office 2008).

New Zealand's political leaders learned a lot from the breakdown of the National–NZ First coalition in 1998. In forming the next government in 1999, Clark and Anderton took a completely different approach, based upon flexible management of the relationship between the political parties, rather than the legalistic and policy-driven agreement of the previous coalition. The 'agree to disagree' provisions in the coalition and 'supply and confidence' agreements established under Helen Clark's prime-ministership allowed supporting parties to express views differing from the government of the day in order to preserve their party-political identities. They act as a political 'pressure valve' for a minor coalition party that fears losing support due to a divisive policy. The National-led government that took office in late 2008 subsequently endorsed the revised Cabinet Manual – as is the convention – thus effectively endorsing the innovations formalised under Helen Clark. The National Party utilised the exemption to unanimity in its own confidence and supply agreements with three minor supporting parties, thus embedding it as a modification to the convention. It is now common to hear a portfolio-holding leader of one of the supporting parties speak critically of a government policy or vote against a government bill. Hence, we can observe how political events, the pressures they create for adaptation and the need to document new approaches have acted over time to modify a constitutional convention of critical importance to the smooth conduct of government.

Conclusion

Observing political change and the formation of durable governments shows us how constitutional conventions have evolved in New Zealand. Some conventions have not changed over the course of a century – particularly the basic convention that the governor-general will appoint as prime minister the individual who leads the party, or coalition of parties, that commands the confidence of the House of Representatives. In contrast, the shift to MMP led to significant relaxation of the formerly strictly observed convention of cabinet collective responsibility. Amidst all of this, New Zealand's Cabinet Manual has gradually evolved into an indispensible and authoritative guide that clarifies conventions and guides ministerial and cabinet conduct. These continuities and developments in constitutional convention are not fully grasped if they are viewed as the unwritten norms of a constitutional monarchy, or as if they were the written law's 'other'. One must understand the messy political context. New Zealand's relatively brief history has seen it evolve rapidly from colony to independent nation, while retaining the constitutional monarchy. It took a radical departure from the Westminster model by adopting the German system of proportional representation. But, as in the complicated three-party politics of the early twentieth century, the political actors and assembled parliaments successfully formed, supported and terminated governments. Governors-general have not had to get their hands dirty with politics. And 'Kiwi pragmatism' has permitted adaptation and extra-legal codification of constitutional conventions.

References

Bassett, Michael 1982. *Three Party Politics in New Zealand, 1911–1931*. Auckland: Historical Publications.

Blick, Andrew 2014. 'The Cabinet Manual and the Codification of Conventions'. *Parliamentary Affairs* 67, no. 1: 191–208.

Blick, Andrew and Hennessy, P. 2011. *The Hidden Wiring Emerges: The Cabinet Manual and the Working of the British Constitution*. London: Institute for Public Policy Research.

Boston, Jonathan, Church, Stephen and Pearse, Hilary 2004. 'Explaining the Demise of the National–New Zealand First Coalition'. *Australian Journal of Political Science* 39, no. 3: 585–603.

Cabinet Office 2008. *Cabinet Manual*. Wellington: Cabinet Office, Department of the Prime Minister and Cabinet.

Church, Stephen 2000. 'Assessing Stability in New Zealand's First Era of Multi-party Politics, 1911–1935'. *Political Science* 52, no. 1: 22–40.

Constitutional Advisory Panel 2013. *New Zealand's Constitution: A Report on a Conversation*. Wellington: New Zealand Government. www.ourconstitution.org.nz/The-Report (accessed April 1, 2015).

Constitutional Arrangements Committee 2005. *Inquiry to Review New Zealand's Existing Constitutional Arrangements: Report of the Constitutional Arrangements Committee*. Wellington: House of Representatives.

Gustafson, Barry 2000. *His Way: A Biography of Robert Muldoon*. Auckland University Press.

Hamer, David 1988. *The New Zealand Liberals: The Years of Power, 1891–1912*. Auckland University Press.

Hardie Boys, Michael 1997. 'Continuity and Change: The 1996 General Election and the Role of the Governor-General'. *Waikato Law Review* 5: 1–16. www.waikato.ac.nz/law/research/waikato_law_review/volume_5_1997 (accessed April 1, 2015).

Joseph, Philip A. 1998. 'Commentary'. In *The Constitutional Implications of MMP*, by Alan Simpson, 121–8. School of Political Science and International Relations, Victoria University of Wellington.

Joseph, Philip A. 2007. *Constitutional and Administrative Law in New Zealand*. Wellington: Brookers.

McGee, David 2005. *Parliamentary Practice in New Zealand*. Wellington: Dunmore.

McGrath, John 1999. 'The Harkness Henry Lecture: The Crown, the Parliament and the Government'. *Waikato Law Review* 9: 1–22.

McLeay, Elizabeth 1999. 'What Is the Constitutional Status of the New Zealand Cabinet Office Manual?' *Public Law Review* 10, no. 1: 11–17.

Palmer, Geoffrey 2004. 'Muldoon and the Constitution'. In *Muldoon Revisited*, by Margaret Clark, 167–214. Palmerston North: Dunmore Press.

Palmer, Geoffrey 2006a. 'The Cabinet, the Prime Minister and the Constitution'. *New Zealand Journal of Public and International Law* 4: 1–36.

Palmer, Geoffrey 2006b. 'The New Zealand Constitution and the Power of Courts'. *Transnational Law and Contemporary Problems* 15, Spring: 551–77.

Palmer, Geoffrey 2013. *Reform: A Memoir*. Wellington: Victoria University Press.

Stockley, Andrew P. 1999. 'Constitutional Law', *New Zealand Law Review*, no. 2: 173–90.

United Kingdom Political and Constitutional Reform Committee 2011. *Constitutional Implications of the Cabinet Manual: Sixth Report of Session 2010–11*. London: House of Commons, HC 734.

United Kingdom Select Committee on the Constitution 2011. *The Cabinet Manual: 12th Report of Session 2010–11*. London: House of Lords, HL 107.

White, Nicola 2005. 'Deconstructing Cabinet Collective Responsibility'. *Policy Quarterly* 1, no. 4: 4–11.

Young, Audrey 2012. 'McLay: My Plan to Replace Muldoon'. *New Zealand Herald*. www.nzherald.co.nz/news/print.cfm?objectid=10830093&pnum=1 (accessed November 7, 2013).

13

Codifying conventions

PETER H. RUSSELL

Practices, principles and rules that are not inscribed in any court-enforceable legal instrument have long been a vital component of the Constitution of the United Kingdom and countries that derive their parliamentary systems of government from the British Westminster model. This component of these countries' constitutions is usually referred to as the 'unwritten conventions' of the constitution.

In recent times there has been a movement to produce an authoritative written version of much of this informal part of the constitution. This movement has led to the production of cabinet manuals in New Zealand and the United Kingdom, and stimulated interest in doing something the same in Australia and Canada. These projects constitute what is spoken of as 'codification of constitutional conventions'.

Why now?

The question arises of why after getting along for so long without 'codifying' constitutional conventions is there an interest in doing so now? In Australia and Canada, political crises arising out of disputed uses of the reserve powers of the Crown were the immediate stimulus of efforts at clarifying constitutional conventions in some authoritative written form.

In Australia, the controversy aroused by Governor-General Kerr's dismissal of Prime Minister Whitlam in 1975 stimulated interest in writing down many of the constitutional conventions relating to the parliamentary-cabinet system of government. The Constitutional Convention, a State/Commonwealth series of meetings dealing with various proposals to reform the Australian Constitution, at sessions in 1983 and 1985, 'recognized and declared' forty-two constitutional conventions (Russell 1988). But the written formulation of these conventions did not have the support of all delegates and did not become accepted by commonwealth or state governments as an authoritative statement of constitutional conventions. It is also important to note that it did not deal with the central issue of the 1975 crisis – the governor-general's power to dismiss the prime minister.

In Canada, a parliamentary crisis occurred in December 2008 when the governor-general acceded to Prime Minister Harper's request to prorogue parliament in order to avoid a vote of no confidence that appeared to have the support of a coalition of opposition parties who had a majority of seats in the House of Commons. Not only was there deep controversy over the convention governing prorogation, but further over whether, if the recently elected minority Conservative Government were defeated on a confidence vote, it had the right to call a new election. These disputes over constitutional conventions prompted the author of this paper to suggest that 'the time has come to bring those spooky unwritten constitutional conventions down from the attic of our collective memory and try to see if we can pin them down in a manner that is politically consensual and popularly accessible' (Russell and Sossin 2009: 136–49).

In the United Kingdom, it was the anticipation of the 2010 general election resulting in a 'hung parliament' that triggered efforts to produce a cabinet manual similar to New Zealand's (UK Cabinet Office 2010). The main concern was uncertainty about the roles of party leaders, the Crown and the public service in the formation of government process following an election in which no party held a majority of seats in the House of Commons (Hazell and Paun 2009).

The first edition of New Zealand's *Cabinet Manual* emerged quietly in 1979 as 'a consolidation of the rules, procedures and conventions of Cabinet' (New Zealand Cabinet Office 2008). It was not until 1996 that it became available to the public. By then it would seem to have grown considerably beyond cabinet procedures, for it is frequently cited as playing a useful role in providing the public and politicians with guidelines as to the process of government formation following an election giving no party a parliamentary majority – a virtually certain election outcome following New Zealand's adoption of proportional representation in 1994. Thus, while the creation of New Zealand's Cabinet Manual had nothing to do with a constitutional crisis, real or apprehended, the existence of the manual with its politically consensual guidelines on government formation may well have prevented constitutional crises occurring in New Zealand.

A major source of the concern about avoiding constitutional crises is an important change in the party structure of the Westminster countries and indeed of most western democracies. As the editors of this volume point out in their introduction, the vote share of the two largest parties in each of the Westminster countries has decreased by between fifteen and thirty-five per cent. Two-party systems have given way to multi-party systems in which the prospect of any party winning a majority of seats in the elected house of parliament has significantly declined. This is the case even in Canada and the United Kingdom, which still use first-past-the-post simple plurality electoral systems. The usefulness of New Zealand's Cabinet Manual in providing guidelines on the process of government formation following elections resulting in hung parliaments has stimulated UK and Canadian interest in developing cabinet manuals for their countries.

The 2010 federal election in Australia produced a House of Representatives in which the governing Labor Party and the opposition Liberal/National Coalition held an equal number of seats, with a handful of independents holding the balance of power – Australia's first hung parliament in a great many years. Although there was no constitutional crisis, it took three weeks of political bargaining to establish that there would be sufficient support in the House for Labor to carry on as a minority government. The experience, added to questionable interventions of state governors in post-election efforts at forming governments, may have revived Australian interest in clarifying constitutional conventions (Twomey 1985).

There is a larger reason for considering the provision of an authoritative written text on some of the matters that heretofore have been in the realm of 'unwritten conventions'. This is the deep societal change in the character of the electorates that has taken place in the Westminster countries since the days when eminent Victorians such as Walter Bagehot and A.V. Dicey wrote so clearly and confidently about the conventions of the constitution. In part, but only in part, this societal change is ethnic. The citizenry of all four Westminster is becoming extraordinarily diverse. Nearly 50% of the residents of Toronto, Canada's largest city, where I live, were born outside Canada, most of them in countries that did not practice Westminster-style parliamentary democracy. In the citizenship orientation they undergo there is no document that can answer a question as basic as explaining how Canadians determine who will be prime minister of the country.

But the societal change I refer to is much deeper than the growing diversity of our citizens' ethnic backgrounds. Unlike the propertied male electorates of Bagehot's and Dicey's time, the electorates of the

Westminster countries today are mass electorates, most of whose members have virtually no schooling in the traditions and practices of parliamentary government. The problem may be compounded in Canada by the proximity of the United States and the extent to which accounts of its presidential/congressional system dominate the popular news and entertainment media. I am frequently asked by members of my own generation to explain the difference between the American and Canadian systems of government. To believe that the citizens of today's parliamentary democracies carry around in their heads a knowledge of the conventions of parliamentary and cabinet government is to believe in fairy tales. For the citizens of a democracy to not know the rules and principles by which the most powerful institutions of government are supposed to operate, and further, for them not to have a convenient and authoritative source to turn to for information about these matters, is to have a serious democratic deficit. Reducing that deficit could be the most important benefit of 'codifying' constitutional conventions.

That may well be the most important lesson to take from the Canadian experience. It was the constitutional crisis arising out of Prime Minister Stephen Harper's advice to Governor-General Michäelle Jean to prorogue Parliament that provoked Canadian interest in 'codifying' constitutional conventions. However, it turns out that a codification of constitutional convention is not likely to provide a satisfactory solution to regulating prorogation. The larger civic education rationale may be the best reason for attempting something like a cabinet manual in Canada – even if it cannot settle the disagreement that sparked interest in the project.

Canada's prorogation crisis

On Thursday, 4 December 2008, millions of Canadians watched a gripping political drama play out in their nation's capital as, glued to their electronic viewing devices, they saw Conservative Prime Minister Stephen Harper wade through throngs of journalists and TV cameras to enter Rideau Hall, the residence of Governor-General Michäelle Jean (Valpy 2009). Three days earlier, on Monday, 1 December, leaders of the three opposition parties had unveiled a formal written accord setting out plans for a minority coalition government between the Liberal and New Democratic Party (NDP). Led by Liberal leader Stéphane Dion, it was agreed that, with the support of the Bloc Quebecois, it would govern until 30 June 2011. The opposition parties had been provoked to do this by the Harper government's sudden announcement of plans to remove women's rights to seek pay equity and the right of federal public-sector unions to strike. These measures were included in the minister of finance's 27 November fiscal update statement, in effect a mini-budget. There had been no mention of them a week earlier in the Throne Speech when the government met parliament, to avoid defeat on a no-confidence vote five weeks after the 15 October federal election. The opposition parties now seemed determined to defeat the Harper Conservatives and they had the votes to do so.

To counter that possibility Prime Minister Harper announced that he would ask the governor-general to prorogue parliament before it could vote on a no-confidence motion. It was with that purpose in mind that Harper took the short drive from his residence to Rideau Hall on that bitterly cold December morning.

Prorogation? What on earth is that? Canadians were now asking. Most of them were completely unfamiliar with the term. Prorogation was, however, a term familiar to parliamentarians. It is the way of ending a session of parliament without dissolving parliament and having an election. Its normal use is to end a session that has been running for a long time with most of its business done. After a break (often for the summer holiday period) a new session opens with a Throne Speech setting out a new government agenda. The circumstances under which Mr Harper was advising a dissolution were totally different. A newly elected parliament had just begun its first session. Prorogation was being sought by the government to escape a vote of no confidence.

To find anything like this use of prorogation historians had to go back to 1873 when Canada's first prime minister, Sir John A. Macdonald, requested prorogation in order to halt the work of a parliamentary committee investigating his party's improper acceptance of campaign funds. Lord Dufferin, the governor-general, granted the dissolution, reluctantly, but set a strict two-month limit on it (Gwyn 2011: 244–6).

Now Canadians also discovered – and for many this would be a revelation – that legally the power to prorogue lay with the Crown, and that many years earlier Canada's governor-general had been authorised to exercise the Crown's power to summon, dissolve and prorogue the Canadian Parliament. This immediately provoked two questions: Can the governor-general say 'no' to such a request from a prime minister? Should the governor-general say 'no'? These were the questions the nation pondered for the two and half hours the prime minister met with the governor-general.

When Prime Minister Harper finally emerged from Rideau Hall, he told the mob of journalists, and through them the nation, that the governor-general had agreed to prorogue parliament but on condition that a new session of parliament would begin on 26 January 2009 just ten days after the normal Christmas season recess, and that when it opened his government would submit immediately to a vote of confidence regarding a budget designed to be palatable to at least the Liberals, the official opposition. That is indeed how events unfolded. When the new session of parliament opened on 26 January 2009, the Harper government introduced a budget significantly revamped from the Finance Minister's earlier mini-budget to win the support of the Liberals.

The political crisis was over, but the constitutional debate had just begun. Most constitutional scholars agreed that the governor-general could have said 'no'. The debate was over whether Madame Jean should have declined the prime minister's advice to prorogue parliament (Russell and Sossin 2009). A number of respected constitutionalists argued that granting prorogation, with a no-confidence motion pending that would likely carry, was a denial of responsible government. Others considered that the prime minister's willingness to submit his government to a confidence test a few days after the usual seasonal break meant that the confidence principle was not seriously breached. Besides considerations of principle, the governor-general's defenders thought it appropriate for the vice-regal officer in exercising her discretion to take into account the political crisis that would likely occur if the governor-general swore in a controversial coalition government (Harper's ministers were branding such an eventuality a *coup d'etat*) and the serious consequences for the Canadian economy if such a political crisis occurred at a time when Canada was grappling with the worst international fiscal crisis since the Great Depression. The debate continues to this day.

The one thing that was – and is – clear is that there is no consensus among the political players, the constitutional experts or the people on what considerations, if any, would justify the governor-general's refusing a prime minister's request for prorogation.

Lack of agreement on the Crown's power of dissolution

The prorogation crisis sparked debate on the proper use of another of the Crown's reserve powers – the power to dissolve parliament. When Prime Minister Harper was first confronted with the possibility of his government's defeat on a no-confidence motion being followed by Liberal leader

Dion being sworn in by the governor-general as prime minister of a Liberal/NDP coalition government, he stated that:

> Liberal leader Stéphane Dion does not have the right to take power without an election. Canada's government should be decided by Canadians, not backroom deals (MacCharles et al. 2008).

This gave the impression that Mr Harper was of the view that a change of government could be effected only by the electorate giving an opposition party more seats than the governing party. Political scientist Tom Flanagan, at the time one of Mr Harper's closest advisers, in a widely read newspaper column, argued that in its arrangements for choosing the executive of the national government Canada should move beyond 'the antiquated machinery of responsible government' inherited from the pre-democratic age of the nineteenth century. This means, he argued, that 'the voters must have a meaningful voice in that decision'. In particular, a coalition government, such as the Liberals and NDP had planned to form, must be approved by the electorate before it could be sworn in by the governor-general (Flanagan 2009).

Whether Prime Minister Harper and his advisors believed that *any* change of government had to be approved by the electorate or only that a coalition had to be approved, it seemed to many constitutional observers that these were new rules that broke with established constitutional convention. Many – probably most – constitutional scholars continued to subscribe to the position that after an election, the right to form a government (coalition or unitary) depends on which party leader or leaders command the confidence of the newly elected parliament.

Who was right and who was wrong in this wrangling over the most important 'unwritten convention' of parliamentary government – the principle and rules relating to the formation of government – is less important than the fact that among the relevant political actors there was no agreement on 'unwritten convention' in this area. Lack of consensus about crucial aspects of parliamentary government was by no means confined to political elites. According to an Ipsos Read poll published in the midst of the crisis, fifty-one per cent of Canadians believed that the prime minister of Canada, is directly elected by the people (Ipsos 2008). One hopes that the other forty-nine per cent held to the belief that the elected house of parliament determines who will be prime minister.

These were the circumstances that provoked me to write the words cited above about the need to consider writing down in some authoritative way crucial conventions of parliamentary government, and to initiate a process for doing just that.

The search for consensus

The classical texts that have discussed the nature of constitutional conventions do not use the word 'consensus', though they imply that the effectiveness of conventions depends on their being accepted by those who are involved in operating the institutions of parliamentary government.

A.V. Dicey, for example, wrote that the conventions are one element of the constitution that 'consists of maxims or practices which, though they regulate the ordinary conduct of the Crown, of Ministers, and other persons under the constitution, are not in strictness laws at all' (Dicey 1961). Later on he refers to them as 'a body of constitutional or political ethics'.

Similarly, the test set out by Sir Ivor Jennings for identifying a constitutional convention, a test adopted by Canada's Supreme Court (1981), indicates the need for agreement among the relevant political actors. To identify a convention, Jennings wrote:

> We have to ask ourselves three questions: first, what are the precedents; secondly, did the actors in the precedents believe that they were bound by a rule: and thirdly, is there a reason for the rule? A single precedent with a good reason may be enough to establish the rule. A whole string of precedents without such a reason will be of no avail, unless it is perfectly certain that the persons concerned regarded them as bound by it. (Jennings 1959).

Jennings' statement draws our attention to the fragile nature of constitutional conventions. A rule based on constitutional convention works to regulate the politicians and officials operating the institutions of parliamentary government only when all concerned feel bound by the rule. If one key actor feels not bound by what others regard as the rule, the convention ceases to do its work, and in effect ceases to exist. This certainly could not be said about laws. A law, be it one based on legislation or a written constitution or the common law rulings of courts, does not lose its effectiveness simply because a person who appears to be bound by it no longer regards herself as so bound.

It was the apparently rule-less situation that so alarmed me when Canada's prime minister and his constitutional advisers, on the one hand, and the opposition parties and their constitutional advisers, on the other, seemed to disagree on the constitutional convention that should apply in forming a government following an election resulting in a hung parliament. As a person who is sometimes consulted by the governor-general on these matters, I felt it put the governor-general in an impossible position of being an umpire in a game in which the players did not agree on the rules. When I learned of the work that the Cabinet Manual did in New Zealand to provide acceptable guidelines for forming governments after elections in that country – elections that always produce hung parliaments – I grasped at the cabinet manual idea as a possible answer to Canada's situation. I published an article in the *National Journal of Constitutional Law* inviting my constitutional law colleagues to contact me if they thought the idea had merit and, if they did, what should be the first step towards developing a cabinet manual at the federal level in Canada (Russell 2010).

An academic/practitioner workshop

The response to my article was positive enough to organise a workshop on the subject that would bring together leading constitutional scholars, advisers of political party leaders and individuals with experience and ties to the Crown, cabinet and parliament. It was to be truly a workshop, not a conference. Instead of presenting papers, participants would work at the key issues with a view to exploring where consensus was possible and where it was not.

The workshop would focus on the question of whether it would be worth working towards a New Zealand–type cabinet manual in Canada. In considering that question, participants inevitably would discuss controversial matters related to important aspects of parliamentary/cabinet government that are governed by constitutional conventions. If a group such as this one were divided on these issues, there would not seem much point in moving ahead with the project of developing a Canadian Cabinet Manual.

The workshop was sponsored by the University of Toronto's Asper Centre for Constitutional Rights (Milne and Russell 2011). It took place for a day and half in February 2011. Eighteen of the twenty-six participants were leading scholars almost equally divided between political scientists and law professors. The advisors to political leaders covered all five parliamentary parties, including Conservative Tom Flanagan. A former Clerk of the Privy Council, the Law Clerk and Parliamentary

Counsel and a representative of the governor-general's office completed the Canadian contingent. Robert Hazell, the UK constitutional scholar who played a leading role in initiating the Cabinet Manual project in the United Kingdom, gave a public lecture preceding the workshop on the role the Manual played in providing guidelines to the media, the public and the politicians on the process of forming a coalition government after the May 2010 election.

To ensure candour among the participants, the workshop was not open to the public. But the co-chairs, Professor Cheryl Milne and myself, published an account of the workshop and its conclusions approved by all participants. It is an indication of the extent of consensus among this knowledgeable and multi-partisan group on difficult issues concerning constitutional conventions. The workshop participants agreed that, in an era when hung parliaments may frequently be the outcome of elections, 'There would be much less risk of a parliamentary crisis following an election in which the result is not clear if there were an authoritative set of guidelines such as New Zealand and the UK now have in their Cabinet Manuals' (Milne and Russell 2011: 11). But before moving forward with a full cabinet manual project the workshop thought there was a need for 'more public engagement and engagement with community and public policy oriented organizations' (Milne and Russell 2011: 11).

On one matter governed by convention the workshop thought there should be immediate action. That was caretaker government. Mel Cappe, a former Cabinet Secretary and Clerk of the Privy Council, told the workshop that the Privy Council Office (Canada's cabinet office) has guidelines on when government is in caretaker mode and what the limits on caretaker governments are, but he was not at liberty to make them public. Workshop participants agreed that these guidelines should be made public.

The workshop's discussion of the very difficult questions concerning the discretion of the Crown in exercising the reserve powers to dissolve or prorogue parliament indicate the limits of any possible 'codification' of constitutional conventions. All participants agreed on the confidence convention 'that the right to govern depends on maintaining the confidence of the House of Commons'. There was agreement that the House's choice of who should govern is not constrained by a rule that would permit only the leader of the party with the most seats to form a government, and that there was no settled convention that coalitions must be approved by the electorate. But beyond that participants could only agree 'that there is a large number of factors that the governor-general must take into account in responding to a request for dissolution in the early months of a new parliament (Milne and Russell 2011: 6).

As for prorogation, none of the participants questioned whether the governor-general retained the reserve power to decline a prime minister's advice to prorogue parliament. In March 2010, the House of Commons voted in favour of a motion by NDP leader Jack Leyton that a prime minister's request to prorogue for more than a week must have majority support in the House. But the workshop noted that the fact that Layton's motion had been opposed by the Conservatives indicates prorogation is a matter that cannot be regulated by constitutional convention. It appears that the only way to put some limits on the use of prorogation is through legislation.

Two controversial prorogations since the 2008 crisis have stimulated interest in doing just that. On 30 December 2009, Governor-General Jean acceded to another request from Prime Minister Harper to prorogue Parliament until 3 March 2010. Mr Harper said he needed to prorogue to give his government time to 'recalibrate' its economic program (Leblanc 2009). The opposition parties and many in the media thought that the real reason was to terminate an inquiry by parliamentary committee into troubling facts about the treatment of detainees by Canadian Forces in Afghanistan. The second incident occurred in the province of Ontario when, on 15 October 2012, Ontario's Liberal Premier, Dalton McGuinty, shocked the province by announcing his own resignation and the prorogation of the legislature so that, before he stepped down, he could concentrate on negotiations with teachers' unions (Howlett and Waldie 2012). Again the opposition and much of the media thought the real reason for advising the lieutenant governor to close down the Legislative Assembly was a pending vote of censure over the government's failure to disclose documents relating to two cancelled power plant contracts.

There is a precedent in Canada for legislation regulating prorogation: Section five of the province's *Legislative Assembly Act*, originally passed in 1879, states that 'it is not necessary for the Lieutenant Governor in proroguing the Legislature to name a day to which it is prorogued' (Government of Ontario 1990). Premier McGuinty's controversial use of prorogation has sparked a further legislative initiative to control the use of prorogation. Bill 24, a private member's bill introduced by an NDP member of Ontario's Legislative Assembly goes further than Jack Layton's 2010 motion. It prohibits a premier from advising the lieutenant governor to prorogue the Legislative Assembly without a resolution of support adopted by the Assembly and recommending the approximate date when the next session of the Legislature should begin (Government of Ontario 2013).

Bill 24 is likely to receive majority support in Ontario's Legislative Assembly. It may be challenged in the courts as an attempt to bind the Crown in the exercise of its reserve power – even though it does not purport to do so. To rule that elected legislatures cannot control their closing down would be a damaging blow to Canadian democracy.

Gathering support

Serious efforts were made to carry out the workshop's recommendation to stimulate public discussion and engagement with the cabinet manual project. The well-connected Ottawa-based Public Policy Forum (PPF) hosted two roundtable meetings on the proposal. These were attended by experienced government officials, constitutional scholars and leading members of the media. At the second of these, Sir Gus O'Connell, Secretary of the Cabinet in the United Kingdom, explained how the UK Cabinet Manual was developed and its value for parliamentary democracy in the United Kingdom (Public Policy Forum 2011). Although the PPF meetings focussed on the role of the manual in government formation, they registered a high level of support for a more comprehensive set of publicly accessible guidelines on the operation of parliamentary government.

Other meetings on the cabinet manual proposal included a public forum in Toronto sponsored by the Churchill Society for the Advancement of Parliamentary Democracy, and discussions at the annual meetings of the Canadian Political Science Association and the Constitutional Law Section of the Canadian Bar Association. All of these meetings elicited high levels of support for the proposal. There was some media coverage and comment – most of it positive. Dan Gardner in the *Ottawa Citizen* suggested that the Cabinet Manual, 'a sort of pocket guide to Canadian parliamentary governance', would be a worthy way of honouring Jack Layton, the NDP leader who died in 2011 (Gardner 2011).

By the fall of 2011, there had been sufficient public discussion to bring the proposal to the attention of senior officials in the Prime Minister's Office. While members of the Privy Council Office appeared interested in proceeding with the project, they could not do so without the prime minister's approval. If a Canadian Cabinet Manual is to follow roughly the same path of development as in the United Kingdom, it must be seen and be understood to be an official but non-partisan project which eventually is opened to input from parliament. It would be difficult to initiate such a process without a formal announcement by the prime minister (or perhaps the minister for democratic reform), explaining the nature and purpose of the manual, as well as the process through which it would be developed. So far there is no sign of that happening.

I have suggested that Mr Harper's initiation of a project that gives Canadians access to a clear and authoritative description of the principles and practices of parliamentary democracy 'would be an important part of the prime minister's legacy to the country' (Russell 2012: 364). However, I must admit that this project does not have much popular appeal. Whenever I talk to the general public about constitutional conventions, I can sense eyes glazing over. The public can understand laws, and the absence of laws. But the in-between world of constitutional conventions is a strange and mysterious realm to most of them. Of course that is the very reason why something like a cabinet manual is needed.

Conclusion

The Canadian experience demonstrates that while a constitutional crisis may well trigger efforts to clarify constitutional conventions, the resulting effort may do little to settle the issue that was at the heart of the crisis. That should not be surprising: the very lack of consensus that created the crisis prevents a solution to the issue through constitutional convention. Prorogation – more precisely, the circumstances in which the Crown's reserve power should be used to deny a prime minister's advising prorogation – cannot be resolved through constitutional convention in Canada.

That does not mean that prorogation cannot be democratically controlled. Assuming the Bill now before the Ontario Legislative Assembly passes, and survives court challenge (if there is one), then prorogation will be subject to constraints that are clear and democratically based. It would be most unfortunate if the courts were to rule that this legislation constitutes an unconstitutional regulation of the Crown. Such a ruling would mean that prime ministers and premier are vested with an absolute and unaccountable power to shut down parliaments whenever they wish – like the absolute monarchs of old.

As to the classic controversy concerning the Crown's reserve power to refuse a prime minister's request for dissolution in the early months of a new parliament, an authoritative consolidation of constitutional conventions is not likely to move beyond the consensus position reached at the Asper Centre workshop, namely that 'there is a large number of factors that the Governor General must take into account' in these situations. Canada would benefit if the government formation guidelines of a Canadian Cabinet Manual went as far as New Zealand's and the United Kingdom's in making it clear that when an election results in a hung parliament, the onus is on party leaders, not the Crown, to work out which party or combination of parties can command the confidence of the House, and that in these circumstances the leader of the party that won the most seats is not the only person who can be prime minister. But I suspect that Mr Harper, who is a tough political player, is wary of such guidelines because they would reduce his options. He would prefer to be free to make the case for his own view of constitutional convention, if that is the only way he can stay in power.

It is unfortunate that so much of the discussion of a Canadian Cabinet Manual has focussed on contentious issues surrounding the use of the Crown's reserve powers. Those who take the time to read through the New Zealand and UK documents will find that most of what they contain – their bread and butter – deals with mundane issues that are not particularly controversial. These publications are designed to be primarily descriptive of existing practice and long-accepted principle. They include matters already covered by law and some that are simply statements of established practice that are not significant enough to be considered constitutional conventions. A recently published book on government transitions discloses that without any public announcement, Liberal Prime Minister Paul Martin and his Conservative successor, Stephen Harper, have discontinued the practice of permitting senior public servants to respond to requests of opposition party leaders for information about the feasibility of policy proposals they are considering for inclusion in their party platforms (Zussman 2014: 64). One wonders if the Canadian first ministers would have done this had the practice of their predecessors been included in a Canadian Cabinet Manual.

Much of what a Canadian Cabinet Manual would contain can be found in the *Manual of Official Procedure of the Government of Canada* that has existed in Canada's Privy Council since 1968. But it is a document many hundreds of pages in length, containing guidelines and protocols for dealing with routine functions of government and special occasions, and not written in clear and accessible language. There is good Canadian scholarly writing on constitutional conventions but this writing is just that, 'scholarly', and not written as a guide for practitioners, journalists and the public. Andrew Heard's book is the leading text (Heard 2014). As for texts at a more elementary level, the high school civics texts are woefully inadequate on the operation and principles of parliamentary government (Tidridge 2012). Moreover, the work of private scholars and teachers cannot have the authority of a document issued by government and accepted by an all-party committee of parliamentarians.

The greatest benefit of a succinct, well-written and digitally available account of the principles, rules and practices of parliamentary government issued by government and approved by parliament would be its contribution to civic literacy in Canada. If the support for such a project is not forthcoming at the federal level, one of Canada's provincial governments might be persuaded to take up the idea. New Zealand and the United Kingdom have recognised that the Westminster model of parliamentary democracy cannot rest on its laurels. Until Australia and Canada follow suit and produce similar guides to the operation of parliamentary democracy their citizens will know considerably less about how they are governed than citizens elsewhere throughout the parliamentary world.

References

Canada Supreme Court 1981. *Reference re Amendment of Constitution of Canada*, 1 S.C.R. 753, 880.

Dicey, A.V. 1961. *Introduction to the Law of the Constitution*, 10th ed. London: Macmillan.

Flanagan, Tom 2009. 'Only Voters Have the Right to Decide a Coalition'. *The Globe & Mail*, Toronto, 9 January 2009.

Gardner, Dan 2011. *'A Proper Tribute to Jack Layton'. Ottawa Citizen*, 24 August 2011.

Government of Ontario 1990. *Revised Statutes of Ontario*, ch. L 10, s.5.

Government of Ontario 2013. *Legislative Assembly Amendment Act, 2013* (Bill 24).

Government of the United Kingdom Cabinet Office 2010. *The Cabinet Manual – Draft. A Guide to Laws, Conventions, and Rules on the Operation of Government*. London: Government of the United Kingdom.

Gwyn, Richard 2011. *Sir John A. Macdonald: His Life and Times, vol 2: 1867–1891*. Toronto: Random House.

Hazel, Robert and Akash Paun (eds.) 2009. *Making Minority Government Work: Hung Parliaments and the Challenges for Westminster and Whitehall*. London: Institute for Government.

Heard, Andrew 2014. *Canadian Constitutional Conventions: The Marriage of Law and Politics*, 2nd ed. Toronto: Oxford University Press.

Howlett, Karen and Paul Waldie 2012. 'McGuinty Resignation Shocks Ontario'. *The Globe & Mail*, Toronto, 16 October 2012, A1.

Ipsos 2008. 'In Wake of Constitutional Crisis, New Survey Demonstrates that Canadians Lack Basic Understanding of Our Country's Parliamentary System'. http://ipsos-na.com/news-polls (accessed December 2008).

Jennings, Sir Ivor 1959. *The Law and the Constitution*, 5th ed. London: University of London Press, 136.

Leblanc, Daniel 2009. 'Harper Suspends Parliament to Recalibrate'. *The Globe & Mail*, Toronto, 31 December 2009, A1.

MacCharles, Tonda, Bruce Campion-Smith and Joanna Smith 2008. 'Harper Scrambles to Retain Power Against Opposition'. *The Globe & Mail*, Toronto, 29 November 2008, A1–A23.

Milne, Cheryl and Peter Russell 2011. *Adjusting to a New Era of Parliamentary Government*. Toronto: Asper Centre for Constitutional Studies, Faculty of Law, University of Toronto.

New Zealand Government, Cabinet Office, Department of Prime Minister and Cabinet 2008. *Cabinet Manual*. Wellington: Government of New Zealand. www.cabinetmanual.cabinetoffice.govt.nz.

Public Policy Forum 2011. *Government Formation: The Need for Clear Guidelines*, Ottawa, 1 June 2011.

Russell, Peter H. 1988. 'The Politics of Frustration: The Pursuit of Formal Constitutional Change in Australia and Canada'. 6 *Australian – Canadian Studies* (no. 1), 3–32.

Russell, Peter H. 2010. 'The Need for Consensus on Fundamental Conventions of Parliamentary Democracy'. 27 *National Journal of Constitutional Law*, 205–15.

Russell, Peter H. 2012. 'The Principles, Rules and Practices of Parliamentary Government: Time for a Consolidation'. 6 *Journal of Parliamentary and Political Law*, 353.

Russell, Peter H. and Lorne Sossin (eds.) 2009. *Parliamentary Democracy in Crisis*. University of Toronto Press.

Tidridge, Nathan 2012. *'Ontario's Civics Textbooks and Their Errors Concerning the Crown'*. Paper presented at The Crown in Canada Conference, Johnson-Shoyama Graduate School of Public Policy, University of Regina, 26–28 October 2012.

Twomey, Anne 1985. *'The Governor General's Role in the Formation of Governments in a Hung Parliament'. Legal Studies Research Paper No. 10/85*. Sydney Law School, University of Sydney.

Valpy, Michael 2009. 'The Crisis: A Narrative'. In Peter H. Russell and Lorne Sossin (eds.), *Parliamentary Democracy in Crisis*. University of Toronto Press, 3–18.

Zussman, David 2014. *Off and Running: The Prospects and Pitfalls of Government Transitions*. University of Toronto Press.

14

Constitutional reform

ANDREW BLICK

Conventions are a vital part of any constitution. Often they go unnoticed, but this lack of visibility serves, paradoxically, to underline their importance. They are most noticeable when they fail, or threaten to malfunction. We realise how much we need the service they perform when faced with losing it. As well as being essential to the operation of the system as it is, conventions can play a prominent part in efforts to change it. And just as the potentially amorphous nature of conventions can cloud assessments of them, so too can it make a consideration of their association with constitutional reform a challenging task. This chapter considers attempts to improve the system that have a connection with conventions. It does so taking into account the country-specific chapters that have preceded it in this book: by Andrew C. Banfield on Canada, by Nicholas Barry and Narelle Miragliotta on Australia, by Grant Duncan on New Zealand and by Robert Hazell on the United Kingdom. It also draws on the academic research of the author (especially Blick and Hennessy 2011; Blick 2014a, 2014b), and his previous experiences as researcher for a member of parliament in the UK House of Commons, adviser to a Commons select committee, and intern at Number 10 Downing Street. The present chapter encompasses changes directed specifically at conventions; and circumstances in which conventions play a secondary role in other alterations. A key purpose is to discern the common features identifiable across the different constitutions, despite their differences. It considers why such change comes about: what are the motives and rationales, and what circumstances are conducive to it? There is then an assessment of the different types of reform that are involved. Finally, the chapter discusses the benefits and complications associated with these assorted kinds of action, before drawing conclusions.

Though all grouped under the general heading 'Westminster model', there are clear differences between the constitutions analysed here. Two (Australia and Canada) are 'written' – that is, their fundamental arrangements are contained in a specific text with special legal status expressly labelled the constitution, though the documents – as is often the case with written constitutions – leave important gaps, particularly as regards the role of the monarch. The other two have 'unwritten' constitutions. Many parts of the constitution may exist in written form, but there is no single document equivalent to that of Australia or Canada. New Zealand and the United Kingdom are often cited, alongside Israel, as the only significant democracies in the world not yet to have fundamental texts of this sort. The two countries with written constitutions are federal. New Zealand has a unitary system. The position in the United Kingdom is more complicated. Though traditionally a centralised system, in the late 1990s it introduced devolution to Wales, Scotland and Northern Ireland, suggesting movement in a federal direction, though not a complete process. The constitutions concerned differ in other ways, such as electoral systems. They have varied arrangements in place to accommodate their particular national, ethnic and cultural diversities. The systems of each country have also altered over time.

These particular qualities and dynamics of development have had a close connection with the reform of constitutional conventions. But there are important similarities among them as well. The historic constitutional legacy, deriving from the British Empire, is clear. This past has bequeathed a common institution: each country remains a monarchy (and they share the same monarch), though in 1999 Australia held a referendum on whether to become a republic, rejecting the idea on this occasion. This shared characteristic is linked to other similarities: in particular the existence of parliamentary government. The commonality of monarchy is also of pronounced importance from the point of view of constitutional conventions. The monarch is formally the font of important prerogative or 'reserve' powers (vested in representatives such as governor-generals in Australia, Canada and New Zealand). To reconcile this strict legal position with the requirements of post-colonialism and democracy, mediating conventions are required, relating, for instance, to the appointment of prime ministers and the granting of dissolutions. They apply in all four constitutions assessed here, 'written' and 'unwritten' alike. Mutual characteristics, then, are identifiable. A wider exploration follows.

Drivers of reform

Pressure for change involving conventions can develop for a variety of reasons. It may occur because of some kind of dysfunction calling into question the appropriateness of existing arrangements. Nicholas Barry and Narelle Miragliotta have assessed an exemplary example of a predicament involving the use of conventions: the Australian constitutional crisis of 1975. The most notorious occurrence in this chain of events was the decision by Governor-General John Kerr to supplant the Labor Prime Minister Gough Whitlam, appointing Liberal Malcolm Fraser in his place. A 'double dissolution' and election followed, with a victory for the coalition that Fraser headed. Other issues raised during this crisis involved questions about what was appropriate conduct by the Senate and the appointment of replacements for outgoing members of the Senate. The account Barry and Miragliotta provide suggests that there are certain characteristics associated with the role of conventions in a constitution that may make them liable to generate systemic difficulties: differences over how to interpret conventions; conflicts between conventions; and disparity between conventions and the written constitution. In the 1975 instance, it was possible ultimately to resolve the conflict, these authors suggest, through a mutual commitment to underlying constitutional stability among different players.

The events of 1975 contributed to change, though in a complex, indirect fashion. They produced demands for the codification of conventions, including those determining the respective positions of the prime minister and the governor-general. Ultimately, in 1985, a process of recognising and declaring eighteen conventions took place, though they were not incorporated into the Australian constitutional text. While the position of the governor-general provided impetus for this exercise, the process established did not ultimately deal with the status of this post. A call for further change arising from the 1975 difficulties – a constitutional amendment to remove the ability of the Senate to deny the government supply – made no practical progress. The impact of a constitutional wobble of some kind can be more direct and immediate than was that of 1975 in Australia. As Grant Duncan shows, following an election defeat in 1984, the outgoing New Zealand Prime Minister Robert Muldoon sought inappropriately to continue to exert policy influence, trying to prevent a currency devaluation. This difficult circumstance prompted the establishment of a caretaker convention for New Zealand. It also encouraged the introduction of the *Constitution Act 1986*, drawing together key constitutional arrangements into a single statute, though not amounting to a full written constitution. A more recent incident in Canada that Andrew C. Banfield describes has once again induced reform proposals. In 2008 Canadian Prime

Minister Stephen Harper sought and obtained a prorogation from the governor-general as a means of avoiding a forthcoming confidence vote that the government was set to lose. This controversial episode has led to a call for the introduction of a Canadian cabinet manual that codifies key conventions, as discussed in Peter Russell's Chapter 13. However, it has not yet materialised.

Another source of encouragement for change can be that rather than responding to a difficulty, policy-makers foresee a problem, and seek to pre-empt it. New Zealand was due to hold its first election under a proportional system (mixed-member proportional or 'MMP') in 1996. In the knowledge that a period of coalition forming would follow, the New Zealand *Cabinet Manual* included a new section describing 'caretaker' conventions, which outlines the rules covering how incumbent ministers conduct themselves pending the resolution of negotiations. The text also came to include detailed stipulations about the limitations applying to the governor-general in any potential exercise of the 'reserve powers' in such circumstances. Similarly, in advance of the May 2010 UK general election, there were signs that, for the first time since February 1974, the outcome would be inconclusive, with no single party commanding a majority in the House of Commons. Given the unfamiliarity of this experience in post-1945 UK history, the Cabinet Office, early in 2010, issued a statement of the conventions it felt applied in such circumstances: the first proper official description of the rules in this area. The primary intention was to create understanding and confidence among the wider public, as well as to guide those operating within the system. This account later formed part of a larger text, the Cabinet Manual, the contents of which included descriptions of a range of constitutional conventions, a number of which, once again, had never before appeared in a public, official statement.

A further driver of reform can be the requirements of the institutions involved in the operation of the constitution. The introduction of documents such as *Questions of Procedure for Ministers* (QPM) in the United Kingdom (since 1997 known as the *Ministerial Code*) and the *Cabinet Manual* in New Zealand, both of which set out conventions, came about initially as a means of providing guidance to ministers and officials in their day-to-day work. Initially, such texts may be intended for internal use only, and not for introduction into the public domain. However, pressure can build for their publication. Though QPM was not a public text before 1992, its existence had become widely known and some of the contents had leaked. Following the UK general election of this year,

Prime Minister John Major published it, in line with encouragement he had received to do so. This kind of reform can point to a wider expectation of greater openness in government, that the public are entitled to know the rules applying to those who govern them. In accordance with this trend, some statements of conventions, rather than beginning as internal texts which may then receive wider circulation, are designed with public consumption in mind from the outset. The purpose may be to enhance awareness of and confidence in the system, as with the UK *Cabinet Manual.*

These kinds of motivations for change may be part of a wider climate of constitutional reform, which can have further impact upon conventions. Demands for specific alterations may manifest themselves. In the United Kingdom, around the time of the invasion of Iraq of 2003, the idea of a convention for government consultation with the Commons over military action began to gain salience, and has gradually become part of established practice (Blick 2014b). It is also possible for criticism to centre on the very concept of conventions as a component in systemic regulation. The various examples considered here demonstrate that some may hold that conventions need to become more clearly defined; more enforceable; or perhaps that at least some of them should be eradicated altogether, with the rules they prescribe placed on a different constitutional footing. Reforms not directly engaging convention may take place, that in turn lead on to developments in conventions. The passage of the *Constitution Act 1982* in Canada triggered an effort to seek clarification through the courts of the position of the provinces with respect to constitutional modification. In New Zealand the use since 1996 of the MMP system in parliamentary elections has made coalition or minority administrations the norm. Consequently, as Duncan recounts, conventions have had to adapt, with attention focusing on the handling of the uncertain circumstances of post-election negotiations, and a loosening of the principle of collective Cabinet responsibility. Potentially, Duncan goes on, direct intervention from the governor-general may take place in an effort to resolve a future parliamentary arithmetical deadlock. This prospect implies a further forced development in the conventions of government formation and continuity. Another reform triggering consequential change came in the United Kingdom with the introduction of devolved government in the late 1990s. Like MMP in New Zealand it rested on statutory enactment, but has necessitated the establishment of conventions to regulate the relationship between the Whitehall/Westminster centre and the newly formed devolved institutions.

Forms of change

Just as the motivation for reform involving conventions can take many forms, so too can the type of change that takes place. It can involve an instant occurrence. In 1984, New Zealand Deputy Prime Minister Jim Mclay persuaded Prime Minister Robert Muldoon to accept a new 'caretaker convention' as a means of resolving the difficulty facing the political system at this time. It gained acceptance because it seemed a reasonable response to the circumstances. This development involved a swift, deliberate action. Other changes can take place over a prolonged period of time, with no clear moment of decision, and no formal declaration at the time of their coming into force. A good example of this kind of shift is the convention, which developed during the course of the twentieth century, that a UK prime minister must sit in the House of Commons and not in the House of Lords. Between 1902, when Lord Salisbury stood down from the post, and 1963, when it was clear that whoever succeeded Harold Macmillan at Number 10 could not do so if they wished to remain in the second chamber, this transformation took place. But precisely when it occurred is probably impossible to establish; and no one individual or group proclaimed it. Yet it is still correct to describe this transformation as a reform in the sense that an underlying and strengthening set of values – derived from the idea of the Commons possessing a democratic legitimacy that the Lords does not – drove its appearance.

Change may involve the extension of an already existing principle. For instance, the UK *Cabinet Manual* of 2011 asserted that the restrictions on ministers introducing substantial new policy measures immediately before a general election also applied during any period of post-election negotiation. Modifications to existing conventions may take place. Both New Zealand (in the post-MMP environment) and the United Kingdom (since 1975, drawing on a precedent from 1932) have seen the relaxation of collective responsibility to accommodate political realities. Sometimes a completely new convention can appear, as with the aforementioned 'caretaker' principle created in New Zealand in 1984. In the United Kingdom around the time of the 2010 general election a principle was established that it was possible for the civil service to provide support to coalition negotiations in the event of an inconclusive general election. This rule did not exist before. Similarly, there now exists in the United Kingdom an acknowledged convention that, whenever practically possible, the government should seek the express approval of the Commons in advance of the deployment of the armed forces on operations overseas that actually or potentially involve hostilities.

A further possible form of change is that of clarification. As previously noted, in 1981 three Canadian provinces referred to the courts the question of whether the passing of the Constitution Act would violate the constitution. Their complaint was that their approval had not been obtained for this change: they sought to establish what the position was. Elucidation may involve public iterations of some kind. Following the introduction of MMP in New Zealand, Governor-General Sir Michael Hardie Boys made a number of public interventions intended to make clear the principles surrounding the establishment of governments. A related practice is the production of official documents setting down conventions in writing. The New Zealand *Cabinet Manual* is an example of such a practice. So too is the Australian 'recognise and declare' exercise of 1985. It may involve iterating already-existing rules that previously lacked formal textual expression or generating new conventions through writing them down. Such declarations may be for internal consumption within the institution that creates them, or their authors may deliberately introduce them into the public domain. The creation of such texts – available in public – has become an industry in the United Kingdom over the past three decades. Many of them relate to the functioning of the executive; but they have also encompassed its dealings with other institutions, such as parliament and the devolved administrations, and its interactions with the public. Other branches of the UK constitution have issued codes, such as parliament, the devolved legislatures and executives, and the judiciary (Blick and Hennessy 2011).

Arrangements previously dealt with as a matter of convention may acquire a statutory basis. One of the stipulations of the *Constitution Act 1986* in New Zealand was that only individuals who hold seats in parliament could be appointed to ministerial offices or to the executive council, a rule which was previously only a convention. In the UK the *Constitutional Renewal and Governance Act 2010* gave conventions surrounding the impartiality of the civil service a new statutory basis. It also provided for a convention known as the 'Ponsonby Rule' (modifying it in the process) that granted parliament an admittedly limited role in the ratification of treaties. The Fixed term Parliaments Act of the following year dealt with further functions previously left to convention. It regulated the calling of general elections in advance of the five-year maximum and created a framework for Commons motions of no confidence and confidence in the government. In countries with written constitutions, when seeking to reform conventions in some way, another option is to alter the fundamental text. Some in Australia thought that the Senate violated convention when it blocked supply to the government in 1975. But it was deploying a power that, in strict legal terms, it was entitled to under the constitution. From the point of view of the Labor party, convention had failed in 1975. This spurred advocacy of change to the constitutional document, to make it reflect the arrangement they claimed the Senate should have recognised as prevailing in practice in 1975, and to make it more firm and legally binding. This goal has not come about.

Reform may take place involving new means of upholding and enforcing conventions. Bodies may appear with a role in the implementation of particular conventions, such as the Independent Adviser on Ministerial Interests in the United Kingdom, who advises ministers on compliance with the *Ministerial Code* and can, at the request of the prime minister, investigate alleged breaches of the rules. Involving the courts is a bigger step and the judiciary tends to be circumspect in this regard. When the Canadian Supreme Court considered the constitutionality of passing what became the *Constitution Act 1982* it provided a dual response, concluding that a constitutional but not legal violation had taken place. Nonetheless, the consideration of conventions by the courts is significant. It has developed in the United Kingdom also, and may one day occur in New Zealand.

Alterations may take place in the processes by which conventions themselves develop. Official bodies charged with identifying them may be created. Those who produce codes may choose to consult on them, privately or publicly. Parliamentary committees can become involved in scrutinising these texts. Issuing a statement or text can become a means of forcing the development of a convention that might otherwise have been allowed to appear without conscious intervention of this kind. Codification can also modify the very idea of what a convention is, entailing a shift away from more traditional perceptions of conventions as tacit rather than express understandings. Conceptual transformation can arise in other ways, for instance if conventions governing relationships between institutions become enforceable by third parties, where once they were seen more as self-imposed rules.

Consequences of reform

Changes of the sorts discussed here potentially offer certain benefits. They can facilitate systemic development, enabling continued operation without more formal and cumbersome legal change being necessary. The New Zealand 'caretaker' conventions are an instance of such a development. Reforms can make it possible to prevent crises from occurring, or from taking place again if they have already happened. Conventions around the formation and operation of coalition governments are an example of useful devices in this area. Developments in conventions can also be a means of ensuring that other reforms function effectively. The non-statutory rules that have appeared in post-MMP New Zealand and have congealed around devolution in the United Kingdom perform this role. Clarification of the meaning of conventions can help those directly involved in the working of the constitution. It means that in difficult circumstances, under public scrutiny, they can act with confidence that they are behaving appropriately. It also makes violation of the rules easier to identify, and creates a deterrent to abuse. The publication of codes brings the potential gain of wider public understanding of rules that might otherwise seem obscure. Cabinet manuals are well placed to fulfil this objective. In the immediate wake of the 2010 general election in the United Kingdom, constitutional commentators found the text helpful when providing accounts to the media about how the government-formation system operated.

Alongside substantive alteration, some of the processes used to bring it about may be advantageous in themselves. The tendency in all the countries discussed here has been for deliberate acts, such as statements by officials, the production of documents or legal proceedings all aimed at clarifying, developing or creating conventions. These practices can create greater certainty and transparency around not only *what* conventions are, but *how* they come into being and are modified. It is also possible through these procedures to widen participation in the management of conventions, through parliamentary inquiry and public consultation. Finally, the possibility of new enforcement mechanisms has attractions. Conventions involve some of the fundamental features of a democratic system, and it may be appropriate to introduce additional means of ensuring adherence to them.

However, the reform of conventions can entail complications and drawbacks. While transparency may be a goal, issuing public statements can create confusion if they appear to conflict with each other. Duncan has described how in 1998 the Cabinet Manual and the agreement underpinning the particular coalition in office at the time were not congruent. The then-Prime Minister Jenny Shipley acted on advice from senior officials that the former document took priority over the latter.

This event leads to a more fundamental issue: the source of conventions. As I have argued elsewhere, an iteration or text cannot by itself create or provide the basis for a convention: it can only achieve this objective through interacting with a wider social environment. If key players reject or ignore an asserted convention, for example, it will not take hold (Blick 2014a). In a sense, this limitation on the ability to determine the nature of conventions is a useful safeguard against abuse. But it means that the text may not always be the reality. Actual conventions may be different to the description offered in a document; and the document cannot account for all their possible applications, given the multiplicity of possible circumstances. Conventions may not exist at all, despite what a code or statement claims. They may change in future despite the text – and their ability to do so is essential to the flexibility regarded as vital to their effectiveness.

However, there is evidence that it is possible consciously to bring about the fabrication of conventions, if circumstances are conducive. Indeed, though texts such as cabinet manuals may claim they are only asserting existing principles, they are likely to bring about change even if their authors wish to avoid doing so. In the case of New Zealand, the *Cabinet Manual* has at least established a principle that it should be reissued by each new government. Moreover, it has asserted firm stipulations regarding the possible exercise of the reserve powers by the governor-general. The UK Manual, too, has encouraged change. Sometimes the modification or creation of conventions may be deliberate. When arguments break out over the precise nature of conventions, or whether a particular convention exists at all, reform can be a means of settling the argument in one direction or another. In other words, it can enable participants on one side of a dispute to put beyond doubt that a rule they believe exists – or think ought to exist – is adhered to in future. This attitude manifested itself in the Australian Labor Party in response to the serial crises of 1975. In this instance, the party did not achieve what it wanted. However, this episode demonstrates the possibility of an urge to alter conventions in a way that suits a particular interest. More recently in the United Kingdom, governments have sought to expand the scope of the so-called Salisbury-Addison convention. Traditionally it requires the House of Lords not to seek to block legislative measures prefigured in the manifesto of the party that won the previous general election. The executive now asserts that it applies to the entirety of the government programme.

The idea of conventions becoming subordinate to the requirements of particular groups is democratically unsatisfactory. The rise of the practice of codification presents dangers in this respect. In some cases a particular player, such as the UK executive, can be predominant in the process of producing a code, raising questions about its legitimacy. However, even though particular institutions may be able to exercise heavy influence over the contents of these texts, the possibility remains that the same institutions will be held accountable against these documents in public if they are in some way perceived as having violated the rules they have proclaimed for themselves. Furthermore, the possibility of judicial intervention cannot be ruled out. Indeed, Nicholas Barber has argued that codification can contribute to a process where conventions come increasingly to resemble laws (Barber 2010). One option for judicial engagement is that taken in Canada in 1981: to deem the constitution, but not the law, to have been violated. Another is to give conventions legal force, but only as a means of considering the actions of a public authority in judicial review. To go further and seek directly to assert a convention would be a more dramatic step. It could well be regarded unfavourably by other participants in the system and could pose a further threat to the flexibility of conventions as a constitutional source. Indeed, if experiments in the codification and enforcement of conventions become too successful, it might prove necessary to evolve another set of tacit, more malleable conventions, the observance of which depend on self-restraint more than formal external mechanisms, for the system to function satisfactorily.

Conclusion

It is clear that there are many common features across the different developed Westminster systems. They involve the motives for change, the alterations themselves, and their consequences. Sometimes development in one state has influenced another: the caretaker convention in New Zealand drew on thought elsewhere in the Commonwealth; and the UK *Cabinet Manual* followed the New Zealand example. Certain further observations present themselves. In each case, reform in conventions may serve not to bring about change as an end in itself, but to preserve an underlying constancy in the system. Conventions change so that other constitutional fundamentals can survive. In particular they engage functions such as the appointment of governments and the holding of elections that ultimately derive from the head of state. Forbearance in the exercise of these powers is essential because of their monarchical origin. This sensitivity suggests that, while efforts to justify the existence of an unelected hereditary head of state often focus on the idea that it is a source of stability, it is prone to becoming associated with crisis. Other parts of the system may be supporting it, rather than vice versa.

A noticeable division between the four constitutions considered here is that two of them, Australia and Canada, are provided for in a single written text; while two, New Zealand and the United Kingdom, are 'unwritten'. The commonality already established between the four demonstrates that crude binary differentiations between 'written' and 'unwritten' constitution are not appropriate. A constitution is always more than a single document, and perceptions of any system should not solely use the prism of its possession or lack of it. However, alongside this realisation it is important to recognise the widespread existence of a powerful urge to express fundamental arrangements in writing for all to see. This imperative has intensified in an age of mass literacy, widely and instantly available information, and steady pressure towards openness and transparency. It is surely not a coincidence that the United Kingdom and New Zealand, in the absence of written constitutions, have acquired documents serving as proxies for them: in the United Kingdom, the numerous constitutional codes, and in New Zealand both the *Cabinet Manual* and the *Constitution Act 1986*. Perhaps eventually one or both of these countries will come into line with most other democracies and introduce full constitutional texts. Yet conventions will remain in some form, with or without a written constitution.

References

Barber, Nicholas W. 2010. *The Constitutional State*. Oxford University Press.

Blick, Andrew 2014a. 'The Cabinet Manual and the codification of conventions', *Parliamentary Affairs* 67: 191–208.

Blick, Andrew 2014b. 'Emergency powers and the withering of the Royal Prerogative', *International Journal of Human Rights* 18 (2): 195–210.

Blick, Andrew and Hennessy, Peter 2011. *The Hidden Wiring Emerges: The Cabinet Manual and the Working of the British Constitution*. London: Institute for Public Policy Research.

Conclusion

In this volume we have articulated and applied a political approach to understanding conventions, and their legitimacy, stability and – with recent challenges – adaptability. This political approach is a direct response to decades of legal scholarship that has relegated or simply ignored conventions. Yet without conventions in these countries there would be no working political system to make laws. Most key political institutions and actors are governed at least partially by conventions.

In the first chapter we provided an overview of the key theoretical contributions of both political philosophers and constitutional lawyers to understanding the character and status of conventions. We observed that conventions are both implicitly and explicitly recognised by elites and citizens as fundamental parts of the political system, as written constitutions are not extensive and the monarchy retains a symbolically powerful role. Conventions bind political actors to behave in ways that ensure political stability, but can adapt to accommodate some difference through negotiation. Yet challengers are essentially co-opted into the dominant practice more than they are genuinely accommodated through changes to conventions.

In Chapter 2 Nicholas Aroney continued to interrogate the definitional, conceptual and theoretical debates in the constitutional law literature, while drawing on key cases to further distinguish between law and convention, with a focus on enforceability by courts. Conventions are not enforceable like written constitutions or law, which at least partly explains their perceived inferior status. Yet debates over the application of conventions often represent more fundamental concerns about the political systems, which can only be resolved through politics rather than judicial review.

Of the three branches of government, it is the executive that is subject to the most conventions and therefore has the most potential to cause controversy. Nevertheless, as Brian Galligan discussed in Chapter 3, there is broad agreement on the core conventions of parliamentary responsible government despite significant crises such as the 1975 Australian constitutional crisis and the 2008 Canadian prorogation dispute. Such crises are charged political affairs that expose differences in how conventions are viewed and how they should be applied. Despite calls for greater clarity through codification, ongoing political differences preclude such resolution and there is no judicial arbiter to settle matters. For most of the time, executive conventions function in predictable ways that structure government and limit the involvement of the monarch and her representatives.

The fourth chapter continued the focus on the executive, with Patrick Weller examining the political conventions surrounding cabinet government. Two levels of conventions exist here: expectations of ministers in relation to the cabinet, the government and the parliament, and the codified rules and routines that give practical effect to those expectations. The question of whether any of these are strictly binding, though, is open. For these sets of conventions there often is an authoritative arbiter – the prime minister – who can also adapt or even ignore certain practices. However, this power is curtailed by other political norms that serve to foster-conservatism.

Jennifer Menzies and Anne Tiernan returned to one of the central issues of this volume in Chapter 5, where they analysed a subset of conventions necessary for orderly changes of government. The executive is of course not just the cabinet, but the broader government and public or civil service, and in this instance public officials are the authoritative interpreters and in a sense, guardians. Again, written codes have helped to clarify appropriate forms of behaviour in a period when political sensitivities can be heightened and certain actors seek advantage.

Chapter 6 concluded the focus on the executive and more closely addressed the question of how conventions can remain stable yet adaptable. Scott Brenton charted the weakening Westminster majoritarian model of democracy, and how the major parties have been largely effective in retaining their dominant position in the face of changing voting trends and the rise of the new challengers. These cases of minority and multi-party government demonstrate how strong conventions actually are; even when the major parties are in a weaker bargaining position, they are still able to contain potentially more radical demands for changes to the political system. While conventions provide more flexibility than a written constitution, their influence is no less significant, and even when minor adaptations are made the original convention is acknowledged and mostly upheld.

J. R. Nethercote explained in Chapter 7 the main institutions that structure the workings of parliaments. Beginning with Westminster, parliamentary practices have a long history and cover a variety of usages, forms, customs and precedents. Many of the more important ones are covered in treatises that are regularly updated by the clerks of the respective houses, and provide the most instructive and detailed accounts of how parliaments function. Despite differences in some of the practices, the similarities among these four Westminster parliamentary systems are striking, including not only such notable institutions as the opposition and ministerial responsibility but also the architecture and colour green of all the lower houses. If conventional practices are clear enough and ensure fairly predictable operational procedures, they remain flexible blueprints or guidelines for parliamentary practitioners.

In Chapter 8 Campbell Sharman compared and contrasted the appointed upper houses of Canada and the United Kingdom with the elected upper houses in Australia. In all cases the role and powers (and very existence) of the upper house can be a source of tension and again highlight the important role of political parties in determining how the institutions has evolved, and continues to evolve. The conventions surrounding responsible government, which advantage the governing party, continue to be the most influential.

Four country-focused chapters highlighted some of the key differences and the importance of particular factors in each of the countries. Robert Hazell chronicled a twenty-year constitutional 'revolution' in the United Kingdom in Chapter 9, where each recent, successive government has responded to calls for regulation and decentralisation of political power, particularly in relation to the executive. Various forms of codification have been used, including legislated devolution, and while the incentives for executives to drive such a reform agenda may not be immediately apparent, they can be seen to placate demands for a written constitution. The executive has to concede certain powers or be subject to scrutiny, but retain more control than if the codes became part of a written constitution. While enabling some power-sharing and democratisation, the major parties are still setting the agenda.

Andrew Banfield's Chapter 10 on Canada provided further clarity on some of the foundational issues raised in the first chapter and also examined the role of the courts raised in the second chapter. Firstly a distinction was made between conventions and customs, with customs being symbolic rather than acting as binding rules. In many respects, Canada has accommodated some extraordinary circumstances with conventions remaining remarkably stable. Rather, evolution has often served to reinforce and strengthen existing conventions. The Supreme Court of Canada has even acknowledged the importance of constitutional convention in upholding the political system.

In Chapter 11, Nicholas Barry and Narelle Miragliotta looked at the most significant case of constitutional conventions being breached. Australia's 1975 constitutional crisis is also an example of the major parties being unable to agree on the 'rules of the game' and demonstrates how much the stability of Westminster-derived political systems depends on this tacit understanding and acceptance. While constitutional reforms to codify the governor-general's reserve power remain elusive, one important convention has become part of the Constitution. Vacant Senate seats must be filled by a member of the same party as the departing senator. It is noteworthy that two of the biggest constitutional crises have occurred in the two countries with written constitutions, Australia and Canada. In both cases the opposition was attempting to remove a government using unusual political tactics.

Grant Duncan's Chapter 12 on New Zealand recorded a constitutional revolution comparable to that of the United Kingdom. The smallest, most centralised and constitutionally conservative country has become the most radical in recent decades. Yet with a comprehensive *Cabinet Manual* in some respects substituting for a written constitution, and an electoral system leading to multi-party governance arrangements, the position and authority of the leaders of the major parties – who alternate in the prime ministership – remain fundamentally intact. In both the process of codification and the evolution of multi-party governance arrangements, most conventions have been explicitly upheld.

In Chapter 13 Peter Russell critically examines the Canadian case and controversy over the governor-general's proroguing the Canadian parliament in 2008. The governor-general effectively saved the day by acceding to the advice of a minority prime minister threatened with a no-confidence motion that he seemed likely to lose. The alternative option was to reject that advice and commission the leader of the recently formed coalition of combined opposition parties. With the matter hotly disputed by commentators as well as politicians, Russell makes the case for greater certainty through codification.

As Andrew Blick made clear in Chapter 14, constitutional reform can take many forms. Yet despite some notable differences across the four countries, Blick identified the many more common features. Each country does look to the others for guidance and clarity, in a way that few other groups of countries can. Reforms or adaptations of conventions ultimately preserve the fundamental tenets of the political system.

INDEX

Lightning Source UK Ltd.
Milton Keynes UK
UKOW06n1919280216

269267UK00006B/91/P

9 781107 100244